# THE WAY OF RŌNIN

# THE WAY OF RŌNIN

DEFYING THE ODDS ON BATTLEFIELDS,
IN BUSINESS AND IN LIFE

## TU LAM

HANOVER
SQUARE
PRESS

HANOVER
SQUARE
PRESS™

Recycling programs
for this product may
not exist in your area.

ISBN-13: 978-1-335-49086-5

The Way of Rōnin

Hanover Square Press
22 Adelaide St. West, 41st Floor
Toronto, Ontario M5H 4E3, Canada
HanoverSqPress.com
BookClubbish.com

Printed in U.S.A.

This book is dedicated to the most important women in my life: my wonderful mother, and my loving wife, Ruthie. You are the light that guides me through the darkness.

# THE
# WAY
## OF
# RŌNIN

# PROLOGUE

I sat on the edge of my bed in the darkness. Another restless
night. Try as I might to avoid it, I could feel my old friend anxiety moving in. And as it did, my heart felt as if it was about to
pound through my chest.

Hoping to control it, I slowly walked over to where my sleeping wife lay and kissed her as softly as I could, hoping neither
the touch of my lips on her smooth, warm cheek nor the sound
of my heart pounding would wake her. After I started to walk
toward the deck adjoining the bedroom my cairn terrier, who
I named Little Rōnin, hopped off the bed to join me.

It was a cool summer morning in the Colorado Mountains.
A light breeze touched my face as I sat on my meditation mat.
The soft sound of aspen leaves flowing through the air swirled
into my ears. I was hoping, as I did every day, that today the
peaceful views, feelings, and sounds would somehow soothe my
soul. But once again, no such luck.

So I sat, enveloped by the dark stillness of the morning, and
wondered why and why not. I had sat there almost every day
for five years searching for inner peace. I was not going to give
up. I never had before, and I wasn't about to start now—not
after what I had already been through.

I focused on my deep breathing, trying, as I was taught, to

put my agitated mind into a state of trance. But, just like the other mornings, it didn't quite work.

Little Rōnin sat quietly and waited. I was grateful that the terrier did not share my anxieties. Thankfully she seemed to take after my wife. As I attempted again to meditate, I could feel her warm little body push up against mine.

When I finally opened my eyes, she kissed my hand, seemingly knowing that I had been in a very dark place for a very long time. But she, like my wife, also seemed to know that all along I had been searching for the light.

It was ironic because during this search, which had brought me all over the world, I had taken on the mantle and responsibilities of a rōnin—the famed, and infamous, Masterless Samurais of one of the most noble and turbulent eras in Asian history. And it was by traveling down that path that I became, I'm told, the light for so many others seeking their escape from pain.

I looked at my watch. It was 3:05 a.m. The hour of the tiger had arrived and, with it, the memory of my mother's continual admonition.

"Smile," she always told me, "and be brave."

My mother was born in the Year of the Tiger. I, too, was born in the Year of the Tiger. According to the Chinese zodiac, one of the main attributes of those born under this auspicious, powerful sign is bravery. I couldn't disagree, especially when it came to my mother. She had survived things that had killed many others, and she had carried me with her.

I left the deck and went inside. If I couldn't find inner warmth this cool morning, I could at least find some outer warmth. I lit the fireplace, and soon felt its comforting heat stroke my skin.

It was the fourth day of the eighth month during the hour of the tiger. I should have been able to harness and direct its power to find a path through my unease. But like the thousands of previous days, the way was obscured by memories that flashed past my mind's eye like shrieking wraiths.

First the horror of war and the torment of escape. Then bullying and racism that continued all the way through military training, followed by years of terror and tragedy that exploded all around me as I tried to set things right.

I saw glimpses of attacks, assaults, and gunfights that went on for days, continuing for years. There were flashes from special reconnaissance, special operations, and special missions, as well as memories of battles in Africa, Asia, America, Arabia, and even *mano a mano* no-holds-barred fights.

And through it all: "Smile and be brave." But even that wasn't enough to completely soothe my soul.

Yes, I had survived it all, but the shrapnel it had implanted in my mind was deep, sharp, and ample. And the worst irony was that, even after I seemingly had left it all behind, I found the aftermath and recovery could be just as bad, if not worse—no matter how many accolades, awards, accomplishments, and acclaim I accrued in what some might call my *peacetime*.

I knew that it had already taken years for me to even start to defuse all the land mines in my brain, but, as ever, I was not going to stop when the going got tough. So in this hour of the tiger, by the glow of a warm fire, I finally reached out—not for what I knew but for what I didn't know.

I reached out for my very first memory. It was the five-year-old me looking out onto a refugee camp. At that time, I really hadn't known what had happened to me previously. What were the character-defining and personality-shaping experiences that led to that first memory? What made me who I was, am, and would be? What was the first step in my journey of a thousand miles or more?

It was within that hour of the spirit of the tiger—the time when the brave can travel from the physical to the spiritual world—that I truly began to face and explore the darkness that came before my transformation into a rōnin. But what had started it all was a terrifying story my mother told me to get my mind off what had been, up until then, my very worst day.

# 1

Even in the refugee camp, my mother had taught me that chaos was needed to make way for calm.

"Without chaos," she said, "there will be no mountains to climb, armies to fight, or dragons to slay. Without chaos, how can there be a realization to one's actual truth?"

Like some other things my mother told me, I didn't understand it then. I learned the hard—and easy—way that my mother's words planted seeds in my mind that could bloom, whether it was hours, days, weeks, months, years, or even decades later.

But on that particular day, I was still a poor Vietnamese refugee boy living in North Carolina, raised by a family who had been forced to start over after losing our freedom and our country. The Vietnam War was unpopular in America, and my family and I were the very image of that hateful conflict.

In 1981, through a sponsorship from my American military uncle who fell in love and married my aunt while he was recovering from wounds in Vietnam, my family and I were relocated from an Indonesian refugee camp to a town in the southern United States called Fayetteville. Fayetteville is a small military town right outside of Fort Bragg, the country's largest Army base. It housed more Army commandos than any other base in America. Fort Bragg was even home to the Special Operations Command.

When my father, mother, brother, and I first came to the United States, we lived with my aunt and uncle, who was a American Special Forces Green Beret officer. His wife, my aunt, took care of us until we were able to move out on our own.

My parents settled us into a one-bedroom apartment in the poor part of town. There we had only one piece of furniture—a used full-size mattress that my whole family slept on. The language barrier made my parents unqualified for higher-paying jobs, and the lack of money caused them to argue. We were so poor, in fact, that my brother and I often went days without eating.

Even so, we made the best of it, led by my mother's indomitable spirit. After all, as bad as it was, it was better than the Indonesian refugee camp had been.

On one warm Sunday, I was playing in the front yard of our small apartment building when my mother pulled up in a car I had never seen before. She was positively beaming and honked the horn as she pulled up. She had been so proud that she had been able to pass the American driving test and now was so happy that she got to put her license to good use.

"Get in," she told me. I wasn't about to turn down that offer.

Somehow my mother had convinced my aunt to let her drive the family car that day. By the time we went two blocks to a local Piggly Wiggly supermarket, we were both smiling. My mother held my hand as we walked into the grocery store together.

Poverty and prejudice had already taught me many things, but it had also rearranged my priorities. I didn't care about sports stars like so many American kids. No, the superstars in my eyes were the ones who didn't go hungry. So I'll never forget walking into that Piggly Wiggly.

My eyes widened, and maybe my mouth even fell open, when I saw the seemingly endless rows of food. That might not mean much to many Americans who were already used to this sight, but when you have starved to the point of nearly dying, that moment meant everything. That moment, to me, meant America.

My mother packed a shopping cart, went through the cash register line, then we pushed the cart toward the car. As she loaded our groceries, an older man walked up. I should have been prepared, but the food had lowered my defenses. Besides, I was only nine years old.

As I looked up at his red eyes, ready to share my happiness, he spit in my face.

His spit smelled of cigarettes and alcohol. As I tried to wipe the saliva off, he pointed his middle finger at my mother and spewed more bile.

"You chinks don't belong here," he snarled. "You need to go back to Vietnam."

Not only didn't he know the difference between China and Vietnam, he did not know my mother at all. Rather than cowering or retreating, this woman, who had faced an entire army who were filled with unreasoning hate, rammed the man with her shopping cart.

She hurt him enough to make him run. Even so, she had learned that racist cowards often came back with other racist cowards, so we got into the car and drove away.

On the ride home, I felt abused and defeated. But my mother said, as ever, "Smile and be brave." Then, with a knowing smile, she added, "After all, it's a beautiful Sunday afternoon."

That set the stage for my first year of American school. There, the richer and more privileged kids would often remind me of how poor I was. I was also reminded daily of how my clothes smelled like fish. The small holes in these supposedly fishy garments were gleefully ripped into bigger holes for the pleasure of degrading and laughing at me.

As we continued to live in North Carolina, we did the best we could, shared what happiness we had, and just kept going. I made it through first grade, then second. It could be very rough, but I remembered what my mother had taught me. I tried to smile and be brave.

But during the third grade, it got even rougher. "Substitute teacher day" was the worst. My Vietnamese name is Tú Tuân Làm. I give my American name as Tu Lam so people can pronounce it without getting too frustrated or angry. But on one particular day, a substitute teacher was overly insistent on trying to pronounce my name correctly.

His many failed attempts inspired my classmates to greater heights of derision, led by our class bully, Jake. Jake had a bad mouth along with a bad temper. He relished the very sound of profanity. His bad words and bad attitude had him repeating the third grade for disciplinary reasons, which is how he ended up in my class. Lucky me.

Jake took advantage of the situation and began convincing a majority of the class to throw trash at me while yelling racist names. The overly persistent substitute teacher finally had all he could stand.

"Enough!" he interrupted. "Be quiet!"

His hands trembled as he stood up. He pointed at the bully but then pointed at me too.

"You need to go with Jake to the principal's office," he shouted.

Confused, I pointed at myself to confirm that both the bully and the victim were being pointed at.

"Report to the principal's office!" he yelled, now in a legitimate rage.

Confused as well as embarrassed, I packed my books in my yellow hand-me-down backpack. Walking behind Jake down the hall, I couldn't help but feel unjustifiably punished, and having come from refugee camps, I knew what unjustifiable punishment felt like. Humiliated and scared, I entered Principal Duncan's office.

Principal Duncan was an old white man in his midfifties with a ready-to-retire attitude. He was wearing tight brown checkered slacks, with a short-sleeve buttoned shirt, in which he proudly wore his pocket protector. Standing up behind his desk, Mr. Duncan ordered that we sit and wait for our parents to pick us up.

I knew that, for me, would be a long wait. My mother did not have the time, freedom, or motor vehicle to pick me up. She was too busy trying to make ends meet.

Jake the Bully sat on the far left side of the principal's waiting room while I sat on the far right, hoping to survive the rest of the school day without further humiliation. No such luck. I looked at the floor, seeing my worn, scuffed, refugee, hand-me-down shoes. That was the moment I began to realize how truly defeated I felt.

Then I felt the tears begin to well up. *No, no, no, no,* I told myself. *Don't cry. Not here, not now.*

Holding back my tears as best I could, I tried to distract myself by listening to the office secretary hunt-and-peck away on her old typewriter. The rhythmic click-clack sounds of the manual machine blended with soft thuds as the occasional teacher walked in and out of the office to go about their business.

Still focusing on the ground, I then heard a sound that was new to me: the sound of high heels walking sharply and loudly across the hallway's tile floor. The noise quickly approached us like bullets slapping cement. Finally, the door swung open, and the bully's mother plowed in, yelling at everyone in the office.

"What is going on? Why did I get a call to pick up my son?"

The principal dropped his pen and stood up. Taking off his glasses, he said, "Your son Jake has called this Chinese boy here a chink."

Although I was not Chinese, the degrading word hurt me all the same. Even so, I continued to stare at the ground. I heard the high heels clack toward Jake. Out the corner of my eye, I could see her grab her son's hand, but instead of going away, she came over to where I sat.

"Look at me," I heard her say.

I looked up at her towering over me—a third grader staring up at an angry mother gripping the hand of her bullying child.

"Jake is right," she said. "You kind of people don't belong here. Go back to where you came from."

Now with the support of his mother, Jake laughed as they left the office together, leaving me to sit there, stripped of all dignity, and berated in front of everyone. Not only that, but the very people who were empowered to support, defend, and educate me ignored it.

Finally, the injustice and abuse of these illogical and hateful years welled up and burst out. I cried harder than I ever had before. I cried so hard I began to hyperventilate. My bawling got so loud that the principal finally looked up.

But instead of helping, he simply snapped, "Wait in the hallway."

His dismissive attitude actually helped me muster up the small remainder of pride I had left. I managed to make it out to the hall and control my weeping enough not to get any more attention. I still knew that my mother couldn't come get me the way Jake's mother had, so I simply stood there, trying not to cry, until school was out and I could catch the bus home.

I was so upset that I decided it was best not to tell my mother what had happened. After all, she had enough on her plate just trying to provide for our family.

Arriving home, I went straight to our one bedroom. Sitting alone, I reflected on my horrible day. I said nothing about it to my family, despite the upsetting memories of my hateful classmates. Instead, I finished my homework and prepared for bed.

I was sitting on the edge of the mattress when my mother walked into the room. She always knew when something was wrong, so she smiled and sat next to me. For a moment we just sat there, mother and son, her smiling patiently at me, the room, the town we lived in, and life. Then she spoke.

"There will always be bad days," she said softly, "but what do we learn from these bad days? How can we expect to find deeper meaning in life unless we first experience bad days?" Her smile grew wider and brighter, and she hugged me. "We should be grateful for each moment of each day no matter how bad," she told me, "for we should have died many years ago."

First I had to take in my mother's words. Then I had to try to fully understand them. But I couldn't quite yet.

"What do you mean?" I asked her, honestly confused. "Why did we almost die, Mom?"

On the edge of the used mattress, staring into the small apartment, she seemed to make a decision that she had been waiting for until this very moment.

For the first time, she told me the story of the life I didn't remember.

# 2

Back in the 1960s, according to the pictures I've seen and the family I've talked to, my mother was a young, beautiful, feisty woman who lived out in the Vietnamese countryside. Although she was considered pretty by everyone, her reputation was that she was as wild as a tiger.

Therefore, she was often beaten by her extremely strong mother. My grandmother's strength came from carrying buckets of water and rice sacks through the village every day to supply the roadside restaurant she ran.

My mother told me that my grandmother had knocked out grown men in the village and would often try to do the same to her. But even though my mother was beaten, she continued to get in trouble in school. She had a wild spirit and would often get into that trouble by trying to protect her weaker classmates from bullies.

My grandmother had to be tough to survive and, either consciously or unconsciously, had raised her daughter to be just as tough. So, fed up with both the verbal and physical abuse her mother consistently dished out, my mother left the village as soon as she could to find some sort of life in Saigon.

My mother had worked with my grandmother in a restaurant serving pho—Vietnamese noodle soup—so she was able to find similar work in Saigon. My father was an engineer, helping to rebuild our city after more than nineteen years of war, and often frequented that restaurant.

One thing led to another, and they became husband and wife and had their first son, my older brother, in 1971—just in time for the United States to withdraw its troops from the country. My mother skipped over the story of the following few years, as if those tumultuous times were nothing new, and came to me. Mine was hardly an auspicious beginning.

According to her, I was born on a cold cement floor in the basement of a Saigon hospital on December 17, 1974, in the Chinese Year of the Wood Tiger, within the hour of the tiger, while bombs fell around us. She said she was shielding her new-born baby from incoming artillery fire.

My mother rarely went into details. I've pieced together this entire story over the years, and it was not an easy story for me to hear at any age, or for my mother to tell—especially since she's only gotten more strong-willed over the decades.

So, according to her, I came into this world while fragments of the hospital fell down around us as Saigon was bombarded. Rather than dwell on our personal danger, my mother said she saw families holding on to one another as their homes collapsed around them. Rather than tell me of my screams, she said she heard other children's screams echoing through the streets as they tried to wake up their dead parents.

But 1974 was more than the Year of the Wood Tiger. It was also one of the worst years of the Vietnam War for the South Vietnamese, of which my mother and I were just two. The American troops had left the country, and I was born on the losing side. Unbeknownst to me, within three months I had lost all the freedom I never knew I had to the Communist North Vietnamese.

The occupying North Vietnamese Army (NVA) poured into our city of Saigon and immediately executed anyone they thought opposed their Communist occupation. And according to evidence from television, newspapers, movie documentaries, and my mother, that was putting it mildly. But those sources seemed to be quickly forgotten by those outside the conflict. For my family, the persecution and fear went on twenty-four hours a day, seven days a week, for years.

I realize now that I was actually lucky to be so young and able to forget so much so easily.

In truth, I really wasn't even aware that North Vietnamese soldiers would break into the homes of innocent civilians to loot, abuse, and worse. These soldiers took money and valuables from anybody they decided to target, and anyone who tried to stop them, in words or action, would be killed on the spot. Or if the soldiers wanted to make an example to intimidate the neighbors, they would be dragged out onto the street and murdered there.

People who tried to protect their family and belongings were set upon and repeatedly stabbed by the NVA soldiers' rifles' fixed bayonets. As my mother said, the screams of their unarmed victims echoed through the city as the Communist regime forcibly stripped away all freedoms, seeking to violently break the will of Saigon residents.

I was only three months old and cradled in my mother's arms as NVA soldiers kicked open our front door. Our third-floor apartment was immediately overrun with soldiers screeching commands as they stabbed their bayonets at us. Although my mother was in her twenties, small and slim, she stood her ground and showed the soldiers no fear as she continued to hold me while reaching down to find my four-year-old brother's hand. When she spoke, it was only for her eldest son, not for the soldiers.

"Be brave," she said. Understandably the "and smile" was absent.

My father stood in front of my mother and pleaded with the soldiers not to harm us. He was answered by the nearest soldier, who hit him in the face with the butt of his rifle. Then the other soldiers joined in and beat my father to the floor.

Emboldened, another soldier grabbed my brother and yanked him away from my mother. My brother cried out as the soldier hurled him to the ground. By this time my father was beaten so badly that he was unable to stand. Still holding me, my mother kneeled to shield my father's beaten body and finally spoke directly to the invaders.

"You can take our belongings and you can kill us," she said, "but I am not afraid, and I'd rather die today with my family than be separated."

That might sound to some like an exaggeration or even self-aggrandizement. But you don't know my mother. And you haven't heard anything yet.

She told me that the soldiers screamed at her as they grabbed her hair, then pulled, pushed, and beat our family down the stairs and into the street. The smell of gunfire, burning buildings, and dead bodies saturated the air as my family was thrown to the pavement. Four stories above us, my grandfather prepared for what he knew was coming.

According to my mother, her father was a remarkable man. He lived on the top floor of the building, and just by the growing sounds of clomping feet and snarling commands, he knew that the soldiers were getting closer to his apartment. Even so, he stayed where he was, in front of his saltwater aquarium, making sure his beautiful, exotic fish had one last meal before the soldiers entered. With his experience and streetwise wisdom, he made an unforgettable first impression. So he sat in front of his fish tank and waited for the NVA to arrive.

Any aquarium in 1974 Saigon was notable, but apparently my grandfather's fish tank was truly imposing. Not only was it massive, taking up much of the room, but the aquatic life within it was even more beautiful. My grandfather would travel where he needed to, and spend whatever he could afford, to outfit his aquarium as he wanted. And what he wanted was awe-inspiring beauty.

His wife would often argue about the time and money he put into his hobby, but my grandfather didn't pay her much mind. He wanted what he wanted, and he had his reasons—reasons we would learn at a very important moment in our lives.

So my grandfather was sitting in front of his aquarium when the soldiers kicked in the door. The NVA shoved in, shouting, but he simply continued to admire his aquarium and ignore them. And while they yanked him out and hit him as they hustled him down to join our family in the street, they did not wreck or even touch the aquarium—which they could have easily done.

My mother comforted my grandfather and us all as the NVA soldiers put the collected captives into groups on the street. A North Vietnamese Army officer then appeared. He had a list of names. He called them out, one by one. If someone responded, he continued. If someone didn't respond to a name being called out, the soldiers beat people until someone identified the person whose name was called.

My family stiffened in dread as my uncle's name was called. He was a South Vietnamese officer who had served alongside the American military. My family watched as the soldiers dragged him from his home. He was thrown into a group of people considered to have political power, higher education, and, worst of all, a history of working with the American armed forces.

My uncle's family screamed in horror as an NVA squad prepared for the execution. This was not a firing squad. There were no blindfolds or last requests here. These were sadistic soldiers preparing for a cold-blooded slaughter of unarmed Saigon citizens.

As NVA soldiers put the group onto their knees, my mother looked at me and my brother, smiled, and said, "Close your eyes and be brave."

Of course I don't remember if we did. I don't even remember the machine-gun fire. But my mother will never forget that, when the smoke cleared, what remained was my uncle's corpse splayed among many other bullet-riddled bodies.

She also remembered that the heat from the war-torn streets had become almost unbearable by then. The smoke from nearby burning buildings hurt my family's tearing eyes. The hot concrete burned through our knees as we hopelessly waited for the next horror. We didn't have to wait long.

An NVA officer called out another list of names. These were the names of anyone they decided had supported the American government. At first their fates seemed merciful when compared to what had already happened. After all, they weren't executed on the spot. Instead, they were all sent to so-called re-education camps in the surrounding jungle.

Only later did I learn that these were, in reality, torture camps where the NVA would brutally break a person's body, mind, and will. It's no secret that hundreds of thousands were imprisoned there, and many died from starvation, abuse, and hard labor— which they ironically called the living conditions in these camps.

So my family survived that awful day, but there were more awful days to come. The old South Vietnamese government was replaced by officials from the north. These officials created laws to restrict the freedoms of the South Vietnamese people. Higher taxes were imposed to support the new government's Communist agenda. But none of this curtailed the NVA soldiers' greed, sadism, and power-lust. Once they got a taste of looting and pillaging under the guise of collecting taxes, they did not give it up. Anyone who had a problem with that got a ride to the re-education camps, a bayonet to the body, or a bullet in the head.

Not surprisingly, these orders usually came for the poor who could not afford to pay the heavy taxes imposed by the new government. There were stories of families enslaved by the North Vietnamese to carry out hard manual labor at these camps. Prisoners who were injured or sick from the terrible conditions were brought out to the jungles and executed.

I now know that several of my uncles were prisoners at these camps. My mother told me the story of one who had escaped.

He was even able to make his way home to his pregnant wife. My aunt quietly asked my mother for help. My mother traveled at night after curfew to visit her brother—an infraction that could have resulted in her capture, assault, torture, or murder if she had been caught. But she wasn't caught, and brought them money and food to help them attempt an escape.

Since her brother was already a fugitive, they couldn't wait long. My uncle and pregnant aunt started out in the darkness. Their plan was to walk through the jungle into Cambodia, with the hopes of eventually making it into Thailand. They traveled as light as possible, with only a few personal belongings.

All major roads and bridges were manned with armed NVA guards so they needed to make their way through the wilderness, which was also heavily patrolled by NVA soldiers, already well trained to capture the fleeing refugees who had tried to escape before them. Some South Vietnamese hired guides, but no one knew where these self-proclaimed guides' loyalties lay. Once someone escaped from the camps, their names and rewards for their recapture were announced, so many so-called guides would take the escapees' money and turn them in anyway.

Traitors and guards were not my aunt and uncle's only problem. The NVA didn't have hundreds of land mines to plant, but they knew how to prepare tiger traps throughout the wilderness. These were leaf-covered pits, filled with sharpened punji stakes, which were all too easy to step onto during the night.

My aunt and uncle trudged blindly through the hot, steamy darkness, but it was all for naught. Although they tried the best they could, they were eventually recaptured and then brought to the camps. My aunt was interred in a fetid prison cell, while my uncle was sent to a labor camp.

The punishment for trying to escape was barbaric. They took enough flesh from the bottom of my uncle's foot that he was unable to run or barely stand. When he wasn't locked in a bamboo-covered pit, he was chained among the animals. He was swarmed with mosquitoes until he contracted malaria.

Meanwhile, my aunt lay on a cheap mattress atop a bamboo bed in a dark, freezing cell made up of green mildew-covered walls, with just one red bucket in the corner. There, she gave unassisted birth to a daughter, on a cold wet concrete floor.

Somehow they survived, but they were never the people they had been before their attempted escape. Still, their tragic example only convinced my mother that anything was worth the risk of fleeing such cruel stupidity.

Once the collaborators were killed and the sympathizers sent away, we were allowed to return to our homes, where we now lived under Communist rule. My mother recalled this as the oppression years.

Even so, I was told I still had somewhat of a normal childhood. I grew up in that third-floor apartment we had been dragged out of, one floor down from my grandmother, my grandfather, and his aquarium. We survived as best we could on my parents' income, but danger always seemed close by.

One warm summer night in the city, when I was about three years old, my mother was cleaning up the restaurant when a government tax collector arrived, accompanied by a bunch of NVA soldiers. Although my mother was upset that the new government allowed the soldiers to take funds and supplies from any business they wanted, she gave the civil servant her earnings for that day because she knew what happened to workers who didn't. The soldiers then told her that they needed more money and that they would be following her home to get it.

I was home with my father when the soldiers came. They threatened to send us all to different labor camps if they didn't get what they wanted. My father gave them all the money we had on hand—enough that the tax collector and the soldiers left without beating anyone or destroying anything.

That night, for the first time, my mother spoke of escaping Vietnam.

My father reminded her that many of the refugees fleeing the area were either captured and tortured in labor camps, or died of starvation, sickness, or murder. My mother replied that she would rather us die together than allow her two sons to grow up in Vietnam the way it was then. Although my father was understandably hesitant, he well knew the tiger he had married and agreed to try to find an escape route for us.

My father was a quarter Chinese mixed with Vietnamese, came from an educated family, worked in an office near the docks, and was well-liked. After work the next day he met with one of the ship captains, who many locals said had successfully escorted refugees out of Vietnam. My father asked him how much it would cost. The captain didn't blink.

This human smuggling practice was a well-kept but also well-known secret among the oppressed South Vietnamese. The price for freedom was five gold bars for each adult and three gold bars for each child. Then the captain told my father that he would be making the next escape run in two days. He said if we planned on going on this trip, we should show up with only one small bag per family and bring the gold because each refugee had to pay before boarding the boat. Eight at night was the time of the escape, and the captain advised my father not to be late.

At home, my mother immediately agreed and set to work. For the next two days she carefully packed and stealthily went around to say goodbye to her friends and family. Finally, it was the night of the escape. The bag was packed. The gold was ready. My brother and I were dressed and set to go. My mother waited.

My father did not come home on time that night. And when he finally did show up, it was long after eight o'clock, and apparently, he said nothing about it.

But it's not a good idea to poke at a caged tiger. It was no secret that my mother was very upset at my father for making us miss the boat. What was a secret, and one my mother never shared with me, was why.

But a few days later, my grandfather came downstairs to our apartment. He sat quietly and listened to my mother vent.

"I mean, how could he be late on such an important day?" she cried. "What man does that to his family?"

She went on and on until my grandfather quietly interrupted. He told my mother that he had gotten word that the boat we were supposed to escape on had been hijacked by pirates. Everyone on board had been killed.

My mother stood there in shock. She knew the journey was risky, but until then the reality of just how risky hadn't hit home for her.

As my grandfather spoke, she walked over and picked me up. She smiled through her tears and held me as she repeated to him that she would rather die than allow her sons to grow up under this oppression. As silent tears rolled down her cheek, she turned to him and asked for help.

It was as if he had been waiting for that. He said to give him a few days.

My father may have been well-liked, well-educated, and well-dressed, but nothing compared to my grandfather. He was a strong-willed man who had survived the Indochina War and the Vietnam civil war because he was cunning and street-smart and had trusted contacts everywhere.

For the next few days, he sat down by the ship docks, studying the schedule of the weekly escapes, the NVA guards' patrols, and where they went to stop the fleeing refugees. He studied the various options. Making his decision, he contacted a fishing-boat captain friend who had served alongside the American Navy during the war. That friend knew the most direct route to Malaysia and promised he could make the journey in forty-eight hours.

Then they got down to details. The captain acknowledged that the trip would be risky, so he would require seven gold bars

for each adult and four gold bars for each child. He informed
my grandfather that we had less then twenty-four hours before
the escape.

But rather than run back to the apartment and tell my mother
everything, he calmly invited my parents to come by his apartment for dinner. Only during the meal did he tell my parents
about the escape, the deadline, and the details. It would be on a
small wooden fishing boat. We could bring no bags with us—
only what we could carry on our bodies.

Finally my grandfather told my father the cost. After repeatedly paying off the NVA "tax collectors," my parents no longer
had that kind of money. My parents sat there hopeless and helpless, seeing their best chance to escape go up like so much smoke
from one of my grandfather's hand-rolled cigarettes.

As he looked on my parents' sad faces, my grandfather stood
and walked over to his couch. He reached for a small, artfully
designed and painted tin can on a Chinese-style coffee table.
From the can he pulled out his favorite rolling paper, then a
pinch of his favorite tobacco. Slowing filling the paper, he seemingly casually rolled his cigarette. Then, crossing his legs and
sitting back, he lit it.

Only after a few satisfying puffs, did he stand and go over to
his favorite place in front of his aquarium. By this time both my
parents had seemingly forgotten about their troubles and were
staring at him. And, as they watched, my grandfather started to
take apart the water tank's black frame.

Pulling off the side of the aluminum, he revealed his biggest
secret. So many times, the Communist soldiers had entered my
grandparents' apartment. They were looking for money and
valuables but were always distracted by and admired his collection of exotic marine life. Little did they know that the aluminum frame that lined the aquarium was hiding bars of gold.

He disassembled the frame as my parents stared in amazement.
Gathering the gold bars for our escape, he told my parents that

the ship would be leaving at nine o'clock and that we should not be late. He made my mother promise that if we were to survive this escape she would do what she could to ensure that the family became Americans.

He then told my mother the story of her older sister. During the war, a Green Beret officer's Special Forces camp had gotten overrun by NVA soldiers, and he had been stabbed in the ribs with an SKS bayonet. He said the soldier had been sent to a Saigon hospital, where my mother's older sister met him.

During his recovery my aunt would often visit him. Although my grandfather did not think the officer would survive his wounds, the Green Beret proved him wrong. Not only did he survive, he fell in love with my aunt and eventually married her—unlike so many American soldiers who abandoned the Vietnamese women they said they loved. He even took her back to the United States, despite the racism and hatred many would greet them with.

My grandfather told my mother that the Green Beret was a good man and that he would help.

"But first," he concluded, "you must survive."

# 3

It was the night of a full moon, and the air was warm. My family could smell the ocean as they approached the boat. Like so many others bobbing around the docks, it was a relatively small old wooden fishing boat. What set it apart from the others was that there was a long line of people waiting on the dock next to it. The boat could normally hold forty people comfortably, but tonight it was crammed with close to a hundred.

My mother cradled me in her arms as we boarded. Whatever the captain's relationship had been with my grandfather, it didn't have any effect on our treatment now. Seemingly wounded by years of war, he didn't care about people anymore—only money. To him we were just cargo, so the captain brusquely shoved us into the hold of the boat.

Even though my mother carried me, we were all but crushed by the people crammed around us in the low-ceilinged, unlit, confined space. The captain hissed that we had to pack in tight. My mother quickly found and all but claimed a small space where our family could sit close together.

A haughty woman next to her snapped that there wasn't enough room for us there. My mother apologized, saying that there was nowhere else for us to sit. The woman then informed her that she was a very important person, and we had to move. My mother calmly ignored the lady. After all, how important could she be if she was squeezed into the hold along with everyone else? My mother could have reminded the woman that we were all, literally, in the same boat. But she did not. Instead, she stood her ground.

At that time, many South Vietnamese were trying to escape the country. Many government employees were able to leave on military planes when the American soldiers withdrew. Others were not lucky enough to fly out, but unlike my pregnant aunt and her fugitive husband, they managed to make the dangerous trek across the country's borders. My family joined thousands of others who would soon be termed "boat people."

The full moon reflected on the South China Sea as the little fishing boat we were hidden on started out, heading southwest. In one way we were lucky. Since we were in the dark bottom deck of the boat, we did not see the dangers of the nearly four hundred miles we needed to travel. In another way, everyone older than me was not lucky, since they could still imagine and worry about those dangers.

My mother held me, smiled, and whispered for me to be brave. But all around us, the sounds of fear, desperation, and loss echoed through the darkness. The very important lady next to us was now weeping. My mother reached out and held her hand, telling her that "everything will be okay." The thumping noise of the boat's small engine sounded like a struggling heartbeat as it pushed us deeper into the unknown.

However, for the captain of the ship it was all too known. My grandfather had seen this once-happy man change over the years of Communist control. He went from being a friendly optimist to a selfish pessimist, willing to treat people like animals as long as he had their gold. And now, as he stood at the controls above deck, he could see hundreds of boats in the distance—all with large spotlights searching for fleeing refugees. But he had the experience to avoid this armada and worked with all his knowledge and skill to complete the trip as fast as he could.

At one point, as he skirted the edges of the Gulf of Thailand, he had to shut the engine down because he knew the sound would attract pirates. Like their predecessors dating back to the fourteenth century, these seagoing raiders from surrounding countries like Thailand, Indonesia, and the Philippines soon saw the increasing numbers of South Vietnamese escapees as easy targets.

And it quickly became known that they showed no mercy. Not only would they rob everything but they thought nothing of raping the women before killing everyone, including the children. The success rate of these monsters attracted more criminals to take advantage of the helpless refugees. So the captain knew that there were literally hundreds of pirates waiting to profit from our escape and did everything he could to avoid them—knowing that he would not be spared if they attacked.

Thankfully, the captain's experience saw us through. Our boat arrived off the coast of Malaysia in just two days. Everyone was thankful, but also exhausted. The captain had not stored enough food or water, choosing to use that space for more paying passengers. The boat was already reeking of excrement, urine, and sweat as the Malaysia Coast Guard approached.

Within moments, the relief turned to terror as the coast guard cutters started shooting. They announced that we were not welcome in their country, and Malaysia was no longer accepting refugees. The stunned passengers could only stand and stare as the coast guard personnel boarded, attached a thick rope, and used it to drag our fishing boat back out into the South China Sea—for hours!

Finally, when they thought it was far enough that no current or tide could bring us back to land, they destroyed the fishing boat's engine, cut the rope, and left us adrift.

In these waters, at this time, in this condition, leaving us adrift really meant leaving us to die. We had been so close to escape and rescue, but now we were close to death. Within hours, there was virtually no food or drinkable water. Some passengers started to turn on each other. What started out as a short trip to Malaysia had now turned into a desperate struggle for survival, but with no engine, sail, or oars, there was nothing anyone could do.

After all these years, I'm grateful I don't remember such terror as our boat drifted farther and farther into the unknown sea. But my mother will never forget the growing stench of urine, feces, fish, and salt water as days turned to weeks. Soon even the crying had stopped as the passengers were too starved to have the strength and too dehydrated to create tears. But the coughing only got louder and more frequent as sickness spread.

The heat of the sun, combined with the lack of water and food, led to death. The corpses were thrown overboard. Even in desperation no one wanted to eat human meat. The important lady who had yelled at my mother that first night became ill. My mother did what she could to comfort her.

The only relief came from the small buckets of water my mother told me she had put out to catch whatever rain fell, which was too little, too seldom. On the night of our thirtieth day adrift my mother stared at the last almost-empty bucket, then looked over to where my brother and I slept as if in comas. Our lips were cracked from the heat, and our bodies were starting to form ulcers due to the lack of blood flow. She did not know how long she stared at us. The dehydration and starvation weakened her so much that she fell in and out of consciousness.

That night my mother said she cried tearlessly, in silence. She looked up at the moonlight coming through the rotting deck of the boat. Then she woke up my brother. She told him to drink half of the remaining water in the bucket. My mother then touched my seemingly lifeless body, waking me up to drink the last water she had.

Later that night, there was a huge storm. The captain worried that we would capsize as the wind and the waves pulled the boat farther into the dark sea. But the next day my mother thanked the heavens for filling the buckets with drinking water, allowing our family and the few other survivors to live a few days more.

That night my mother said she held me, her legs in pain from sitting for a month. As we lay dying she told me to smile and be brave. She then reached out into the dark to hold the hand of the angry lady, but the important woman's hand was now cold. She had died in the darkness moments before.

Exhaustion and weakness had us all drifting in and out of consciousness—each time making my mother wonder if this would be the last time she would see us. Finally, one night she closed her eyes, and they didn't open again until the miracle happened.

Light woke her up. Light opened her eyes. But it was not sunlight. It was from a search beacon coming from the deck of a Russian supply boat.

It had been coursing out from Vietnam when it spotted us. The same Communist ideology that had ripped apart our country, the same ideology the South Vietnamese people had fought against for many years, now held our lives in their hands. The Russian captain had a decision to make. He could leave us to die since we were ostensibly the enemy, or he could help us.

He chose humanity. That morning, the Russian medical crew boarded our boat and carried the remaining survivors to their sick bay. The smell of human waste was so foul that it made some of the Russians vomit. My mother held onto me when the Russians finally made their way down to the lower deck.

My mother and father were unable to walk due to being lost at sea for so long. My mother was so weak that she could barely hold me. Finally, as the Russians helped us, she collapsed onto the urine-soaked floor.

She woke many hours later on a Russian sick-bay bed, screaming for her family. She tried to get up but fell, ripping an IV from her arm. A Russian nurse quickly helped her back to bed. My mother asked the nurse for her family. The nurse did not speak Vietnamese but left the room and quickly returned with us, and we sat by my mother's bed for the next few days as she recovered.

Happy ending? Not quite. After the Russian crew staved off starvation and death for we few remaining survivors, they loaded us back onto our boat. They informed the captain that the motor could not be fixed at sea. They would have to pull us along. The captain thanked them for saving us.

"You were lucky that we were coming out of Vietnam," the captain explained. "If we had spotted you going in the opposite direction, we would have been duty-bound to pull you back into Vietnam. But because you were going in the other direction, maritime law gave us no choice but to help you."

Even so, the smell of waste and sea salt still filled the fishing-boat air. We all struggled to breathe because of that and the almost-unbearable heat. My mother pulled me close to her as the engines of the massive Russian ship roared. The vibration from the huge vessel shook our small boat. Suddenly, we felt a violent tug as the Russian ship started to pull our fragile lives to safety. Our little boat bounced along as this mammoth vessel ripped through the China Sea.

After a day, the Russians pulled our boat to a dock located on one of the southern islands of Indonesia. The Indonesian military were waiting. They weren't happy, but they weren't homicidal. People in uniform ordered us to quickly load their buses. Those buses transported us to what seemed to be a hastily created refugee camp between a dirt road and a beach.

The cool sea breeze gave us a little comfort as it provided a flow of air through the open windows. A small lady then stepped onto our bus, and my mother was pleased to see that she was Vietnamese rather than Indonesian. Maybe she would try to be more understanding. The woman yelled as loud as she could, advising us that soldiers would escort us to a processing area.

As we got off the bus, sullen, seemingly uncaring, and reluctant Indonesian soldiers ordered us to move to the beach. Once there we were ordered to sit down in groups until they could process us. The Vietnamese woman went to a little grass hut that she used as an office. Soldiers stood guard to make sure we didn't leave; then, once again, we waited as the hot tropical sun beat down on our depleted bodies.

Refugees begged for water from the Indonesian guards. The pleas were ignored. So, my mother told me, we sat for hours more, wondering if we were about to endure another nightmare.

But then a bus of Indonesian monks arrived. Dressed in orange robes and leather sandals they walked down to our group, carrying buckets of water and food. They asked the guards' permission to help us. The guards begrudgingly gave it by moving aside for the monks to approach. Smiling beneficently, they offered us food and water.

As one monk approached my family, my mother got on her knees, put her hands together in a praying position, and thanked them for their compassion. The monk's smile grew even wider and warmer, then he kneeled next to my mother. He looked around at our family. Smiling and touching my brother's head, he pulled an apple out of his robe and handed it to him. My mother cried, thanking him.

The monk moved on to me. He gently touched the ulcers on my legs and ankles before reaching into his robe again to pull out a medicated cream that he then gently applied to my wounds. Once more, he smiled, only this time he pulled an orange from his robe. Still smiling, he peeled it and handed me a piece.

As my mother thanked the monk again for his blessings, I took a bite. If it hadn't been for my chapped lips I might have forgotten that orange as I thankfully forgot everything else about this terrible trip. But the orange's juice seeped into my cracked lips and cemented a memory in my brain.

I know that I was only a little more than three years old at the time, but I can tell you that, despite its sting, an orange has never tasted so good.

# 4

I remember running.

I don't remember being born during the bombing. I don't remember seeing members of my family executed right in front of us as my mother held me in her arms. I don't remember the weeks I lay languishing from exposure, starvation, and lack of water on a boat drifting at sea. I was too young then.

But I remember running. You could say I was born running, as I came to a child's full awareness in that jungle, surrounded by that sea.

My brother yelled, "Slow down," as I ran barefoot through the jungle toward the beach.

I was five years old, laughing, with both hands holding on to a worn pool flotation toy around my waist. Finally breaking through the foliage, my little feet touched the warm tropical sand. I didn't stop to savor it. I just kept running. My brother stopped at the edge of the sand to catch his breath.

"Stop!" he gasped.

But my tiger spirit was too wild to listen. My bare feet kicked off the hot sand and onto an old wooden pier that looked like the broken ribs of a tree's skeleton. Hardly pausing, I hopped over one torn, cracked hole after another until I finally reached the end of the broken old dock. By then my brother had gotten to the edge of the pier and started yelling again.

"Stop! Stop! Don't jump!"

I heard him, but I didn't turn around. Instead, I stood on the lip of the pier and looked down at the water. What once was fresh ocean was now polluted with trash and even floating human waste.

My brother finally got close enough to speak without shouting.

"Don't jump," he warned.

He said that Mom told him to watch over me. He said that Mom told us not to go into the water. He said we shouldn't even be on this side of the beach because of the riptides—riptides that had already pulled many people out to sea, where they had drowned trying to break away from the powerful currents.

But as I stood there, looking down into the sickening, smelly surface, I could feel the spirit of the tiger flowing through me. Finally, as my brother got even closer, I looked at him and smiled. That smile stopped him dead and filled his face with worry mixed with disbelief.

"Don't do it," he said, half warning and half begging.

Closing my eyes, I leaped off the pier. I felt myself falling. I felt my little legs hit the warm tropical water. I immediately started swimming away from the trash that had accumulated around the dock. I finally made it away from the waste, kicking with both legs.

My brother yelled at me from the pier, but I don't remember the words. All I remember is the feeling of the water coursing around me, getting stronger all the time. He probably saw that too. I didn't see him jump in, but I do remember him swimming to my side, wrapping a worn rope around the flotation device at my waist and dragging me back to the beach.

Soon we were walking toward the camp, the jungle heat drying us faster than any towel could.

"You can't run off like that," he told me, more tired than angry. "Mother would be worried."

He turned his face away to look at the darkening sky. My brother knew the dangers that the night brought to these jungles. Many people had disappeared in nights.

But I was five, surviving in the biggest, strangest playground I had ever seen. I smiled at my brother and then we ran back home. I really didn't understand that home was a refugee camp. I didn't know it was on a southern Indonesian island. All I knew for sure was that I was with thousands of others who looked like me and spoke the same language I did, living in a crowded cluster of grass huts made with wooden posts, wrapped in plastic, and tied together by rope.

We lived on a dirt floor covered with cardboard and more plastic. We slept atop a thin worn stained mattress. What served as our kitchen was located outside, a circular firepit made of stacked rocks, with a bent old wire grill placed on top. There my mother would heat water and cook what she could.

Outside of that, the only area that seemed important was a headquarters hut, where refugees went to receive mail—the more important of which were care packages, and the most important of which was information on which country would accept which nationality of refugee.

Just like everything before the age of five, I found out about this later. My parents told me that refugees had to submit letters to different countries requesting to be accepted. There was only a small list of places that accepted Vietnamese refugees, but those places had long lists of requirements. Still, once the country approved the request, the refugees were given the opportunity to leave the camp and emigrate there. The entire process could take years, no matter whether the answer was yes or no.

Again, I knew little or nothing about that then. But I did know about survival. There were nearby streams that once had fresh water, but now were used for bathing and cleaning clothes, among other things, by hundreds if not thousands of people. So that meant my brother and I had to walk through the jungles every day to gather water from upstream of the camp if we didn't want to get sick.

We also had to search for firewood. Given the large population of refugees, firewood became an issue around the camp. *Issue* is a nice way of putting it. It became a point of contention, jealousy, desperation, arguments, fighting, and even theft. That meant my brother and I had to walk even farther away from the camp to find wood—and then be extra careful on the way back not to get robbed.

It wasn't uncommon to see dead bodies in the jungle. Even I knew that refugees were beaten up, and worse, out there. I didn't go running off on my own.

While my brother and I searched for wood and water, my father worked all day on the docks—the ones away from the riptides—repairing motors for local fishermen. There was little pay, but the fishermen would often give him some of their catch as a bonus. And here, food might have been even more important than money.

Meanwhile, my mother worked at a fruit stand in a makeshift shop area that some more enterprising, skilled refugees had set up to sell food and services to other refugees and any locals who were willing to go among refugees. My mother would often cook and clean there, to make money that she could add to my father's earnings.

Between their jobs, we had enough to barely survive. Even so, there were days we went without eating, but my parents always made sure that my brother and I were fed first—if the jungle rodents didn't get there before we did. The smells from the camp brought in many creatures from the tropical forest.

There were dozens of species of rats, squirrels, and even porcupines in Indonesia. And any one of them who got inside would tear away at our supplies. Worse, not only would they take things, they would leave waste which was filled with disease.

Of course, the wet jungle vegetation was also a breeding ground for mosquitoes which, with thousands of refugees crammed in the camp, feasted a lot more than we did. Malaria was a constant problem that came in only two categories: the ill and the dead.

My mother told us that there was a graveyard outside the camps. But it was a hastily made cemetery where the heavy tropical rain would reveal parts of the corpses shoved into the shallow graves. Local monks would often go there to burn incense and bless the bodies that could not rest in peace.

My mother constantly warned us that we should be respectful of wandering spirits, so of course, I was curious. But I only neared that graveyard once. I'll never forget the first time I smelled a dead body. It will be forever burned into my mind.

There was a small aid station located in the headquarters hut. Voluntary workers and nurses labored around the clock to treat diseases caused by the poor living conditions. Given their lack of funds, they could only give out one mosquito net per family. But even those nets might not help when powerful tropical storms hit without warning.

One windy afternoon, my mother was serving soup to a group of aid workers when an uneasy feeling came over her, unsettling her own tiger spirit. She hastily asked one of her friends to watch over the cooking station while she looked for me and my brother. She ran as fast as she could, looking everywhere. She ran into our plastic-wrapped hovel, calling our names, but we were not there.

By the time she emerged from the hut, the wind had picked up even more. She raced to the docks, running over to our father. He didn't know where we were either, so they immediately rushed around in a panic, calling out our names over and over again. But there was no answer.

I didn't hear them where I stood alone, back on the riptide dock, still wearing a ragged floatation toy around my waist, staring at the coming storm. I was absolutely fascinated. I could see the tides building up. I looked into the storm's face and felt its incredible energy. I was drawn to it. I wanted to feel its power. I wanted to be part of it.

Suddenly I jumped off the dock again. I was back in the water, swimming. The waves were massive this time. Before I had felt alive. This time I felt energized. But the power quickly got too much for me. I tried to go back. I couldn't. Something was pulling me toward the storm.

I turned around in a panic, but I couldn't even see the dock anymore. I couldn't swim back. I kicked frantically with both legs. It didn't work. Almost immediately I was being dragged out toward the storm again. The tides were pulling me out further into the massive ocean. I didn't know what to do.

Then, suddenly, I felt a jerk from my flotation device, pulling me back. I looked around, and it was my brother.

Somehow his presence gave me strength I didn't know I had. We both swam so hard. It seemed impossible, but we got back to shore. We barely made it. I lay on the beach, surrounded by trash, and took great gulps of air until I felt a slap on my head.

"What were you thinking?" cried my brother.

I started crying. I don't know what I had been thinking. How was a five-year-old refugee to know why he wanted to be part of that powerful, commanding storm? I didn't know what to say to him. Thankfully he took care of that.

"We have to go home," he said, helping me up. "The storm is coming."

Somehow, I instinctively knew how he'd found me in the nick of time. Just like me, his energy was drawn to the storm too.

Then my brother and I were running again—running as fast as we could as the wailing wind whipped around us, making the vegetation seemingly come alive and slap at us. We raced back to the camp, slipping and sliding on the muddy ground. My brother grabbed me again, keeping me from falling.

"Let's go!" he urged over the wind's roar.

We ran into the camp, the sight of my mother pushing me on.

"Mama!" I cried, running faster.

She also picked up speed, running to meet me. As soon as she got close enough, she slapped me on the head.

Just as I reacted to that, she dropped down, hugging me, and cried. As she did that, my brother, the rat, tattled on me.

"It's all his fault," he cried. "I told him not to go to that side of the beach!"

My mom picked me up and started to run back to our home, my brother trying to tell my father, or anybody willing to listen, how stupid his little brother was.

That night the storm tore through, ripping the camp apart. Joining the noise of the wind were screams and crying. I heard my mother praying, hoping we could just survive the night.

The next morning the storm broke. The clothes that weren't on our backs were gone. What remained of the camp, what remained of our lives, was scattered around us.

As we waited to see what came next, my mother sat next to me. She looked at me with an expression I couldn't understand and said one word.

"Why?"

When I couldn't explain why, her expression changed. She recognized something in me that was also in her. It was the spirit of the tiger.

"So curious," she said softly. "So fearless." I stared at her, and she stared back knowingly. "We have to be careful," she told me with certainty. "It's such a strong spirit."

I didn't completely understand what my mother was saying, but on that morning, I just nodded.

Life went on in the camp. It was rebuilt, if you could call it that. My father and mother continued to work while my brother and I continued gathering water and firewood, until one day, I went with my mother to the headquarters hut where a letter was waiting for her. It didn't mean anything to me until she cried out, gripped my hand, and started jumping up and down.

"Mom, what is it?" I asked in confusion.

She grabbed me in a strong, happy hug. "We're going to America!" she cried.

Then she ran with me back to our home and grabbed my brother in a big hug too.

"We're going to America!" she repeated.

"What's that?" we asked.

"America is a country," she told us. "During the war your aunt met a soldier who was fighting against the Communists, and he got hurt, so they sent him back to America, and he married your aunt. He helped us, so we're going to America. We're going to be Americans!"

This was all too much for me to comprehend. I understood the storm more than I understood this.

"What's that mean, Mom?" I asked.

"Oh," she said with a relieved smile. "It means you're going to be free, son."

# 5

A small old green bus pulled up at what served as our camp's station stop. Indonesian guards with guns came out and faced a group of refugees. Among them was my mother, my father, my brother, and me.

We had everything we owned, which wasn't much. My mother held an old plastic bag filled with rice that the camp authorities had given her.

"This should carry us for the morning," she said. "This is our breakfast."

She watched as the guards who came off the bus went into what served as the camp office. We watched as the small Vietnamese lady who had met us when we first came here emerged with a list. She started calling out names.

We stood and waited until my mother responded. "That's our name," she said. "Let's go!"

And just like that, my time in the refugee camp was over. I followed my family in a stunned fog. I stared, not really seeing anything, as we were driven away. I snapped out of it when we got to the airport.

I had never seen an airport before. *What is this?* This was new. This was amazing. I wanted to know everything. I don't really remember jumping off the bus, but of course I remember running through the airport, looking at everything. My mother ran right after me.

"Stop!" Her voice pulled me up short. "You're going to make us miss the flight," she said, taking my hand and bringing me to my family at the gate.

I was still excited when we got on the plane. Of course, I had never flown before either, but once I was in the seat, all the years of searching and surviving seemed to catch up with me. I don't remember much about the flight. To me it was just another vibrating, occasionally shaking room. I don't remember falling asleep, but I definitely remember waking up hours later. The first thing I remember seeing was this beautiful American stewardess smiling down at me.

She handed me a drink of shining liquid. It was orange juice— one of the best I'd ever tasted, eliciting a distant memory of the orange that Indonesian monk had given me when we were first given sanctuary. But this was somehow even sweeter.

I also remember the physical and mental jolt when we touched down. I didn't know it then, but this was Fayetteville, North Carolina. All I knew was that it was very different. It looked different, it smelled different, it felt different. When I got off the plane and entered the airport, I didn't run. I was stunned.

*Everyone and everything is so busy*, I remember thinking. *What is going on?*

I tried to hold on to my mother as we moved through the different rooms and hallways, as if the humanity was going to sweep me away like the storm's sea currents. It was all a jumble to me until we got outside, and my aunt drove up. My mother brought me into the front seat with her as my father and brother got into the back of this big American car.

As my aunt told my mother all about America, I stared out the window. *So big*, I thought. *So many buildings. The roads are so smooth. It looks so clean here.*

I must have been in a daze when we got to her house, and she invited us in.

"This is where we're going to be staying," I heard someone say, but I was still in a daze as I walked through a house the likes of which I had never seen before.

Everything was just so beautiful. I had never been around this much comfort. When I turned back to my family, my smile was wide.

"We're going to stay here for a few months until we get on our feet," my mother said.

"We can stay here for a very long time, you know," I replied. "No rush, Mom."

Those first few months passed by in a blur of pleasure. Sunshine. Food. Freedom. There was a lake right across the street. It was beautiful. My mother would go there every day to watch the swans who swam there.

"Those swans," she said, "they're good to eat." According to my mother, everything moving was good to eat. She saw a frog? Good to eat. A fish, a bird? Good to eat.

I seemed to adapt the way any five-year-old might, but at night, when she thought I was sleeping, I would get up. Mostly because my brother snored like a chain saw, but partly because I was still adjusting to this new freedom and comfort.

I would just walk around the house looking at everything. I knew that my uncle was a Special Forces Green Beret officer, and he and my aunt had all these framed pictures on the walls with words on them. I didn't know English, so I didn't know what any of it actually said, but somehow they were exciting, challenging. I knew there was some energy to them. Like the storm, I was drawn to them.

But also on my night walks around the house, I heard my mother crying softly. We stayed in my uncle and aunt's home for a few months, and my mother would quietly cry almost every night we were there. I didn't know why, but I was not going to ask her or anyone else.

Then one day my aunt packed up the car with our bags.

"Okay," someone said. "Time to go."

And with that, I got into the car with the rest of my immediate family, and my aunt drove us to an older part of town. I didn't know where I was before and didn't know now. All I knew was that it looked different. It wasn't as clean.

We went into a small apartment, and I started jumping up and down and running around. I stopped when my mother spoke.

"Don't leave the apartment," she said in no uncertain terms. "Stay here."

As my parents moved our meager belongings in, I looked out a window. It wasn't anywhere near as nice as my uncle's neighborhood. I didn't know it at the time, but there were drug dealers and a lot of crime all around us.

But back then I saw it through a refugee child's eyes and was so grateful. I lived in a small one-room apartment with my father, my mother, and my brother. The only furniture we had was one used mattress. My mother would cook dinner, and we would all eat it together while sitting on the floor. We all slept together on that one mattress. We spent all our time together as a family.

And I was so thankful for it all, because whenever I wasn't with them, things changed.

I was playing in the front yard of the apartment building one summer afternoon when I saw a group of kids, so I walked up to them. I still couldn't speak English, so I said *hi* in Vietnamese.

They looked at me like I was a talking bug.

*Maybe they don't understand*, I thought. So I waved.

One of the kids picked up a rock and threw it at me.

I didn't understand why. I also didn't understand why they all started pressing their forefingers against the upper outer corners of their eyes.

I just stared at them confused, but not the way they stared at me. They understood all too well what they were doing.

I finally got the hint when one kid walked up and pushed me to the ground. Then they all kicked dirt in my face and called me names. I didn't know what they were saying, but I could tell from their voices they were not nice words.

Eventually they moved away from me, laughing. I walked back to my new home. I didn't understand why I was being treated this way. But it didn't end there. From then on, kids would come over and tell me I smelled. I still didn't know what that meant, but I could understand the tone and see the way they held their noses.

I suffered but didn't complain. I already knew oppression, and even inside the small apartment I could tell I wasn't suffering alone. We were so poor. We had nothing. And the burden and stress of life in this new country was getting to my parents. They were arguing now. Always arguing. And there were no other rooms where I could go to hide from it.

"What are we going to do?" my mother would say. "Where are you going to go? How are you going to get a job? You can't even speak the language."

My father would say he'd try harder. But my mother always had the last word.

"How many more days are we going to starve?"

Even my mother needed to escape the oppression of our apartment. She would take me to visit other refugees in the area. They were kind people who would hand out used, but clean, clothes. At that age, I loved going with her. Kids would give me toys. They were third-generation hand-me-downs, but still, they were toys.

I got dolls with no arms. I got a teddy bear with no head— literally no head. It had been ripped off, so they had sewn the neck together. I stood there holding a teddy bear with no head.

And I loved it.

The hand-me-downs included clothes and shoes with holes

everywhere. My mother would go to a local thrift store for cheap needles and thread. Then she would sew all night.

The next day she would hold up her work. "Looks like new, right?"

It didn't look like new. It looked like secondhand refugee clothes. But I knew my mother.

"Yeah, Mom," I told her with a smile. "Looks like new."

Then she would put it on me. "How does it fit?"

My belly button was showing, but I would pull the shirt hem down to cover it.

"Just perfect, Mom," I'd tell her. "Thanks."

Then came school. Somehow, I thought it would be better than the front yard or the sidewalks. I had somehow learned enough English to survive, but growing up as a refugee was hard. I really didn't understand what it meant to be different. I never felt my way was different. I never thought I was any different from any other child. I always thought I was just not accepted.

But once I got to school, I was reminded. Every. Single. Day. I was reminded by my peers of how different I looked. I was reminded by my teachers how poor I was.

"You need to sit in the back of the class. Because you stink. Don't your kind take showers?"

Not sure who said that—a student or a teacher. Ultimately it didn't make much difference.

So I sat in the back of the class. That wasn't the only place I had to sit at the back.

"Go sit in the back of the bus," said the bus driver. I didn't ask why, but he told me anyway. "You stink."

Well, I can tell you from experience who else sits at the back of buses. That's where all the bullies are. That's where all the bad kids are. And that's where all the different kids who get bullied by the bad kids are.

The clothes that my mother sewed wouldn't last long.

It didn't end at the bus stop either. I learned the difference between good and bad kids, as well as the good and bad parts of town. The good parts were not where I or the bullies got out. And the bad parts were not where my parents met me. The bullies' parents did, and neither they nor their children let a day go by when they didn't remind me that I didn't belong.

But at least the one thing I had to look forward to was going back home and basking in the glow of my protective family. Until one day, I didn't even have that.

That was the day my mother moved out. Now I only got to see her once a week—sometimes even less.

I did see my father, however, but that was no help since he had started to drink. At first, he tried to hold himself together, but soon he was drinking himself to sleep every night. All we ate every day was ramen.

But that, too, ended one day when my father told me and my brother to get all our stuff. I made sure I ran to get my headless teddy bear. With no help or hope, I knew how he felt. I clung to him.

"Get in the car," my father instructed us. He drove us to another place. "You're going to live with your mother now," he said.

And there she was. I ran to her, but she said, "You need to say goodbye to your father."

So I went back and hugged him, still holding my headless teddy bear, thinking *So maybe I'll see him this afternoon?* But when I looked at my brother hugging my father, his expression was strange. Something was different. Something was wrong.

We went back to where our mother stood, got into another car, and my mother drove us across town to a house I had never seen before. I looked up at it.

*It's a nice house*, I thought. I knew the difference now.

That was where I met the man who would become my stepfather. I didn't know what was going on. It took me a while, but I learned that being a child of divorce wasn't easy. But so far, what had been?

From then on, my life and growing up became regimented. My soon-to-be-stepfather was an ex–drill sergeant and a Special Forces Green Beret. He raised us with military discipline. Exact scheduling. Dress code. Daily chores. If it was good enough for him, it was good enough for us.

Ever try to cage a tiger? I was not ready. I struggled. Looking back, I went from no discipline to a life of complete discipline. I didn't want to accept it. But what I didn't know then was that my stepfather was giving me strength for a life dealing with racism.

"All right, boys, stand here."

My brother and I were looking at bunk beds in what was now our room.

"Rip off all the sheets."

We ripped off all the sheets.

"This is how you make a bed. Forty-five-degree angle here, ninety-degree angle there. Needs to be snapped. Needs to be crisp. Needs to be perfect. Understand, boys?"

"Yes, sir." We had already learned that it shouldn't be just *yes*. It had to be *yes, sir* and spoken like we meant it.

So we started making our beds. Every day. To perfection. No exceptions. After all we had been through, that was difficult for me. Even tougher for us was that we couldn't watch TV on weekdays, only on weekends. Even so, still I was a tiger. I was always looking to break the rules. I was always looking for loopholes.

"Well, Dad doesn't get home till roughly five," I told my brother. "You can watch out for him while I watch my show."

"Yeah, I can do that," said my brother, "but after you watch your show, I want to watch my show, and then you can look out the window for him."

I loved cartoons. My favorite was *G.I. Joe.* Wow, storm shadow ninjas! I loved it.

"All right," my brother snapped when my show was over. "It's my turn, it's my turn."

We switched places and I kept lookout at the window. I only glanced back once to see what my brother was watching.

"*Sesame Street*?" I blurted in disbelief.

My brother looked back at me with disdain. "Yeah," he said. "It's about learning and being smart."

Then we went back to him watching TV and me watching for our stepfather. We didn't have long to wait.

"He's home, he's home!" I cried. "Turn off the TV. Oh my God, turn off the TV!"

The TV was in the guest room next to our bedroom. He turned it off, we ran next door, closed the door, and opened up our books. We started to pretend we had been studying for hours.

I tried so hard to look interested in my homework. *What was I studying again? Oh yeah, that's right...* In just a minute or two, our stepfather walked in.

"What are you boys doing?" he asked. I should have been alerted by his seemingly casual tone. A good tiger can smell a trap. I wasn't a good tiger yet.

"Oh," I replied, trying to copy his casual tone, "studying."

"Really?" he replied evenly. Then, after a long second, he said drily, "You want to say that again?"

My brother knew the jig was up. But I plunged on.

"Studying!" I repeated, looking encouragingly at my brother. Little did I know our stepfather had touched the top of the television set: back then, any TV that had been on for more than a few minutes got warm.

Busted. But did I learn my lesson? Not really. Just decided to look harder for new loopholes.

We were lucky that we still got dinner that night. The regular routine was that we would eat dinner together and then my brother and I would wash the dishes. Afterward we would shower and get ready for bed.

After all I went through, I'm grateful to my stepfather for the discipline he taught me at such a young age. But back then, I didn't see it. All I saw was how much homework and how many chores I had to do. It was a long tunnel that didn't seem to have an end. So I just kept going and going. If I couldn't run free, at least I could run fast. Years passed, and I was still doing chores and homework.

Then, one fateful day when I was nine, my mother interrupted.

"What are you doing, my son?"

I turned to see her in the doorway. "Oh, hi, Mom. I'm studying." This time I wasn't fibbing.

"Oh," she said in the bright, singsong voice she cultivated. "Looks very hard."

"Yeah," I said, "it's hard." When she just stood there, I turned back to my books.

"Well," she said quietly from behind me, "I have this box for you."

That got my attention. *A box? For me?*

"What is it, Mom?" I asked.

"It's from your father."

I instantly choked up. Like so many other things over these years, I had swallowed my emotional pain to survive. And my father's disappearance from my life had been hard to take. Especially since I had not been able or allowed to talk about what had happened to my father—or, for that matter, my mother—when they had each left us.

But I kept my back turned so my mother wouldn't see my pain. After all the pain she had survived, I didn't want to add any more to hers. I looked down at my homework and saw a tear drop fall onto the page.

My mother leaned over and kissed me on the forehead. Then she left the room and quietly closed the door behind her, leaving the box behind.

I looked at it...then went back to my homework. I kept working on it as more tears fell. It got later and later until I finally closed my math book and decided. *I'm done.* Only then did I look again.

I stood up stiffly and walked silently to the kitchen where I got a knife, returned to my room, and closed the door. I sat there for a good fifteen minutes holding that knife.

Finally, I opened the box and saw four VHS videotapes with labels written in Vietnamese. At this point, I knew how to read in English, but I still didn't know how to read Vietnamese. So I just picked up the first tape, went to the guest room, and rammed it into the videotape machine.

I turned on the TV I shouldn't be watching, even though my brother wasn't on lookout this time. I didn't care. I stared at the rippling lines of the used videotape on the analog television screen.

It said *Budo.* It was a documentary about Japanese martial arts, filled with real masters, but it started with a dramatic re-creation of an entire seppuku suicide ritual. I watched, as if hypnotized, about what it meant to be a samurai—the mindset, the strength, the discipl—

*"What are you doing?"*

My brother had come in. I hadn't even heard him.

"Turn that off!"

I quickly ejected the tape and ran back to our bedroom, but I thought about samurai all night, and even my brother wasn't enough to keep me from putting that tape back in the next day.

I watched more, becoming increasingly mesmerized every moment. The great swords…the great swordsmen…strength comes from within…through struggles and hardship you find your way…seek a life of purpose…Bushido…the way of the warrior. It was so compelling I forgot the other tapes.

At that point in my life, I was really weak. And Bushido was all direct, offensive tactics. The journey of Bushido started with you having to stop the spear. And to do that, you had to be trained. So as a weak child, I realized there was a deeper code to life.

I just didn't understand exactly what that meant. So I watched that Budo tape over and over, trying to truly understand. I tried and kept trying. But first, I mustn't get caught watching, and I still had chores and homework to do. Eventually Budo unwillingly retreated to the back of my mind because I had more immediate concerns to deal with.

My preteen years were set in stone. During the week we went to school. On weekends we would go to work with my stepfather at his welding business. We would clean his offices. We would strip and buff the floors. We would clear the land around the buildings.

But don't think we were just child labor. To a drill sergeant, good work deserved recognition. Our stepfather would reward us by taking us to Putt-Putt golf—where he would sit in his vehicle and wait as my brother and I played.

Make no mistake: Putt-Putt was a great time. When I first walked in there, I thought my eyes would pop. There were so many video-game machines, and we had so many tokens! It was so great, and I was so grateful.

My *Sesame Street*–loving brother would play *Tetris*. I never understood why he would waste time on that thing. *G.I. Joe*–loving me? My game was *Commando*. I was drawn to that game. You jump out of foxholes and kill a bunch of guys, then jump back into your foxhole. What a great game. I loved it.

But Putt-Putt was the exception, not the rule. From nine to ten years old, the rule for me was work. I would work with my brother every day in the house, in the yard, everywhere we were sent. There were chores, assignments, duties, schedules, and discipline. But by the time I got to the age of eleven, I was fearless.

Looking back now, I'm still grateful. But at the time, I was becoming defiant. Not to my stepfather. Oh no, I wasn't that stupid. I saved my tiger defiance for my mother. But no need to worry about her. Where do you think I got the tiger energy from? And where do you think she got it from?

Just as her mother lashed out at her when her tiger spirit roared, my mother responded in kind when my tiger spirit took over. She would slap me on the head, she would throw things, she would even grab tree branches and swing them at me—all the time saying, "You need to control your spirit, demon child!"

I would run from her, but she and I knew we shared that spirit. She'd had it as a *demon child* herself; always curious, always getting into trouble. She recognized that in me.

I never really knew if my stepfather saw it too. But one thing he had to admit: I was a quick study. He learned that well enough when he channeled my love of military toys into the real thing.

"All right, boys," he'd announce, holding a stopwatch after my brother and I were seated at a table in front of him. "One minute."

And then I would disassemble a Colt 1911 semiautomatic pistol in less than sixty seconds. Blindfolded. I'd slap the parts down and cry, "Set!"

"That's pretty fast, son," my stepfather would say.

Meanwhile my *Tetris* brother was beside me, still disassembling, giving *Commando* me his usual look of disbelief.

And so it went. After a time assembling and disassembling pistols, among other similar things, my stepfather would let me join him on his night runs. I would race side by side with him through the backwoods of Fayetteville, the training grounds of the Special Forces, navigating by the stars overhead.

Even so, my brother and I were still being picked on at school. It wasn't as bad as it had been in the poor part of town, but it was still bad. Throughout the grades, I struggled because I was constantly being beaten. It seemed like every time I tried to study a book, a classmate would grab it and throw it into the dirt.

"You need to go sit on the ground," they'd tell me, "because you're a dog."

It was hard to disagree when so many people treated me that way. It got so bad that I couldn't hide it from my mother. Then one Sunday afternoon she responded, starting by calling my name.

"Yes, Mommy?" I answered.

"You need to get dressed," she told me.

"Why?"

"Your uncle is going to pick you up."

My uncle. Her sister's husband. The Special Forces officer. He had a very strong personality. Whenever I saw him, I was drawn to his energy, like I was drawn to that storm. I got dressed quickly.

He picked me up in his rusted old Volkswagen Bug. One of his favorite things to do was fix it up on weekends.

"All right, Tu, get in the car!" he called. "Let's go!" I got in and managed to get the creaking door closed. "Well, you know," he told me, "your uncle wants to spend time with you, so I'm going to take you to Dairy Queen."

"Thank you, Uncle," I said.

As he drove, I looked out the window and said nothing. I remember feeling so weak and confused, still troubled by what it meant to be a refugee, to be different, and in the back of my mind wondering what *Budo* meant, and what it would mean to be a samurai.

But my uncle was always aware, like any Special Forces soldier. His voice cut through my confusion, as if reading my mind.

"Well, Tu…"

"Sir?"

"You know," he continued, shifting gears as we went uphill, "you're going to have your bad days. Some days people are going to flip you off or tell you that you don't belong here. They may even spit on you. So you got to ask yourself something."

He looked directly at me as he finished his statement.

"Do you want to be a fucking commando today?"

Confusion spread across my face. "What does that mean?" I asked plaintively.

My misunderstanding didn't faze him. "One day," he continued, his voice getting stronger and more determined, "when your body aches, you're starving, your bones feel like they're about to shatter because of the weight you're carrying, and you want to quit—" he took only a second's pause "—then you can ask yourself, do you want to be a fucking commando today?"

I knew that he was speaking from experience, but I just couldn't find the words to answer. He didn't mind. He went right on.

"You know," he continued, "a few days ago, it was raining. It was cold and wet. It was four o'clock in the morning, and I wanted to stay in bed. But I knew the right thing to do was to get up and train. Because that's what this country needs me to do. You understand?" He didn't wait for any answer. "You ask yourself, do you want to be a fucking commando today?"

I was taken aback. The energy, the language. My uncle let the question stand in the air as we went to Dairy Queen, but I knew what he meant. My uncle and his teammates would come visit my stepfather, and I would hear what they talked about. I heard about counterdrug wars in South America. El Salvador. Panama.

My uncle, and the Special Forces, always talked about freeing the oppressed. I remembered back when I would walk down the hallways of his house while everyone else slept, seeing all those military awards. I didn't understand them then, but I knew what they meant now. *Freeing the oppressed.*

There was a lot of diversity in Fayetteville, with more military on the streets than anywhere else in America, but still, this was post–Vietnam War North Carolina, so hate came with it—the hate for my people. So many acted like I had started the war, like my mother and father had started it.

That, too, was difficult for me, like so many things. I didn't know how my parents could stand it, until my mother showed me one day. In fact, she showed me almost every week, but I was just too hurt to see it. But on this particular Sunday, she called to me again.

"Yes, Mom?"

"We need to drive. We need to go and visit the refugees today."

"Again?" I complained.

"Yes, again. Load up the car, grab that box of toys, grab this pot, bring that Tupperware…" Where did she get all that food? Well, my mother had four freezers in our home, packed to the brim.

"Mom," I had once asked, "how many more freezers are you going to buy?"

She just looked at me. "Son, if you've starved," she answered, "you'll know."

That Sunday, like all the others, she drove for hours, listening to Vietnamese music, as I sat next to her wishing the day was over. When my mother looked at me, I gave her a tight smile. When she looked away, I rolled my eyes.

This was nothing new to me. She would do it almost every week and would always want me to come along. We would drive hours there, stay twenty to thirty minutes, then drive all the way back. She would always sacrifice her time to help someone—and give the small amount of money she might make to the needy.

For any number of reasons, I was especially irritated that day. My mother knew.

"What's wrong?" she asked me.

Normally I'd say nothing and continue to sulk, but today I answered. "I don't know why we do this every weekend, Mom. They don't even appreciate you."

I was prepared for her to slap me. Instead, she clicked on the turn signal and pulled over.

*Uh-oh…*

But then she grabbed my hand. "Look at me, son," she ordered. "Look at me."

I was surprised, even shocked. It went against Vietnamese tradition, because when someone yells at you, you're supposed to look at the ground in respect. So I knew this was something special, something important. I looked directly at her.

"If we can," she said quietly but intently, "we must help others, so we can create a better world."

For a split second my angry, frustrated mind started to form a snide answer, but then our tiger eyes met. I stayed silent. I might have nodded, but the next thing I remember was arriving at the place where the refugees were staying.

The kids would always run up to me because they knew I would have some of my old toys to give them. I passed on all my secondhand childhood playthings, except one. Meanwhile, my mother gave the adults the containers packed to the rim with the stuffed egg rolls she had made.

Normally we would spend around twenty minutes there, then start the long ride home, but today there was a mother and daughter I had not seen on the other visits. The woman came running up to my mother and gave her a big, tearful hug.

I started to go back to the car as they talked, but then my mother stopped me. She explained that the woman and her daughter had lost everything. They had no father, no brother—everyone else in their family had died.

I looked around and saw the little girl, sitting on a rock, staring down at the ground. Her dress was tattered. Her hands and eyes were empty. She was maybe six years old. She reminded me of where I had come from.

Remembering what my mother had said, I went to the car, opened the door, leaned in, and grabbed the arm of my headless teddy bear—the last thing that reminded me of when my family wasn't broken. Hugging it one last time, I walked over to the little girl and sat next to her. She saw me hugging the teddy bear, but then I smiled and offered it to her.

She immediately saw that it was hurting too, and that they could help each other. Her eyes brightened, her lips stretched into a grateful, even hopeful smile. Then she took my old friend and hugged it like a life preserver. I'll never forget the look on that little girl's face.

Only then did my tiger mother and I start the long ride home.

Later that night, lying on my bunk bed, I remembered my father and the VHS legacy he had sent me. Budo. Bushido. I reflected on what it meant to be a warrior. Then, remembering my uncle and stepfather, I reflected on their goals and achievements. To free the oppressed. To fight for what's right. To be a force for a better world.

It was on that night I decided I was going to follow the path of the warrior. That I was going to forge my body, my mind, and my spirit into a weapon. It was that night that I made a promise to myself that I would fight for others. That I would free the enslaved.

Today was the day I finally answered my uncle's question. Yes, I wanted to be a fucking commando.

I began to make plans. I had some more running to do.

# 6

I was still running. But it was no longer on my own schedule.

The alarm startled me when it went off. My eyes snapped open, staring up at the ceiling from the top of the bunk bed. I heard the door open, the sharp snap and swoosh sounding like an alarm itself.

"Wake up, gentlemen," my stepfather said, also sharply. "Today's the first day of the rest of your life."

I wasn't sure when my stepfather married my mother during our stay, but he did, and that changed nothing for us.

I was thirteen years old now, it was four o'clock in the morning, and we had been doing the exact same thing since I was nine, but I was still not used to it. I guess the reason I wasn't is that I didn't want to be. My tiger spirit did not like to be tamed.

My brother, one bunk down, had no such qualms. I heard him quickly getting up, then almost immediately ripping the sheets off his own bed.

"Six inches between the top edge of the blanket and the sheet," I heard him mutter as he started to remake the bed with the precision we had been taught. "Hold the corner in place and bring the sheet over to form a forty-five-degree angle."

I hopped off my own mattress and landed with both feet atop his.

"Get off my bed!" he snapped. "Stand on your own."

No time to joke with him. We had fifteen minutes before our stepfather expected us in the front yard. My brother was good at the bed-making, but I was better at the next part.

On went our T-shirts, shorts, and running shoes, then off we went into the dark. Our stepfather was, of course, waiting. Waiting as he always was, by the aluminum flagpole in our front yard, with a tightly folded American flag.

He handed it to me. I undid the lines, rotated it, snapped the lines onto the flag's holes, tightly fixing it in a groove hitch. My brother was there, ready and waiting, to help me raise the flag. It unfurled and blew in the hot early-morning summer air.

Our right hands went over our hearts, and we pledged allegiance to God and country—in spirit if not in words. Best not to disturb the neighbors.

Then I quickly followed into the dark of our backyard, using my stepfather's white T-shirt as a beacon in front of me. Nothing was said. It was just another day moving through the dark maze of the backyard.

"All right, boys," he said on that summer morning. "You know the drill."

"Yes, sir," we replied.

The drill was, of course, running. When he opened the backyard gate, I took off with a laugh, because I knew my brother hated this part. It was a half-mile through the woods to the lake. Our backyard brushed up against a dirt road. And on the other side of that road was Fort Bragg, the training grounds of the US Army Special Forces.

I looked at it now in the predawn haze as I ran down the dirt trail, still laughing at my brother.

"Come on," I urged him. "Let's go! Keep up!"

"Slow down," he pleaded behind me. "Slow down!"

You'd think that after all these years he'd have gotten his cardio up. But he'd much rather have his nose in a science or math book than the warm humidity of a breezy North Carolina summer morning.

I could smell the pine-needle scent running through my nostrils as I ran, the vegetation snapping at my ankles. I could feel the low ground starting to harden from the drop in temperature as we neared the water. My inner tiger felt so connected and free. After running this trail every single day for forty-eight months, I was in tune with nature, including my own.

I made it to the lake way ahead of my brother and immediately started back.

"Hey," he said as I neared him up the trail. "You think Dad would know?"

The early-morning air and his dislike of these forced runs was making him uncharacteristically foolish. Of course Dad would know.

"Yeah," I reminded him. "You need to run to the lake and dip your shirt, right?"

Our stepfather hadn't always made us dip our T-shirts into the lake to mark the task's halfway point. No, he did that once he caught my brother trying to cheat by saying he had run all the way to the lake when he hadn't.

I made it back to our yard as the sun was coming up, my soaked shirt dripping in my hands. My brother came sometime after, his T-shirt dripping too. But today, my stepfather was not around to inspect them. He had already left for work.

This was our normal routine. Up at 0400. Make our beds. Wash, brush our teeth, raise the flag, run to the lake and back.

"Win the morning," my stepfather would say, "win the day."

But we were not done. Then came academics. Academics was a big thing in our house.

"Son," my mother had told me, "I made sure that you came to America to get a good education. So you make sure you have a good education for Mommy, okay?"

"Yes, ma'am." It was always "yes, ma'am" and "yes, sir" and

had been from the very beginning of our stay in our stepfather's house.

To my mother, education meant good marks. It meant that to him too, but seemingly just as important to him was a regimented dress code. Clean button-up shirts and slacks to school four days a week. Only on Fridays could we wear blue jeans. Clean blue jeans.

"Boys, you need to lay out your clothes the night before," he told us. "Make sure you include your shoes and have your school bags packed. Lay them all out for inspection."

My stepfather had been a drill sergeant for some time. Later in his military career, he had served as a Green Beret with the Army's National Guard's 20th Special Forces Group (Airborne). In between his service times as a reserve Green Beret, he would help run the family's welding business.

His father had retired from the military after the Korean War and started a company fixing lawn mowers. Soon they expanded to many items, even making the miniature golf obstacles that were in the Putt-Putt place. That explained why he would bring us there as a reward for hard work.

When my stepfather joined the family business he took his Special Forces knowledge with him, and they started making assault ladders that were soon being used by the primary Special Missions Units for the Army and Navy. In fact, even I wound up using them during my military career.

Talk about a small world...but back then, it was even smaller in Fayetteville, the home of the 82nd Airborne Division, the Special Operations Headquarters Command, and Fort Bragg. My brother and I would work at the family's business after school.

He had drilled us at that too. As before, we'd clean the offices, only now we were older, stronger, and better at it. Only after everything was to his exacting standards would we get to go home—to do our homework, and then, of course, finish up whatever chores remained. And, if we thought we were done, there were always more that could be assigned. There was no end to chores until he said so. And soon, not even then.

On the weekends, when the family business was empty of weekday workers, my brother and I would do tasks like remove all the furniture from the offices, strip the floors, and deep-clean everything. Then one fateful day came a new way to look at chores.

"Hey, Dad."

My stepfather stopped what he was doing and looked up at me like I was a fly buzzing around the door of his office. "Yes?"

"I finished buffing the floors. You need me to do anything else?" I only asked that because I was hoping there wasn't.

I should have known better, and I regretted it as soon as he replied.

"Don't ask me what needs to be done," he said. "Look around and see what needs to be done, then do it. You don't need to wait for somebody to tell you what to do next."

I may have blinked. I know he didn't.

"Yes, sir," I said, his words sinking into my brain.

He went back to what he had been doing, and I went back out to the shop floor, looking at it with new eyes.

*You don't have to wait for someone to tell you what needs to be done. Look around and do it.*

I tried to extend those new eyes to school life, but there were always bullies ready to blacken them.

My family now lived in a slightly better part of town, so I was being picked on by a better class of bullies. The rich kids were rich, and the poor kids were poor. Me, with my skin color and eye shape, was in the poorer kid category, despite the fact that I went to a predominantly Black school.

I may have been constantly picked on, but now I was also on a mission. I had learned that if anything bad happened to me at school I would be the one who got blamed for it, so I did the best I could not to let that happen—which meant not letting the teachers know what was going on.

So even though I got picked on, I would still try to get good grades. Academics was important to my mother, so it was important to me. But now my stepfather had given me a new weapon.

*Don't ask what needs to be done. Look around and then do it.*

That ran through my mind as I was walking down a school hallway and saw a bully beating another kid. I moved out of sight, pulled out my notebook, and wrote down the time and place. I started monitoring the bullies' behavior from a safe distance.

Operation Avoid had officially begun.

I watched and learned their movements. I concentrated on the ones I most often came in contact with. I found the ones that prowled certain areas of the school at certain times of the day, and where they cornered and beat up kids. Soon, I saw their patterns. Bullies were creatures of habit, and because I knew their schedules, I could avoid them.

And I needed to avoid them, especially now that my mother was finishing beauty school. She had gone through almost a year and was now working on more of the chemical-based hairstyles. And guess who her guinea pig was?

"Tu? Can you come here?"

She was calling me from her workshop/study in her bedroom.

"Yes, Mom." I ran to her.

She was sitting up in bed, watching TV.

"Can you give me that remote control there?"

I looked from her to the remote control. It was literally an arm's length away from her.

"Yes, Mom."

Right after I gave it to her she said, "And can you get Mommy something to drink?"

"Yes, Mom," I said like the dutiful guinea pig I was. I had been her guinea pig since she started beauty school.

"Come sit down," she said when I returned with her drink. Then she would cut my hair. Up until then, it was great: I always had a neat, professional-looking haircut, but at this stage of the game she needed to learn how to perm.

So in the summer of my thirteenth year, I was walking around in the North Carolina heat with a wavy shiny perm. And that heat and my mother the hairstylist teamed up to create the only boy in school with an Asian Afro. And when it was humid? Then I was the only Asian kid in Fayetteville with a Jheri curl.

It was harder to observe the bullies from a distance after that because they always saw my Asian Afro coming, but it didn't make that much difference, because now, once again, everyone was making fun of me—even the teachers.

I'll never forget when my mother turned me around in the chair after taking out the last curler, had me face the mirror, and gave me her biggest, widest, happiest smile.

"What do you think?" she had asked.

I stared at the reflection, seeing some kind of Vietnamese Michael Jackson impersonator, then looked at my mother's reflection in the mirror over my shoulder.

"Oh," I said, "it looks beautiful, Mom."

Need I remind you that perms last a solid six months. I found out the hard way as I walked the halls of school.

"Oh shiiit!" I heard.

I turned and saw Cole. He was my school friend. The only one. He was a very dark-skinned Black man. Very dark. So dark that even the other African Americans in school would make fun of him. He came from a family of blue-collar workers, so the rich kids picked on him too. I think we gravitated to each other because we were both rejects. But unlike me, Cole had a little jive about him, and I liked his style. He thought I was cool and I thought he was cool, and nobody cared about us except us.

Still, he wouldn't listen to me.

"Oh man," he said, "you're telling me I can't go through there?"

"No, Cole," I told him one day, when he wanted to leave school by the most direct route. I flipped through my notebook and showed him the page with the meticulous timelines. "You can't go through there. Bully number three is going to be there if you take that route now!"

"Man, I ain't going off of your timeline!" he said. "I'm gonna go where I want when I want."

"I'm telling you, don't do it." I was practically begging now. "Crawl through this hole in the fence, and we can go down this way without running into any of them." I turned to crawl through the fence, then looked back, holding out my hand. "Give me your bag, Cole...Cole?"

Of course, he was gone. I pushed back through the hole and started down the alleyway he must've entered. I kept especially quiet until I could hear him from some ways away.

"My bad, man," I heard him say. "I didn't know..."

I came around a curve in the alley. Sure enough, there was Cole, surrounded by bullies.

"What do you mean you don't know?" the biggest, meanest one spat. "You've gotta give me some money if you're going to walk through here."

"Oh man," he said, "I don't have any money." He wasn't lying, for all the difference the truth made.

I quickly checked my pockets. No, I was broke too. Looking up, I watched as they grabbed Cole. They threw him down. Then the jumping started. Four of them, stomping him into the ground.

I was scared. I was crying. But still I came out into view and walked toward them.

They stopped for a second, the biggest, meanest one turning his head toward me.

"What the fuck you looking at, chink?"

All Asians were *chinks* to them, whether we were *chink*, *jap*, *gook*, *flip*, or *dink*. I knew I was going to get beaten, but at least

I could take some of the abuse away from Cole. So I came even closer and let them grab me. Then they beat the shit out of me too.

After they were done with their fun and took off, Cole and I helped each other up.

"I told you," I whispered as I wiped blood from my nose, felt my swelling eye, and tried to fix my hair. "I told you, Cole, you can't."

"Man," he interrupted. "I don't wanna hear that. We got rights too, ya know…"

"Yeah, I know," I said while wiping more blood from my face. That blood was the only real answer to why he should've listened to me. "I got to go home."

"You gonna go home like that?"

"Yeah, I got to go home," I repeated, knowing what was going to happen there too. Sure enough, as soon as my mother saw me, she shrieked.

"What happened? Why your face like that? I told you not to fight!"

"I know, Mom," I answered with total honesty. "I didn't fight. I didn't." It was true. I didn't fight. I got beat up, but I didn't fight.

And just like always, she knew. That was the way it was. That's the way it had always been. But she didn't say anything to me or to my stepfather. She had her own unique ways to help—which I would learn soon enough.

I healed, kept observing, kept taking notes, and continued to learn the difference between breaking the rules and avoiding them. If I broke the rules, I got into trouble. But if I avoided them, maybe not. Over the months, I started to get help. In the same way Cole had gravitated to me, other people seemed to feel the energy of a teenager willing, even wanting, to learn.

In North Carolina, there were a lot of soldiers that lived right outside of Fort Bragg, the biggest base that housed Army Green Berets. But they were Vietnam-era Green Berets, struggling vets dealing with post-traumatic stress disorder. Once called shell shock or battle fatigue, at the time it had only been a few years since PTSD had been accepted as a legitimate medical diagnosis, but not even close to being accepted by a public that still spit on Vietnam vets and called them baby killers.

A lot of them had lost their way, and many more were trying to find a way back. My mother and stepfather were always trying to help, starting, first and foremost, by opening their house to them.

"Did you hear what I just said, Tu?"

"Sir?"

"You hear what I just said?"

"Yes, sir."

"What?"

"You just said you came in on the helicopter, as it landed you jumped off, and you shot."

"Who did I shoot, boy? Who'd I shoot?"

"You shot Charlie."

"That's right! Two rounds! Two rounds in the face! I shot Charlie!"

I was looking at a Vietnam-era Special Forces Green Beret and Son Tay Raider. My stepfather told me he was a legend. A legend, sitting in our living room. Stuck in time, snarling stories.

"Did you hear what I just said?"

"Yes, sir."

"I shot him because we had night vision. You understand? He didn't even see us."

It was after dinner, after my stepfather invited him to our home, understanding that he, like the others, was trying to find his place in this world again. But as frightening and fascinating as all this was, it was beyond my complete understanding at the age of thirteen. I would never forget any of it, though. I could feel their energy. Somehow, I could also feel their pain. Sometimes, though, it was too much for me.

One day soon after, I complained to my mother about our many hours of chores.

"Oh, Mom," I said. "I don't want to do that."

"Oh, you don't want to do that, huh?" she replied with a big smile. "Okay. Meet me in the backyard."

Uh-oh. I had already learned what that meant. It was time for another lesson. Any time I didn't want to do something or I disagreed with my mother, she took it as a sign that she needed to work "with" me some more.

She had a beautiful Zen garden in the back because I was defiant at my age. Every time I disagreed? Garden work. Any time I talked back? Garden work. You'd think I would have learned by now. Or maybe I was subconsciously waiting for this day.

Because, on this day, she came out and said, "Oh, son. You know, Mommy was watching TV last night. Remember that movie that you were watching?"

"What movie, Mom?"

"You know," she said, slicing the air with her hands. "Karate! The Karate!"

"Oh, *The Karate Kid*."

"Yes," she confirmed, her smile widening. "Oh, Mommy liked the Japanese garden in that, you know?"

"Yes..." I replied, realizing what was coming.

"Yes," she echoed, pointing toward our yard. "Shovel's in the garage. Dig Mommy a Japanese pond."

"A pond?"

"Yes," she said, knowing I knew what she was referring to. "Mommy loves you," she concluded and went back into the house.

That weekend I dug my mother one of the biggest Japanese ponds I could. It was beautiful. Its perfection could've been my only reward, but the next weekend came with more evidence that my mother always listened and never forgot.

Usually on weekends, my father would work in the family

business, and on the days he didn't bring my brother and me along, we would sit with our mother and watch movies. It was during this time that I discovered the other three VHS tapes that my birth father had sent me in the box.

They were Bruce Lee movies. Japanese martial arts were already on my mind. Now Chinese kung fu entered. And my life changed again.

"Wow!" I would cry. "You see that? So fast!"

"I don't want to watch this anymore," my brother would complain, but I didn't care.

"Did you see what he just did there?" I'd say, rewinding the *Way of the Dragon* tape to watch Bruce's moves again and again. "Look at that kick! Dragon...whips...his...tail. Oh my God!"

I would keep interrupting my brother as he tried to read the dictionary. Yes, my brother would read the dictionary.

"What do you think he means when he says it's like 'a finger pointing at the moon'?"

"What? What did you say?"

"'It's like a finger pointing at the moon,'" I repeated, doing my best Bruce Lee impersonation as I quoted him from *Enter the Dragon*.

"Uh-huh."

"'Don't focus on the finger...or you'll miss all the heavenly glory.' What's that mean?"

"I don't know," he'd grumble and go back to reading. So I turned to the only other audience member left.

"Mom," I said. "'It's like a finger pointing at the moon...'"

"Uh-huh," she said, smiling and nodding.

"Don't look at the finger!"

"Why not?"

"You'll miss all the heavenly glory!" I cried, thinking that I had the last word, thanks to Bruce Lee.

But then my mother said, "Ohhh. That's Buddha, son. That's Buddha."

"What?"

"Yes," she informed me as if it was the most obvious thing in the world. "It was Buddha who said, 'I am a finger pointing to the moon. Don't look at me. Look at the moon.'"

I blinked. "What's that mean, Mom?" I asked. "Who's Buddha?"

And that started my mother educating me on Buddhism, Taoism, and Confucianism with many hours of incredible stories. But as much as I listened, I couldn't quite get it. That only made my mother smile even more.

"It's like the story of the traveling Buddha and the villagers," she told me. "Buddha was looking for the village, and the villagers kept telling him it was very close, and the Buddha would laugh, because, in truth, the village was never close. But Buddha knew that and would still laugh."

Now totally confused I asked, "But what does that mean, Mom?"

"It means, my son, that Buddha knew that the villagers were only trying to encourage him, and help him on his journey for the truth."

"That makes no sense, Mom."

"It will," she assured me, "one day."

I went back to watching Bruce Lee, thinking it would never make sense. But after we started going to libraries, my mother kept trying to teach me about Taoism and great philosophers. There she showed me the *Tao Te Ching*, a book from the fourth century BCE, supposedly written by a sage named Lao Tzu.

I opened it, thinking I would just look at it to satisfy my mother, but, incredibly I opened it to a sentence that read "the journey of a thousand miles begins with a single step."

Those words seemed to sink into my soul, and they have never left. Thirteen years old in a library, beginning to look through stacks of books because of Bruce Lee: that was my single step.

The next step came one Sunday afternoon. My father was at

work. My mother asked me to step out into the yard. I thought I'd have to go get the shovel again, but instead a man I didn't know was standing by her.

"Oh, son," she said. "I want you to meet someone."

Let's call him Mr. Dukes.

"Hi, boy," he said in a deep, strong voice. "What is your name?"

"My name is Tu, Mr. Dukes."

"Oh, just call me Dukes," he said with a smile.

"Yes, Dukes," I responded.

"No!" my mother chided, "you call him *Mr.* Dukes!" She looked apologetically at the man. "My son's so stupid. But my son's going to help you today."

Turns out Mr. Dukes was a Special Forces Green Beret, with the Military Assistance Command, Vietnam, Studies and Observations Group—also known as MACV-SOG—to this day one of the highest, most sensitive assignments in Special Forces history, as well as the joint task force with the most kills of all the Special Operations Command. They were classified top secret at the highest level of the Special Forces at the time—the military action arm of the CIA.

And he and I were going to move rocks. Well, actually, Mr. Dukes had brought a bunch of boulders in his truck, and we were going to line them around the Japanese pond.

I looked up at Mr. Dukes. I had to. From where I stood, he looked like a giant—a muscle of a man, even at his older age. I could tell he was still powerful, even deadly, by the way he hopped onto the truck bed and started powerlifting those big rocks.

"Well, boy," he said with a smile, "you're going to need to lift with your legs."

"Yes, sir!" I answered, then hopped to help him.

So we moved rocks for a while, Mr. Dukes showing me how to lift with my legs, not my back.

"So," he eventually said, seemingly casually, "I hear you're trying to train in the martial arts. What are you doing?"

"Oh," I answered, trying to be just as casual. "I watch Bruce Lee movies, and I learned how to throw kicks."

The rock-moving stopped. Mr. Dukes straightened. "Show me," he said. "Show me a kick."

I didn't have to be asked twice. I threw my best dragon-whips-his-tail kick. Dukes laughed. I threw another kick, trying not to miss all the heavenly glory, but he only laughed again. He seemed to be chuckling in an understanding, appreciative way. It inspired me to reveal even more.

"I have these rice bags that I filled with sand," I told him. "I hoisted them onto the branch of a tree in the backyard."

"Take me there," Mr. Dukes said.

We both forgot about the boulders. I led him down the dirt trail across from the Fort Bragg training grounds to where I had set up an exercise spot.

"You see?" I asked.

He laughed again in his appreciative way. "Who set up all these sandbags?"

"I did," I maintained. "My mother lets me take the big rice bags, and I fill them with sand to become my punching bags."

"Show me a punch," he said.

So I did. "Bruce Lee punched..." I prepped, "...like this!"

I completed my best Bruce Lee punch, and Mr. Dukes once again laughed. Only this time it was more amused than appreciative.

I wasn't upset by it. Again, I could sense his strength and experience. Consciously or not, I was always looking and hoping for teachers—ones who wouldn't send me to the principal's office.

"Mr. Dukes," I said hopefully, "could you show me a punch?"

I didn't have to ask him twice either. He stepped up to the bag and studied it for a seemingly endless second. Finally, he turned his head toward me.

"Well," he said, "you see this bag dangling in front of me?"

"Yes," I said, not realizing that he was redirecting my attention from the heavenly glory to the finger.

By the time my attention got back to him he had launched a seemingly effortless, pistonlike punch that went into the cloth, through the sand, and out the other side as if it was all made of wet tissue paper.

It looked like a magic trick. An extremely powerful magic trick that I felt from the crown of my skull to the tips of my toes. I stared at the sand, draining down onto the ground like it had become some sort of broken hourglass.

To this day, I've seen many other warriors, but Mr. Dukes was the real deal, with an energy like no other.

He waited until my wide eyes finally went from the sandy ground back to his face.

"Well, boy," he said with a knowing smile, "you going to help me line up those rocks now?"

"Yes, sir!"

Soon after, Mr. Dukes came back. He had learned that I was being bullied. He understood that I didn't fit in. So that summer, he taught me Combatives. That's what the Army called fighting techniques.

"The mission of the US Army Combatives Course," the Fort Benning Maneuver Center of Excellence handbook read in 2009, "is to train Leaders and Soldiers in close quarters Combatives in order to instill the Warrior Ethos and prepare Soldiers to close with and defeat the enemy in hand-to-hand combat."

I didn't know any of that then. I just knew that Mr. Dukes was teaching me martial arts. Not the martial arts of the streets, dojos, movies, or TV. He was teaching me survival martial arts, not show-off martial arts. He taught me what power meant. He taught me what drive meant.

"Tu," he said one day, "could you go and get me some water?"

"Yes, sir!" I ran inside, got the water, and came right back to give it to him. I must've gone faster than he expected, because I saw him just sitting there near the Zen garden staring into space. Actually, it was beyond space. Later, I realized that he was staring into emptiness.

I slowed, stilled, and stared myself, feeling the energy that was coming from him. It was different than the energy I felt the day he'd punched through the sand-filled rice bag. It was similar to the energy I felt listening to the other vets my parents invited into our home. There was pride, there was strength, but there was also always pain.

There was always pain in Mr. Dukes too.

I didn't understand why then. He was always so strong, so powerful, so commanding. What did he have to be pained about?

I waited until the dark cloud cleared from his face, and the water glass emptied, then we went back to work. That summer, the one thing Mr. Dukes taught me through all of our training was to respect the skill of speed and violence.

It made me respect the vets even more, as a lot of others passed through our house. There was one I particularly remembered. He was another legendary Green Beret, another man with pain just below the surface. My stepfather was driving me to work one day when he started talking about him.

"Well," he said, "he's been through a lot. He was a private with the Army's Ranger Regiment during the Korean War. It was said that he was patrolling with his Ranger squad and they got caught up in a blizzard. So they broke into an abandoned building to get out of the wind so they wouldn't freeze to death. But later on that morning they discovered that the building was a North Korean safe haven, and the enemy was cooking breakfast in the next room."

What came next, my stepfather told me, were hand grenades thrown into the breakfast room, followed by speed and death.

That wasn't it for the man. He had also served in the Vietnam

War. He was captured and tortured by the North Vietnamese Army. Somehow, he survived, made his way into MACV-SOG, and served his time in Special Forces. After all his missions, the Army told him "Anything you want to do, anywhere you want to go, anyone you want to be, just name it."

"He could have been anything," my stepfather said. "He could have gone anywhere."

But what he wanted was to be a Ranger instructor in Florida. And that's what he did until he retired—wading through swamps, teaching Ranger students how to patrol, navigate, raid, and ambush. The man was truly a warrior.

These were the type of men I was raised around. They came to the house and were teaching me the larger lessons of life whether I knew it or not. Now I was a little Buddha, and these pain-filled villagers were trying to help me to search for my truth.

Because of them, I knew the Warriors' path very early. So martial arts went deeper to me than just movement. Bruce Lee said it was a life expression. So not knowing any better, I combined the teachings. I saw no reason why Bruce's Chinese approach and the Japanese Bushido approach couldn't be compatible. In fact, they went together beautifully. I was able to express this life expression—my life expression—in the way of Bushido.

Those VHS tapes and these wounded warriors guided me to my life's path.

And it wasn't just about education. It was about deeper understanding through experience. And these were the reasons why I was drawn back to the library and books. But the library didn't have one of the most important books of my life.

I still wonder whether that book came to me or the other way around. Or maybe the warrior spirit sent or drew me there. All I knew was that, one day, seemingly out of the blue, my stepfather drove my brother and me to BJ's Used Books store. It became Fayetteville's oldest bookstore, but then it was relatively new, and my stepfather would often support local businesses.

The library was one thing, but this place was something else. The library was clean and neat; this place looked like a haunted labyrinth made of old books. They were everywhere: paperbacks and hardcovers, small and large, crammed horizontally and vertically into worn, stained bookcases, as well as piled in leaning towers from the floor practically to the ceiling, leaving only just enough space to walk between them.

From the moment we came in we knew they catered to their customers as well as those who donated, traded, or sold their books to them. There were a lot of military people in town, so I immediately spotted books about and from all around the world.

As I gaped, my brother ran in and, as usual, went right for the doctor, medical, and surgery books. I remember at that time he was really interested in the skeletal system. He was trying to learn anatomy so he would search for any books he could find on the subject. My stepfather looked for books about antiques.

I was about to start exploring, but out the corner of my eye I saw something bright and colorful. I saw Storm Shadow. I saw Snake Eyes. They had a comic-book section, and I ran straight for it. Storm Shadow and Snake Eyes were the ninja from the *G.I. Joe* comic books, created by Larry Hama, who I later found out was a Japanese judo, archery, and swordsman who worked as an Army ordnance expert in the Vietnam War two years before I was born.

I had been reading his *G.I. Joe* comics for a while, but on this day it was clear that nobody had wanted to part with more recent releases, so I got bored with the same old issues I had already read. When I looked up from the stacks of comics I saw I was alone in that section of the store.

Normally my brother or stepfather would have to pull me away from the comic books. But on this day it was different. Something was tickling the edges of my curiosity. There was an energy that was drawing me to the main section. Normally I never went there. But now, I moved deeper into the shop.

I turned a corner made of looming stacks, and there were all these used books covered in dust, seemingly surrounding what looked like a light beam cutting a path in the paper towers. I followed the dancing dust in the light through the towering alleyways of used books. Their smell filled my nostrils as I tried to find shortcuts through the paper canyons.

I kept going, fascinated, until something else glinted in the corner of my eye. I almost passed it. I had to stop myself and took three steps back. When I turned around, there was this one book that was shining through. I looked closer at its cover, which was facing outward while all the other books were on their sides.

I saw two blades. I immediately knew what they were: samurai swords. I knew what a samurai sword looked like, and I idolized them. I quickly grabbed this one and looked more closely at it.

*The Book of Five Rings*, I read. What did that mean? I quickly flipped through it. No pictures. I flipped through it some more. *The Book of Earth*, I read. *The Book of Water, The Book of Fire, the Book of Wind, the Book of Void...*

"Hey!"

I looked up and saw my brother looking back at me.

"We looked all over for you, you know," he chided. "We were up in the comic-book section and you weren't there, and then you're not around anywhere. Why are you down here?"

I instantly held up *The Book of Five Rings* as if it were a talisman to protect me.

"I'm going to get this," I told him.

"What is it?" he snapped.

"It's a samurai book," I told him.

"Uh-huh," he answered, grabbing it from me. He stared at the cover as if trying to translate the Dead Sea Scrolls. "It's Moo-Maa-Chee Ha-Moe-Chee," he read. "Who?"

"That's Miyamoto Musashi," I snapped, snatching the book back from him again. I had heard of the man. It was hard not to study Budo and Bushido without hearing of the samurai swordsman considered kensei—a sword saint of Japan. I ran up to my stepfather and handed him the volume.

There was a flicker of recognition on his face. *"The Book of Five Rings,"* he read. "That's interesting." Then, without another word, he handed it over to the person behind the cash register.

On the ride home, I stared at the book. *Wow. Samurai. So cool.* There was nothing in it but text. I tried to read it in the moving car, but it wasn't easy.

"I don't understand why he keeps on talking about a merchant," I wondered aloud. He was writing about the warrior class, and he broke it down into the farmer, the merchant, the warrior, and how everything is the same.

I ran inside when we got home and quickly put the book on my desk as if it were a beautiful trophy. I would wake up every morning from then on, looking at Miyamoto Musashi's *The Book of Five Rings*. I kept trying to read it and I kept not really understanding it, but I somehow knew it was important to me. The one thing I knew for sure, though, was that Musashi was an incredible samurai.

But for all his strength and all the book's wisdom, I couldn't get it to help me in school. Try as I and Cole might, it just got worse there, especially for me. At our school, an Asian always had more bullies than even the darkest-skinned African— especially a Vietnamese refugee. I don't know how my brother handled bullies, but I couldn't bring myself to ask him. He'd probably just call me stupid again.

After a while even my notebook of escape routes didn't help. The bullies had covered the entire school, and the teachers just kept sending me to the back of the class. I was always getting picked on, pushed down, and beaten up. As much as I wanted to fight back, especially because of the martial arts I was learning, the one thing the school had definitely taught me was that if anyone other than me got hurt, I would be punished more than the one who had actually started it. Hell, I already knew very well that the ones who started it probably wouldn't get punished at all.

So keeping my grades steady amid all that pain and injustice, as well as my load of daily chores and extra work at the family welding business, got harder and harder, until one day, I just kind of broke down inside. That was the only reason I could think of for the way I acted in response to the infamous report-card day.

"You get your report card yet?" my brother asked.

I had, but I didn't tell him.

"I got all A's," my brother bragged.

"You always get A's, huh?"

"Uh-huh. Where's your report card?" he asked.

My mental breakdown didn't seem to affect my defenses. Instead I immediately said, "I didn't get it yet."

"You didn't get your report card?" he said with less disbelief than I was expecting. That inspired me to double down on the lie.

"Must be something wrong with my school," I shrugged.

My brother returned the shrug. "Whatever," he said and walked away.

Later that day, my stepfather came home with my mother, and my brother immediately and proudly showed them his report card. My mother looked from him to me. "Where's your report card?"

"Oh," I replied as casually as I could, "I didn't get it yet, Mom. Must be something wrong at my school."

There was an endless moment when she said nothing, her face expressionless, but then she just said, "Oooh. Well, when you get it, show Mommy."

I nodded, but as I turned away I could see my stepfather looking at me suspiciously.

Days turned into weeks. Weeks turned into a month. Every hour I expected the axe to fall, so when it finally did, I knew the game was up.

"Where's your report card?"

"Here," I said. I had it ready and handed it over, my tears already starting. "Here's my report card."

My mother screamed in sadness and disappointment. My step-father shouted in anger.

"Why do you have these bad grades?" he demanded.

For some reason I couldn't tell him I was being bullied; I couldn't tell her the workload was too much. Then they looked at the date that the report had been issued. Now we all knew that I was not just a bad student but a liar as well. I was expecting even louder screaming. Instead I got ice.

"You're grounded," she said. "Oh, Mommy has a lot of work for you in the backyard."

"You're grounded," he said. "Get up to your room and stay there."

I was grounded for that whole summer. Work, home, room, that was it. The whole summer.

One day my brother came into my room, irritated that a downpour had ruined his fun in the yard.

"It's raining," he complained, "but you wouldn't know that, would you?"

I had stopped rising to his bait long before. "Mm-hmm," I muttered. "Thanks for the weather report."

Looking around the room for something to use against me, his eyes settled on the samurai book I still prized like a trophy on my desk.

"What's this?" he snapped. "You need to do something that's going to make you money."

"Thanks for the news report," I said before he walked out, slamming the door behind him.

I slowly pushed away from my desk and walked over to the

book. I picked it up and stared at the cover that had galvanized me in the used bookstore.

*Just you and me now, buddy,* I thought. *For the whole summer.*

It was on that rainy summer afternoon that I truly started reading *The Book of Five Rings*. I'll tell you, looking back, I still didn't understand much of it. But how could anyone that young understand it? The Nine Principles...the Attitudes of Swordsmanship...*The Book of the Void...*

What is that? *Void.* What is that like? What is this emptiness that Musashi was writing about? And how can that be the answer?

I finally realized that in order to really grasp what the book was trying to tell me, I needed to study even more about Japan's feudal period and the samurai era. I needed to understand what everything meant. Finally, in this first year of my teenage life, I was ready, willing, and able to do just that.

Now I tried to do more than just read words on a page. I tried to absorb them, to understand everything they could mean. A lot of my information came from the Special Forces Green Berets—my stepfather's friends, his neighbors, and whoever was able to help. Slowly but surely I began to recognize that emptiness...in my heart, and behind the retired soldiers' eyes...

But it all changed again one Sunday afternoon.

"I have to go, son."

The words hit me hard.

"Say goodbye to your dad," my mother urged.

Visions of leaving my birth father on the street all those years ago, never to see him again, came flooding back to me. It was very hard to understand it then, and it still was now.

"Where are you going, Dad?" I had a hard time getting the words out.

"I'm going to be away for a little bit," he finally told me.

I still didn't understand, even after all his comrades had taught me, that he couldn't say where he was going. The secrecy was part of the job.

We all stood by the front door together. His bags were packed. My mother was crying.

My brother hugged him, but I just stood there. The only thing I could think to ask was, "Why do you have to leave?"

I'll never forget any of it, but as he opened the door and patted me on the head, it was his last words to me that day that reached my brain.

"I will be back."

Then he was gone.

# 7

As I had already learned the hard way, a lot could change in a few months.

My feelings of abandonment were tempered because, since we lived in his house, my stepfather was all around me. Just like when I first arrived, I would wander the rooms, only now I could read English and understand what all the decor meant. Now I could read the inscriptions on all my stepfather's awards and better appreciate his collection of bayonets, blades, helmets, watches, and more stuff from all over the world.

But there was one more very telling thing I knew for sure. My stepfather was gone from this house. For all intents and purposes, my mom was now a single mother, trying to raise her two teenage boys. But without the man of discipline on duty, as far as my brother and I were concerned, the rules went out the door with him. And that meant only one sure thing: we could watch TV any time we wanted!

And we did. Then, one Tuesday afternoon I was staring at a channel and the news came on. I saw the word *Panama*. I saw images and heard about *troops surging*. I leaned forward, trying to grasp what was going on.

I found out what it meant soon enough. It was the prestage of the 1989 US invasion when the Panamanian dictator Manuel Noriega was deposed. The Special Forces mission during that time was to go down to Central and South America to train the resistance to help overthrow Noriega.

I was watching news flashes from then on with the same dedication that I watched Budo and Bruce Lee. I never completely understood what was happening, but there was one thing I was sure of: that was where my stepfather was.

Whether in front of the TV or in my own room, I struggled with understanding it all. As I read *The Book of Five Rings* over and over again, I kept thinking of all the Green Berets who had talked to me. Those vets were struggling to make it. They were not accepted. They were ridiculed by people in their own country. Suddenly I realized the similarity to a certain kind of masterless samurai in *The Book of Five Rings*.

Rōnin.

Today we could simply google it or look it up on Wikipedia and reap the benefit of many experts' knowledge, but then all I had was Musashi. So I had to ask myself: What did it mean for these people to be cast aside and wander at such a young age? What could they do when they were shamed everywhere they went?

They were rōnin.

As I studied more, deeper meanings and connections slowly rose through my own pain. Rōnin set their own schedules. They saw what needed to be done and did it. They observed, planned, and always looked for the smartest and most effective way to accomplish whatever their goals were.

The days kept disappearing, but I didn't care. The more time I had to myself the more I could learn. And plan. The bullies kept at me, but I tried to find better ways to survive them. In truth I survived because of all the new teachers I had learned from. Musashi. Bruce. Mr. Dukes.

I kept going, trying and planning, until my mother interrupted my studies one day.

"Oh, son!"

"Yes, Mom?" I answered.

"I need you to go to my room. I need you to get my purse."

"Okay," I said, but I thought *Why can't she just do it herself?* But I got the purse, went back to where her voice had come from, and opened the door.

My stepfather was standing there.

He was back. He was gone for many months, but now he was back, just in time for my sister's birth. He patted my head like he had when he had left.

"I'm not going to go anywhere for a while, son," he assured me. "You know, I heard you and your brother were good boys while I was gone, and I appreciate that."

"Thanks, Dad," I said happily. I was no longer masterless.

The days had flown by while he was gone. Now, with him back, the years flew by.

One day my alarm went off and I woke up, sixteen years old.

"Wake up, gentlemen," I heard a familiar voice say. "It's the first day of the rest of your lives."

I knew he was saying it out of habit: my brother had already left for college. Now I was the only one hopping up, ripping off sheets, slapping other sheets back on, and raising the flag—my stepfather was not even out in the yard anymore.

The discipline I had tried so hard to deal with had become normal for me. It wasn't difficult raising the flag and running through the backwoods of North Carolina in the dark anymore. I had my own schedule and training plan in place. And when Mr. Dukes visited he always helped.

"All right," he said on one of the many days we worked together. "Let's see how your powerlifting is going."

Shrug shoulders, bend and raise elbows, extend hips, steady bar, clear the bar, powerlift, raise the bar, over!

I reveled in my growing strength and power. Of course, my stepfather contributed too. He seemed to appreciate having a stepson in the house whose nose wasn't always in a medical book.

"All right," he told me. "This truck is full of wood. I need you to split 'em up."

There were piles and piles. All that summer, I split logs for hours, until it became as natural to me as making the bed.

It changed again one morning. At first it seemed like any day. The four-o'clock alarm went off, and I made the bed and mentally prepared for the flag-raising and the run. But I found my mind clearing as I was brushing my teeth. Something out of the ordinary was distracting me. My toothbrush slowed. I lowered it, looking at my own reflection in the mirror above the bathroom sink. As I lowered the toothbrush my eyes followed its descent.

I stopped when I saw something I had truly never noticed before. I stepped back and stared at my torso. I actually said the following words aloud and with complete surprise.

"I got abs!"

I wasn't lying. Seemingly overnight (but of course it wasn't like that) I had developed clearly discernible muscles. All that hard work, all the logs, all the discipline, all the running, all the powerlifting, all of that. Holy shit! I had abs.

I'd never noticed my body like this. I was developing power. I was developing strength. I was developing skill.

"Throw the blow like this," Mr. Dukes said at our next martial art lesson, "over and over again with your hips joined—hit *through* the target!"

I remembered him doing that very thing to my sand-filled rice bag, so I tried repeatedly to do the same on his punching bag, developing strength and speed at sixteen years old. My body was being taken care of. Time to take care of the thing that managed it.

As soon as I could, I joined the Junior Reserve Officer Training Corps—the high school version of the ROTC. You had to be at least sixteen so I joined the day my fifteenth year was done.

That wasn't the only thing I started at sixteen.

"Hey, Dad?"

"Yes, son."

"Do you mind if I go into sports?"

"What sports are you looking at?"

"I want to go into football and wrestling, and I want to run track." Strength. Agility. Strategy. Leverage. Speed. I had not chosen those activities blindly.

"Well, as long as your chores are done and your academics are good, I have no problem with it."

"Yes, sir!"

So that's what I did. I took them all to prepare for my ultimate goal—one I was keeping secret from everyone. The rest of my life was theirs. This secret part was mine. But first, I had something that needed to be addressed once and for all. One day, once I was on the football team, I went in the back after practice to find a lot of bullies hanging around there.

And, unfortunately, they decided to pick on the chink that day.

Yes, unfortunately.

For them.

Let's just say that it was also the day when all my martial arts training came together. And this time, I didn't get blamed for it. I had become too important to the sports department for that to happen anymore.

The football and wrestling fit the bill, but the track running needed to be fine-tuned. Sprints were okay but not advanced enough for what I wanted. So I signed up for long-distance running.

I remember one day after school they had the long-distance running tryouts, and I saw these guys who looked like African kids. Really skinny African kids. The coaches told us that it was going to be a short run today: only five miles.

I had never run five miles before. To the lake and back, sure, but that wasn't close to five miles. And I tell you, I wanted to quit by mile two. It was a completely different kind of pain and required a totally different type of endurance than what I was used to.

But that's why I had switched out from doing quick runs with my stepfather and explosive drills at the track. So my inner rōnin told me to suck it up and keep going. I saw what else needed to be done and I did it. Soon enough, not only did I run five miles, I ran eight miles. Then ten miles.

I walked with heavy backpacks. That was easy because my stepfather had his military gear, so I took the sand-filled rice bags from the tree branches and put them in rucksacks. Twenty pounds, then fifty, and more. I would strap them on my back and walk. Five, seven, fifteen miles. Then I would run with them.

The explosive power that I already had was joined by endurance power. Long before, I had run to the commando video game at the Putt-Putt. Once, I had run to the *G.I. Joe* comic books at the bookstore. Now I was running to *be* a commando, *G.I. Joe*, or both.

And I kept running, until one day, the Fayetteville High School road came to an end. It was graduation day—something I had been preparing for over many months, and probably not in the way my family was expecting.

"Son," I heard my mother say.

I looked down at her, in my shining robe and the mortar board cap signifying a high-school graduate. It was a beautiful day as we stood by the school parking lot. I handed her my diploma.

"Mommy so proud of you, son," she said, waiting to take me back home for a big meal and celebration. "I cook so much food for you today."

"Mom," I said sadly but with certainty, "I'm not going home today."

"Huh?" she said, confused. "What do you mean?"

I turned to look at a man in uniform standing next to a dark car.

"You see that guy across the parking lot?" I asked her.

A man in a uniform was far from unusual in Fayetteville, so he didn't look out of place among all the others in their graduation robes, and all the happy parents taking pictures of their children's big day. But in just seconds, with just a few words, the world went away, and it was just me and my mother standing there.

"After I've said my goodbyes," I told her, "that recruiter is going to drive me to the bus station. I'm leaving for basic training tonight."

I watched as my mother tried to process this.

"Mom," I said, "I know you gave up a lot for me. You risked it all. I appreciate you so much. But I can't be the person you want me to be. I can't be the doctor. I can't be the lawyer. I want to be a soldier."

My mother started to cry.

I knew what she had done to take us out of a life of violence. She wanted me to escape it. That was her tiger. But here I was. My tiger. My path. My energy. My goals. My schedule. My spirit.

"Mom," I said, "I know you always wanted me to graduate college, and I promise you that I will. No matter what happens, I will do that. I promise you. In the Army."

My mother, still in tears, hugged me and kissed me on the head. Then, with a sad smile that turned into a set expression of certainty, I turned around and walked across the parking lot, making my way through the celebrating crowd.

I saw Cole. He was talking with his family and didn't notice me. He wasn't going my way in any case. He had been talking about joining the Navy. Soon he was out of sight.

As I passed my peers, I could hear them cheering.

"Man, are we going to party tonight!"

"Yeah, we're going to get fucked up, right?"

I walked through that crowd and left them behind me. I stepped up to the recruiter.

"You ready, son?" he asked. My bags were already packed and sitting in the back seat of his car.

"Yes, sir."

He got behind the wheel and I got into the passenger seat. He was going to drive me to where I would catch the bus to Fort Benning, Georgia—the home of the infantry.

As I purposely avoided looking in the rearview mirror, I realized that I was still running, but I was no longer running away. Now I was running toward something.

It was the end of my life as a refugee. It was the beginning of my life as a soldier.

# 8

Airborne Infantry. That was my plan. Then, who knew? Maybe a shot at Ranger School, then Long-range Reconnaissance, then a fast track into the Special Forces A-Teams. If all went well, it would take me back home to Fort Bragg, North Carolina, but first I needed to become an Infantry Paratrooper.

"You hear me, son?"

The barber's sharp words snapped me out of my reverie.

"Sir?"

It was the morning after I'd arrived, and it was hard to hear him speak over the buzzing of his electric razor.

"I said I'm a retired Sergeant Major, the 101st Airborne Division!" he barked. "Air Assault!"

Now fully engaged, he stopped cutting my hair altogether. We both looked into the mirror and saw what was left of my mother's flowing hairstylist handiwork on either side of the single line he had mowed down the center of my skull.

"I was a retired Sergeant Major with the 101st Screaming Eagles," he repeated quietly with a combination of fondness and warning.

I took the warning. "Yes, Sergeant Major," I said with all due respect.

The barber next to us stopped his shaving as well and joined in. "What's your contract, son?" he asked me.

"Airborne Infantry, sir," I replied.

"Airborne?" he echoed. "You know, I was a Sergeant Major with the 504th Infantry Regiment, 82nd Airborne Division."

As my hair continued to fall, I heard the war stories. And it was ongoing. It seemed like every civilian on the compound, from barber to taxi driver to fast-food server, said the same thing. "I'm a retired Sergeant Major!"

And I always replied with the same three words. "Yes, Sergeant Major!"

In-processing into the Army took about a week. I stood at the parade-rest position with my left hand extended at the arch of my lower back. In my right hand was the Military's Code of Conduct, also known as the Army's Values book. We had to read and memorize the Army code of conduct, followed by the Army's values, drill instructions, and military formations.

We'd march from one location to the next, singing cadence to synchronize our steps. After a week of inoculations, as well as testing my blood and urine, I felt like a pin cushion. I was issued my uniforms and gear. I had been clearly and thoroughly drilled in keeping myself and the barracks clean, as well as how to march, stand, snap to attention, salute, and achieve "at ease" the Army way. Now the Army's in-processing center was ready to ship us out to our basic training sites.

At that moment I was at full attention staring at the face of a seemingly very angry man no more than fifty millimeters from my face. I had made a rookie mistake. I had looked directly at him.

"What the fuck are you looking at, Private Lam? You think I'm sexy?"

"No, Drill Sergeant!" I barked with all my might, quickly discovering that there was no right answer to that question.

"Why not?" came the immediate, seemingly hurt reply. "What's wrong with me?"

I, like many others before me, had fallen for basic training's catch-22. "Drill Sergeant?"

The drill sergeant barked out my locked and loaded punishment immediately. "Push the floor, Private Lam," he said. "Push the fucking floor until I get tired."

To push the floor was to get into a front-leaning rest position and do push-ups—arms locked, chest hitting the ground on the downward movement. The drill sergeant shouted to the rest of the basic trainees to push the floor too, as if somehow it was all my fault.

"I can't hear you!" he bellowed at us later—much later. "How many push-ups did we do this morning?"

How many push-ups did we do that morning? How many push-ups did we do that afternoon and that night? We lost count. But one thing we knew for sure was that the drill sergeant never got tired.

We did, however, because training started at zero four in the morning. I was used to that. I was even used to immediately making the bed in proper military fashion. But I was not yet used to what came by the time we hit the Fort Benning PT field at zero four-thirty.

In June 1993, it went from sixty to ninety degrees in just a few hours, but no matter what time it was, you could cut the humidity with a knife. We quickly lined up in two formations, then Drill Sergeant Smith took the lead on a five-mile run in full pack.

"Left. Left. Left, right, left…"

We ran in cadence. All too soon Drill Sergeant Smith began to sing a sarcastic, well-rehearsed "recruit's lament."

"Spin me around in a barber's chair," he piped out in rhythm with our steps, "spun me around, I had no hair. But it won't be long till I get on back home…"

Basic training quickly bled—and I use that word purposely—into advanced-infantry training. That's where I learned weapons and tactics at a very basic level.

It was a warm summer night when I low-crawled to the crest of a hill with a fixed bayonet at the end of my rifle. There we remained in complete darkness, waiting for a signal. Suddenly a red flare shot into the air. That began our assault into a bayonet obstacle course.

Mannequins were scattered through a maze of barbed wire and mud pits, as well as high and low walls, forcing the trainees to maneuver through the obstacles while stabbing their bayonets through these mannequins. We heard the concussion of M60 machine guns spit out blank casings as training explosives set off around us, while we parried and stuck our bayonets into the mannequins. We knew we'd done it right when the pig intestines that had been shoved inside these dummies started splashing out.

Even though it took up a full two months, my Advanced Individual Training was a blur of concentrated effort, following orders, and no longer looking directly at drill sergeants. My inner fire kept me going with no problem.

Then airborne school started.

"Jumper, stand by!" the Jumpmaster ordered as the door of the Lockheed C-130 Hercules was opened. The Jumpmaster then hung his body outside the door, gripping the side of the frame. Arching his back, he checked the drop zone. Pulling his body back in, he repeated his order. "Stand by."

It had been busy the past two weeks. Airborne trainees had to go through Ground Week and Tower Week before they got close to an aircraft. Ground week, we completed all physical-fitness distance runs. We practiced proper parachute landing falls. We did run-throughs with mock doors, then graduated up to thirty-four-foot towers, learning how to properly exit the side of a high-performance aircraft.

As I stepped up to the side of a mock aircraft placed on a tower suspended two hundred and fifty feet from the ground, I handed my safety line to the Airborne Instructor, who then snapped in the lines running to my mock parachute. There was another airborne instructor on the ground looking up at me, standing at the door of the drop.

On a jumper's *hit it* command I exited, snapped into a tight body position that would properly allow the deployment of my static line parachute, followed by me shouting at the top of my lungs.

"Airborne!"

That got us prepped for Tower Week, where the structures got higher, while swing landing and mass exit training were added. We had to fully qualify on all of that before we could get close to a C-130.

But once in there, when the Jumpmaster yelled *go*, you went. Tucking my body into the tight position I was taught, I exited the plane.

That was always great. I was flying. I was Bruce Lee. I was Musashi. I was G.I. Joe Storm Shadow. And five jumps later, I was also airborne qualified.

So the drill sergeant's five-mile-run song turned out to be right. It wasn't that long till I got on back home to Fayetteville, North Carolina.

The 82nd Airborne Division mission is to deploy anywhere in the world within eighteen hours of notification, with the ability to strategically conduct parachute infiltration assaults to secure key objectives for follow-on military operations in support of US national interests. And this capability was located just across the road from my secret spot where Mr. Dukes had taught me martial arts. But I didn't even glance at it for days once I reported to the 82nd Airborne Division Replacement Center.

After a short in-processing, I was assigned to my first duty assignment: to Charlie company 2/325th Airborne Infantry Regiment.

"Private Lam, what the fuck you looking at? You think I'm sexy?"

It was a new dance partner, but the same song.

"No, Sergeant," I said, with not quite the same gusto I used back at Fort Benning. The response to my answer was familiar, however.

"Why not? Something wrong with me?"

"No," I said flatly. "Sorry."

"Push the ground, Private Lam."

"Yes, Sergeant."

I did as I was ordered. I already knew about all the abuse that would be heaped on any trainee who dared answering the sexy question with *yes*. Virtually all drill sergeants in earshot would then verbally, and nearly physically, dogpile the guy, heaping abuse on him at volumes that would threaten his eardrums.

"PFC Lam," this sergeant continued at the customary bellowing volume. "You think you're smarter than me?"

"No, Sergeant!" But any answer was always reacted to as an affront.

"Push the ground!" he demanded more loudly.

I was prepared. "Yes, Sergeant," I said. The goal was to keep pushing the ground better, faster, and longer than the last time I pushed the ground.

This new Sergeant was my Bravo team leader on the rifle squad. He was a chubby Black man with a bad attitude that he had learned the hard way. According to him, promotion was slower for a Black man.

"A Black man ain't afforded the same opportunity in advancing his career as a white man, Too-tee," he told me.

*Tu T* was my first name and my middle initial, so it became *Too-tee* in this Sergeant's mouth.

"Yes, Sergeant," I answered as I pushed the ground. But he was preaching to the choir. By then I knew that tune well. He thought it was bad for him? It was. But then try being a Vietnamese refugee. I heard *chink* more times than *push the ground*. And I heard it from everyone, from barrack mates to drill sergeants to the high command.

But at least they didn't spray paint *chink* on the side of a Special Forces building the way they did the N-word. That incident had brought President Clinton down to Fort Bragg from the Oval Office to flatly state he would not tolerate that from the Special Operations soldiers.

But that's just the way it was. Back then they could put their hands on us. They could punch us. They were already shooting at us, so it was very racist at that point because, demographically, the infantry was full of hillbilly-country boys, and hillbilly-country boys said that Blacks couldn't pass a swim test and Asians weren't physically strong enough to get through training.

The trick was to prove them wrong.

Even so, back then I was told that it was rare to see an African, and even rarer to see an Asian. But that was fine with me. I had other things to look at. Like the Green Ramp, when the 82nd was conducting a full-dress, nighttime mass attack with complete combat load training exercise. That meant we would be air-dropping military cannons, followed by tactical vehicles, and then complete infantry—with heavy mortars as well as light and heavy machine guns.

That's what the 325th did—go anywhere in the world at eighteen hours' notice to seize, retain, and defend—and they had been doing it since 1917. And that was not going to change no matter how many Blacks and Asians there were in the ranks. Or how few.

My body shook as the C-130 leveled. My eyes adapted to the aircraft's dim light. Slowly I could make out the whole plane filled from front to back. We were sitting, but stacked right on top of each other, and everyone was loaded down with combat equipment. All our faces were painted in camouflage.

My seventy-five-pound combat load rucksack rested on my knees, cutting off the blood to my legs. An M249 light machine gun was wedged to my side, attached to a rucksack lowering line, which in turn was snapped to a quick-release, which was also attached to my parachute harness.

At this point we were already into a few hours of an infiltration tactic called Map of the Earth, which allowed the aircraft to drop below radar detection. The problem with that was it caused airsickness, followed by the inevitable. If I ever wondered what the inevitable was, I got my answer the first time the man in my rifle platoon yakked up. Nauseated in turn, I fought to keep down my dinner as the smell of jet fuel, military equipment, and body odor filled the air.

"Stand up!" shouted the Jumpmaster. It was zero two in the morning. The Jumpmaster ordered us to hook our static lines to the cable line running from the front to the back of the aircraft.

Sliding a pin through the cable hook, I pushed closer to the open door. We all strained to keep our balance as the aircraft roared through the night. And I stood there during the three-hour low-level flight. I gripped tighter as the aircraft dipped down even lower to avoid radar. The gravity brushes your blood from your head to your feet, causing motion sickness.

I heard a guy next to me throw up. I could hear the gagging as others struggled not to do the same. Even I had to struggle to hold my composure. It wasn't the sound of the puking that was getting to me. It wasn't even the smell of the vomit. I had smelled vomit before. It was the smell of the chewing tobacco in the vomit that was gnawing at my last gagging reflex.

Damn hillbilly-country boys. But, whatever the color of our skin, we were now united by the smell of sweat, fear, and chaw.

"Stand by!"

We moved closer to the door—shuffling to gain balance as the aircraft leveled off. I could feel the blood rushing back up from my feet. I could feel dizziness and vomit threatening me again. I held on to the aircraft.

And then the door ripped open. The wind howled. The static line pulled on the anchor, and the rest of the paratroopers yelled as the engine roared all around us. The Jumpmaster looked at me intently as I collected myself.

"Red light."

I could see the red light at the door from beyond the paratroopers in front of me. Hell, I could feel the glow of that red light. I automatically did a mental rundown of my combat loads. The sixty-five-pound rucksack anchored to the parachute made it very hard to walk because it obstructed your movements from your hip to your knees, pulling your weight forward.

My rundown was interrupted by the red light turning green.

"Go!" the Jumpmaster yelled.

I could see the other paratroopers shuffling to the howling door. I tried to maintain balance, moving as fast as I could. To my eyes, the paratroopers didn't fall out the door, they completely disappeared. They would step forward, then be gone as if they had never existed—one after the other, disappearing, disappearing...until it was my turn to disappear.

Out into the darkness, completely in my own world. Tight body position. I could see a line of jumpers falling out of both doors of the aircraft. *Snap*, my parachute opened. Only then did I look to check my surroundings. There was a full moon. I could see layer upon layer of aircraft stacked on top of each other, thousands of paratroopers coursing down all around them.

I couldn't enjoy the view for long because I had to prep for landing. This meant looking around, above and below, while unsnapping the weapons case that housed my M249 squad machine gun and lowering it to the rucksack still attached to the front side of the parachute harness. Looking below to clear my gear, I released the rucksack, which dropped to employ my lowering line which would safely lower my weapon and equipment to the ground. Judging the drift of my parachute, I grabbed the suspension lines to counter the wind, slowing down my descent enough to not injure myself on impact.

All too soon I hit the ground—hard. I uncased my machine

gun, bagged up my parachute, harness, and rucksack, then quickly moved with all items to an assembly area. Tracer rounds were firing around us to simulate the airfield-seizure training scenario we had been taught.

As paratroopers, we were taught to hit and move with speed. This military tactic required the kind of aggression that led to forcefully and successfully taking an airfield, as well as key control points, to secure a safe passage for following military forces. The 82nd Airborne Division's main mission was to parachute-assault into denied areas. Every paratrooper took this mission seriously, and everyone from superiors on down agreed we were damn good at it.

Airfield seizures were big back in the nineties. The 82nd was called upon to do it during the Panama War. So that's what we were there for. We had to take this airfield, which meant we had to move to the assembly area as fast as we could. Once the platoon got up to seventy percent force at the assembly area, we would move to do what we were ordered to do.

We did. We blocked certain positions, set up other ambush positions, cut off roadways, and secured airfields. Mission accomplished.

You may have noticed that I got a bit sketchy there. Get used to it. National security takes precedence, even in an autobiography.

We moved to face our superior officer. Captain Ohura was our company commander. He came from West Point. Very educated man. Very driven. He was a Ranger.

"Laying behind my machine-gun position," I heard, "get the men ready to move, forced-march formation."

It was going to be a twenty-five-mile trek back to the barracks. Full combat load. Sixty-five pounds on my back and a twenty-pound-plus M249 squad assault weapon around my neck as I got into formation.

There were four new recruits that came from the Replacements Center with me, so I joined them as we started moving. It was a hot summer day. I could feel the humidity and smell the pine trees. The dirt was so thick that the heat was baking our feet inside our boots.

It was only minutes before the sixty-five-pound rucksack was digging into my shoulders, and the machine gun was dragging down my neck as if auditioning to be a guillotine. No matter. I had my orders. Move. Move as fast as you can. Move until some-one with a higher rank commanded you to move into a tactical-halt position.

Upon that order, we immediately went into "rucksack flop position." That meant we just dropped and sat down on our rucksacks like they were weapon-filled beanbag chairs. Once there, I gathered my thoughts, using mind over matter while chugging as much water as I could.

It wasn't working as fast as I wanted it to. I took a second to breathe and noticed other paratroopers who were worse off than me getting injected with hydration IVs. I knew it wasn't going to be long before I went down as a heat casualty, so I went right back to drinking as much water as I could as fast as I could. This early in the training, I did not want to be pegged as a paratrooper who couldn't do what needed to be done.

"Captain Ohura," I heard, "the men are ready."

"All right, move them."

Rising from that rucksack was tougher than the rest of the mission. The ruck went from a seat to a sixty-five-pound alba-tross on my back. The second part of the march was worse than the first. I started seeing guys dropping out. Not just quitting—literally dropping.

"Captain Ohura," someone said, "the men are not going to make it."

Ohura made a soft sound of disappointment. "Let the fallouts go into a fallout formation," he said flatly. "I want to see who's not going to quit on me."

That had the effect the captain was probably aiming for. Everyone started again with determination, but before too long, one by one, paratroopers started dropping again.

The senior guys continued to push. The leaders continued to push. I continued to push. I kept staring in front of me until I slowly realized I was the only one left of the new recruits. The only one. But that realization didn't prevent the blisters from filling on the back of my heels.

*Dig deep*, I heard myself think. *Keep moving.*

I followed orders—the leaders', senior guys', and my own—until finally I could see the barracks.

"All right, guys," I heard. "Drop your rucks, drop your rucks."

We dropped right in front of the barracks, and, as my ruck went down, I could feel the blood across my shoulders and inside my socks. But even that wasn't as bad as the sensations returning to my limbs. During the march I went numb. Now the numbness was being replaced by what felt like needles going into every pore and muscle.

"How many of the new recruits are here?" I heard Captain Ohura ask.

"Just Private Lam," said an officer.

The Captain only paused for a second. "I want to see all of the new recruits in my office at 0900," he said.

So we were ordered to get redressed because the commander wanted to see us. It was nine in the morning—rotating off the airborne mass attack, forced road march, and no sleep for more than twenty-four hours—when we moved into a meeting room, the first sergeant yelling at us every step of the way.

"You're a piece of shit."

"Yes, First Sergeant." Well, I certainly did feel shitty.

"You don't know what the fuck you're doing."

"Yes, First Sergeant."

Captain Ohura then popped his head in.

"Attention!"

We snapped up. Captain Ohura looked sternly at all the new recruits. Then he looked at me...with a slow, small smile.

"I have one question," he said. "Who wants to go to Ranger School?"

All the other new recruits just stood there. I raised my hand.

"I want to be Ranger-qualified," I said. The blisters and blood were still there, but my exhaustion was all but gone.

Captain Ohura looked knowingly at the first sergeant, then turned, left the room, and closed the door behind him. But before it shut I could see the smile was still on his face.

The First Sergeant was not smiling. He looked at me as if I was a particularly annoying maggot.

"So," he said, "you want to be Ranger-qualified?"

"Yes, First Sergeant!"

He immediately yelled at the other new recruits. "Get out!"

He slammed the door behind them. When he turned back to me, his tone and demeanor had changed.

"You sure you want to be a Ranger?" he asked as if giving a condemned man his last chance at reprieve.

"Yes, First Sergeant!"

He glanced out the window. Just a normal Airborne day in the infantry battalion.

"Okay, then," he said. "Get into your full combat gear and come right back to my office."

I did as I was told, and then the first sergeant had only one question for me.

"So you want to be Ranger-qualified?"

"Yes, First Sergeant."

"Push the ground."

I pushed the ground—for an hour—until the vomit I had swallowed during the march spewed up all over myself. Through my embarrassment and irritation I heard a voice. "So you want to be Ranger-qualified?"

"Yes, First Sergeant," I said around the puke.

So he had me pick up my weapons and run through the obstacle course for the next hour. After that, he asked the same question and I gave him the same answer. "Yes, First Sergeant."

Then came the mud pits.

"So you want to be Ranger-qualified?"

"Yes, First Sergeant."

Next, combat load, moving through the back hills of North Carolina, before he ran out of new places to torture me. Then he just started having me repeat the sites out of order—obstacle course, up and down drills, mud pit, whatever. Five hours of this.

I didn't ask myself how I survived. I didn't ask why all the other new recruits dropped out and I didn't. They decided to stop. I decided not to. As long as my body didn't collapse, I simply kept going—blisters, blood, vomit, and all.

But after all that, First Sergeant gave me a chance to have the last word by subtly changing his question.

"What," he asked me, "do you want to be, Private Lam?"

"I want to be Ranger-qualified," I answered without hesitation. "First Sergeant!"

And that was it. One week later I was in Pre Ranger. Not Ranger. Pre Ranger. Ranger training was not going to be that easy.


"Get the fuck off my bus!"

That bellow from the driver was followed by explosive training pyrotechnics and yellow smoke. Through the yelling, blowing horns and smoke we dropped our duffel bags and rucksacks on the side of a dirt trail road. I couldn't even see the end of it. So I looked to my right. There was a sign. It said "RECONDO."

A waiting Ranger instructor came up to us.

"Grab all your bags," he ordered. "Move down the road to the Ranger compound."

I had a rucksack and two duffels. They filled both my hands and I moved as fast as I could down this dirt road. A mile later we were at the compound.

Ranger School, and earning a Ranger tab, is important in the infantry world. This school trained students to be effective infantry leaders in a simulated combat environment, complete with lack of food and sleep. In Pre Ranger, they taught us individual Soldiers Skills and Small Unit Tactics—including Ambushes, Reconnaissance Operations, Formations, Movement Techniques, and Troop Leading Procedures. At the conclusion of the course, we had better be, as the school site states, "prepared to represent the Division at the U.S. Army Ranger school."

That's where I learned basic small-unit tactics. That's where I learned land navigation, warning orders, and operational orders. I learned how to be a leader in a combat stress environment. We slept roughly one hour a night and were supposed to eat one meal a day. We tried, at least, because they gave us almost no time to do it.

We pushed our minds and bodies to the breaking point, but I graduated Pre Ranger at the top of my class.

A week later, I had loaded onto another bus in Fort Bragg, North Carolina. It was time to leave my American hometown again. It was time for Ranger School.

"All right, guys, pack it in," I heard as I got on the government bus contracted out to take us to Ranger training at Fort Benning, Georgia. "It's going to be a large class, right?"

I remember sitting there wondering what was to come. Just getting the First Sergeant's permission to get into Pre Ranger had been tough enough, and Pre Ranger pushed me to the breaking point, so what was Ranger planning?

"Combat is easy," I once heard somewhere. "Ranger School is hard."

There was a high washout rate, supposedly fifty percent. The guys who were physically fit could fail mentally and vice versa. You could fail in a leadership evaluation role. You could fail after one too many bad patrols. There were a lot of things outside your control that could sink you. If anything was borderline, they'd rather wash you out than risk you. This course wanted the best infantryman—the best leader in the infantry.

"Rangers Lead the Way." That was their motto. That was what was on their crest.

Thankfully the eight-hour drive across almost five hundred miles to Fort Benning gave me a chance to stop worrying. The Southern humidity helped me to doze off, and a good thing too: I had been pretrained with one hour of sleep a day, and I didn't expect anything more once we got there.

Fittingly, what woke me up was a bump in the road. When I opened my eyes, there was a huge rock filling my vision. It was painted black with gold letters on it.

*This is not for the weak or fainthearted*, it read.

I blinked to make sure I wasn't dreaming. I wasn't. I prepared myself as we pulled into the Ranger camp, knowing that training started tomorrow.

Despite all I had already gone through, Ranger School seemed new to me. Everything the instructors said or did was gospel. I didn't know anything better then. And I didn't care. I wasn't there to please myself. I was there to please them.

"Damn, Ranger Lam!" I remember one of them once said to me. "Why did you put together that machine gun so fucking fast?"

"Because you told me to, Sergeant."

I'll never forget the look of appreciation on that man's face and what he said then. "Damn, you're a fine Ranger." I didn't hear that often.

A less flattering highlight for me was when we were going to jump from a C-130 over Fort Benning and do a forced march to Camp Darby, which was eighteen miles out. Despite being a *damn fine Ranger*, the lack of sleep had somehow made me decide that this would be a great time to break in a new pair of jungle boots.

I exited the aircraft and landed, already moving toward the assembly area. I could hear the Ranger instructors. They were big bulky barrel-chested guys in black T-shirts. They had Ranger tabs on the chest of their shirts, and on top of that were white name tags. They ordered us to move into a tactical movement formation column, with our M16 machine guns in front, and sixty-five-pound rucksacks in back.

"Move! Pick up the pace."

Soon after that I started seeing some Ranger students dropping back. They knew the slogan as well as I did. *Walk or die.*

In this formation, you have to keep equidistant from the Ranger in front and the one behind. If any of us dropped back more than an arm's length from the student in front of them, we were a failure on forced march.

We moved as fast as we could toward Camp Darby. The heat index that midsummer day was around a hundred degrees. Even as top in my Pre Ranger class I, too, was trying to just keep up with the man in front of me, while all around guys were quitting, stepping off to the side of the road and dropping their rucks. As we tried to keep up the pace, the Ranger instructors were pulling out guys who dropped more than one arm's length away.

There were even Ranger dogs walking next to us. These were working military dogs wearing black Ranger T-shirts. And like the human instructors, they had a bad attitude. Even for canines, if you didn't meet the standards, you'd be pulled from training.

The foolishness of my foot gear decision came back to bite me under my feet and across my heels. It seemed that, for every student who was dropping out, there was another blister that was broiling up inside my new boots. I could feel the skin breaking, peeling, and ripping off. It felt like I had no more skin on the bottom of my feet. I could feel the blood soaking my socks.

The heat index had become almost unbearable. Almost. I wanted to drink as much water as I could, but trying to grab, unscrew, and drink from a canteen while running at the pace we were pushing, as well as holding a machine gun with no sling in front of you, while a sixty-five-pound rucksack was dragging you down from behind, was nearly impossible. And the instructors knew it. It was all I could do just to keep going.

Finally, the dirt trail road led what was left of us into Camp Darby—the final phase of our march. At this point, the heat index was more than a hundred degrees. The blood was now sloshing around in my boots. I could barely see because of all the dust and sand the other Ranger students were kicking up. Even though I was getting dizzy, I concentrated on continuing. Walk or die...

"Ranger?"

I looked over to see an instructor had come up beside me. I could see by his expression that I was barely making it.

"If you fall back one more inch," he warned, "you won't be able to touch that Ranger's rucksack in front of you..." He leaned in, his face swimming in my cloudy, dusty eyes. "One more inch," he said, "and you fail."

"Yes, Sergeant," I managed to say, feeling the heat soaking into my brain.

I was losing it. My consciousness was slowly seeping out of me as fast as my blood was soaking my boots. I felt the heat casualty coming on, and I knew I was going down. I was about to become a literal sleepwalker. And then a failure. After everything I had done to get here, I would fail.

So what did I do? What could I do? I couldn't open my canteen, but I could punch myself in the face. So, still holding my machine gun, that's what I did. I punched myself in the face. I punched myself in the nose. I punched myself in the eyes. I punched myself in the chin.

It seemed like a good idea at the time. And, unlike the new boots, it worked.

The instructor, who may have already been in the process of writing me off as a lost cause, turned around.

"What the fuck?" he said as I continued to hit myself. With a disbelieving smile he leaned back in. "Drive on, Ranger," he told me. "Do whatever the fuck you need to do."

So I did. I punched myself in the throat and I punched myself in the ear, all while my bloody feet kept moving in rhythm with our pace. I finally reached the finishing point, still equidistant from the Ranger in front of me and the Ranger behind—not one inch too close or one inch too far.

I crossed the finish line and dropped my rucksack but not my gun or myself. I just stood there, snot all over my lower face mingling with the blood from my nose and what was left of all the dirt that I hadn't beaten off. Then my feet made themselves known to my addled brain.

Only then did I drop. I could barely take my boots off because of the blood. I noticed that all the other students splayed around me felt the same way. We were all physically shattered.

"All right, guys," I heard. I looked up to see a Ranger instructor standing among us. It was obvious that this was far from the first time he'd seen this sort of thing. "We got medics coming by, going to give a look at you. Make sure you put fresh socks on. You got one MRE in your rucksack. Go ahead and eat that. You got ten minutes."

Ten minutes. Ten minutes to get the blood off my heels, patch up my feet, powder them, and put fresh socks on. Then after that, maybe get to the Meal Ready to Eat in my rucksack or at least rehydrate. Because, in ten minutes, patrol phase started.

"All right, Rangers," I heard as I was trying to stay conscious, as well as recover from the heat. "What you guys are going to do is put your machine gun in the elevated position on this road. If you look at how this road bends, that'll force a vehicle to slow down on the bend, putting the machine gun at the most casualty-reducing point. Do you understand, Rangers?"

"Yes, Sergeant!" we barked.

My blood and exhaustion were forgotten. Or, at least, dealt with. We conducted day raids. We conducted night raids. We had one hour of sleep. I woke up the next morning to conduct more patrols and raids during the day, then ambushes at night. That prepared us for desert phase.

We loaded up into an aircraft, and airborne-infiltrated Sand Hills, New Mexico, where we conducted live-fire training, raids, ambushes, leadership training, and learning orders during the hot desert days and the cold desert nights, with hardly any food or sleep at all. Then came mountain phase, and, finally, the swamps of Florida.

That was at Eglin Air Force Base near Okaloosa County in the western panhandle of the state. We were moving down a dark river, half of my body outside of a Zodiac inflatable boat. The other half of my body and a stack of Ranger students were in the Zodiac as we moved through the darkness. We were heading to our drop-off location, which was on the edge of a maze of thick vegetation that was called the Weaver.

Once we entered, Rangers would silently roll off into the water, half submerge, and start moving through the dense swamps—most with the sixty-five-pound rucksacks and heavy machine guns. I got the added pleasure of carrying heavy mortars as well.

That was no surprise to the instructors. Every phase was meticulously planned, and since they had been conducting this course eleven times a year for decades, virtually nothing shocked them. Except maybe for a student who punched himself. Maybe not.

In any case, the swamp was usually the most dangerous phase. Students had died of hypothermia in it. At this point of the training, the students' bodies were so weak and depleted from one hour of sleep, one rushed meal, and at least five thousand calories burned every day for seventy-two days that we were zombies.

We set up into a tactical night moving formation as we slogged through the dark. I could barely see my teammates because I was falling in and out of consciousness. Finally, we arrived at what was called the prison camp. It was a foggy, humid morning in the swamps of Florida.

As we set up into a raid position, I scanned the sector of fire through the hanging fog around the camp. We put our fire-support position out—60 mm mortars and an M60 machine gun mounted on a tripod—to give us the most accurate precision into the interlocked sectors of fire on the kill zone of the camp.

We Ranger zombies moved to our locations. I was still fighting to stay awake, but at this point, raids, ambushes, and patrols were normal. We'd done them so many times in the harshest conditions that you could say that we could almost do them in our sleep. Almost.

At this phase of the game, it was about survival. Our bodies were so depleted, you could smell the muscles burning from our bones. They smelled like moldering tires. But at least there was no chewing-tobacco stink.

As I waited and watched as best I could, the dawn started to break, nearing the time of the raid. Looking down at my watch, I cleared the mud from the dial and my mind. One minute.

At that point of the operation, we didn't even have communications. Everything was run by time and written out on this sequence of events. We were already trained on what to do and how to do it if there were no communications.

Through the mist of the dawn and the fog of my mind, I looked at the prison, scanning my sector and my kill zone. Right on time, the machine gun position opened, spraying down predetermined targets. I joined in on schedule, spraying down the mannequins that were moving across my sector.

After a minute of violence we heard "Cease-fire."

I scanned through the smoke. We all stopped, looked, and listened for threats, movement, and life. If the Patrol Leader felt that there were more threats, then we interlocked this kill zone with another minute of bullets and explosive projectiles. Left- and right-side security locked down this road for a thousand meters on each side with Anti-Tank weapons. The enemy could come into the killzone but nothing left.

Through the fog, smoke, and gun powder, I heard "A-Team, move forward!"

On a rifle squad, there are two fire teams, broken down into an A- and B-Team. A-Team moved forward while B-Team served as their support-by-fire. Then B-Team moved forward as A-Team returned the support-by-fire position, and it kept going like that as we leap-frogged forward, setting up an "L"—which is the Limit of Advance Formation.

The Limit of Advance is when we conducted weapon reload—evaluating personnel, weapons, and equipment. This status was given to the fire-team leaders, then to next chain of command. This allowed the patrol leader to understand his combat capabilities if there were any enemy reinforcements to our ambush. We knew we lost the element of surprise by going loud on the guns, therefore it was about speed.

Moving through the village, we searched for any living and for all the dead. We killed, and swept all guns from, the enemy.

"Five minutes on target."

We set up explosives on any enemy material that required it. We scanned through the area for any enemy intelligence, weapons, or maps. We erased our trails. And then we started getting into a moving formation.

"Four minutes."

At four minutes, Rangers were moving into a wedge formation toward an exit point. It was a good thing that it was all clockwork, because despite all the action, we were still zombies.

That morning we finished our final patrol. All that was left of Ranger School then was graduation. I was nineteen years old.

# 9

From my position as part of the Ranger class #7-94 graduation formation, I saw my stepfather and my mother sitting with all the other parents on the wooden bleachers. When the ceremony was over, my maternal grandmother—the one who was infamous for knocking out grown men back in Vietnam—came rushing up to hug me. I don't think she even knew what the significance of being a Ranger was. She was just proud of her grandson.

My stepfather, however, knew what being a Ranger meant. He was Special Forces. He understood how hard this training was. Even so, I turned to my mother.

"Mom," I said, "could you pin the Ranger tab on me?"

She put the emblem on my shoulder with pleasure. I looked at her with equal pleasure. She was the one who'd got me there. But now it was time to leave this family and get back to my new family.

As a Ranger School graduate, I returned to the 82nd, where I was a fire-team leader, and then went on to become a scout sniper within the Division. By then I no longer thought that anything and everything a superior said or did was gospel. I had learned enough to make my own judgments. I now had my own orders to follow.

"Command Sergeant Major Garrett wants to see you."

Garrett was the battalion command Sergeant Major. When

you went to see him, you were either in trouble or he wanted
to reward you for something. I knew he didn't want to reward
me for something. If anything, he wanted to punish me because
I had the audacity to want to leave the 82nd Airborne Division.

This was not going to be great. I was aware that I was one of
the men that they were most proud of. I had graduated Ranger
School. I had proven myself to be an exemplary leader. They
had already given me sniper training. They had big goals for me.

And here I was, an ungrateful child. Even so, I took the high
ground.

"Sergeant Major, I want to try out for F Company, Long
Range Reconnaissance Team."

Garrett took the low ground. But I was expecting that.

"Who the fuck do you think you are? You know how much
fucking money we put in you?"

"Yes, Sergeant Major!"

"Beat the fucking ground!" he barked.

As ever, I did what I was told and pushed the ground as fast
and sharply as I could. It didn't last as long as the other times.

"Get back up," he said with irritation. "Why do you want to
leave? You know you have a future here."

"I know, Sergeant Major," I answered, "but I want to be
something more."

No one ever said I was insincere. Or tactful.

"You don't think that this is *more*?" he retorted indignantly.
"You think that the LRSD teams are more?"

The LRSD, pronounced *lurst*, were Long Range Surveillance
Detachments. They were the descendants of the infamous LRRP
teams—Long Range Reconnaissance Patrol—which were dis-
banded after Vietnam. I had heard of their inventive, imagi-
native, and effective accomplishments, and it was something I
wanted to do. I guess because of my upbringing and training, I
wanted to be more than the best. I always wanted to be better.

"Sergeant Major," I replied without answering his question.

I didn't want to go from being honest to being stupid. "They're having trials. I really want to try out."

Sergeant Major Garrett looked at me in disbelief. "Who the fuck do you think you are?" he repeated. "You're going to clean my fucking office. And you're going to clean the whole battalion area. You're going to strip the floors and you're going to wax them, and you're going to buff them, and you're going to clean the urinals. You understand me?"

"Yes, Sergeant Major!"

So I did. It brought me back to the days doing the same in my stepfather's offices. The next morning Sergeant Major Garrett came back in.

"What the fuck?" he said with surprise. "The floors are so damn shiny! Sergeant Lam?"

I was right there. "Yes, Sergeant Major."

His tone and demeanor changed. He suddenly went from being my superior to being a peer.

"You know," he told me, "I'm on my way out." He stared at me for a few seconds before continuing. "Why don't you try out for it," he said quietly, "and we'll see how it goes."

"Yes, Sergeant Major," I replied, dropping the toothbrush I had been cleaning the urinals with.

All too soon I was listening to another noncommissioned officer. "Sixty-five-pound rucksack," he said. "You understand the standard?"

"Yes, sir." I was standing on the foothills of Fort Bragg, on the outskirts of the LRSD training grounds, with a bunch of other candidates.

"It's going to be an eighteen-mile forced march. Move as fast as you can. Everything's timed."

They also gave us a so-called map that looked like it had been drawn by a child who didn't know much about longitude or latitude.

"You're going to move through the foothills along the dirt

trail roads and the backwoods as fast as you can, carrying sixty-five-pound-heavy weapons. You understand, candidate?"

"Yes, Sergeant."

There were fifteen candidates, moving as fast as they could, following that scrawled-out map. Fifteen candidates were scattered out, with imposed timelines of twenty minutes each. Scattered out so we couldn't rely on each other. That was fine with me.

*Individual task*, I thought. *Move.*

By this point in my career, I was physically fit. Highly trained at the 82nd Airborne Division level. But not, it turned out, at the LRSD level. And I found that out really fast—but not as fast as I hoped. All too soon, other candidates were moving past me.

I couldn't understand why. I was moving up this hill as fast as I could, but it wasn't enough. Finally, I accepted the fact that I didn't have the speed, strength, or stamina to walk as fast as some of the other candidates. I quickly realized that, if I continued at this pace, which was as fast as I could walk, I was not going to make it in time.

As I moved up a steep hill, I suddenly realized that the operative word was *walk*. Sure, I couldn't run up these hills, but I sure as hell could run down them. So I did. For eighteen miles. And then I started passing the candidates who had passed me—walking as fast as I could uphill, then running as fast as I could down, not to mention running as fast as I could on flat ground.

When I finished, another noncommissioned officer said, "That's a pretty good time. Drop your ruck. All right, next phase."

There was no pause between tests.

"All right," he repeated. "Low crawl to the marked position. Set up a claymore. You understand the task conditions standard?"

"Yes, sergeant." A claymore was an antipersonnel device that we had to prepare in a specific sequence of events. This phase was pass or fail.

I passed. The third phase started immediately.

"All right. Set up this field expedient jungle antenna to initi-
ate basic communications. You understand the task?"

"Yes, Sergeant."

I passed again, because this was what I wanted. And by this
point, when I wanted something, I didn't give up. I didn't stop
until I got it. They wanted to see if we were able to accomplish
our goals, not just through extensive directions and training but
by thinking ahead, extrapolating on what we already knew, and
using our wits. They wanted a different type of soldier. So did I.

"Get the fuck up."

All of us jumped off our bunks, ready to move out. I was now
at the US Marine Corps's Amphibious Reconnaissance School
in Fort Story, Virginia. The LRSD teams would often send new
members to the Marine Corps Force Recon Amphibious Training School, so within minutes, we were conducting our morning swims. Sure, it brought me back to my childhood morning
runs to the lake. But now I was twenty years old, and I had to
dip in more than my T-shirt.

The morning swims soon moved on to pushing a Zodiac over
the horizon and navigating by boat to a release point off the coast
of Virginia Beach. Training was conducted all day. Swimming
to the Zodiac, we loaded our weapons and guns. Exiting into
the water, we judged the tides and how best to penetrate to our
designated infiltration point.

Next came infiltrating by Helocast at night, which required
us to push out a Zodiac from a helicopter into the water, then
quickly jump out after it. We climbed onto these Zodiacs and
navigated toward the coast to a release point. It was dark, windy,
and so cold. My teeth were chattering as my teammates observed the drift in the tide. Navigating with the flow of the
current to our beach-infiltration point, we finally arrived at
our release point.

I felt a squeeze on my shoulder. I quietly rolled out of the

Zodiac and entered the water. I had my weapons, fins, goggles, snorkel, and flotation device. I was a scout swimmer at this time, trained on amphibious reconnaissance. I quietly swam in with a compass man, scouting for a landing point. We moved toward the beach, penetrating the curve of the waves, watching for any movement.

As we neared the coast, a teammate quietly moved himself into a weapon-ready position, scanning the beach as I turned and took off my fins—snap-linking them to my belt line. I provided cover as we moved onto the beach. We looked, listened, and even smelled for anything out of place. Then we started penetrating the beach, sweeping our sectors, looking for a landing for the Zodiac, and a location where we could hide it. Once we did, we went back to the release point and signaled to the team leader.

"All clear."

The Zodiac came into the landing position nice and quiet. They pulled up the outboard motor and slid the Zodiac right onto the beach. We grabbed the Zodiac as my teammates jumped out, dragging it right into the caché point, concealing it, then moving up into a reconnaissance position.

Another test passed.

At this point in my career, I was trained on more advanced forms of military communications than those on the infantryman level. I understood how to cut jungle antennas. I understood high frequency ranges and how to push, as well as encrypt, communications. I understood how to push gain antennas. I understood how to patrol through jungles, woods, and urban areas as a long-range reconnaissance teammate.

As a team member, our tactics on patrol were different than regular infantry. They trained us to operate in a four-person reconnaissance team. We moved in a stealth-with-tactics approach derived from what the military had learned from Native Americans throughout American history.

I was a paratrooper. I was Ranger-qualified. I was LRSD.
And all through that I heard that the white man would oppress
and suppress me. All the way I heard *chink*. But my response was
not to complain, argue, or defend but to rise above that. Prove
them all wrong. Yes, I faced racism the whole way, but I just
kept going. I graduated.

I got promoted ahead of my peers because I took training
that others turned down because it looked more than dangerous. It looked frightening. It *was* frightening. I was frightened
the entire time. But there was something in me that was fearless.
Frightened and fearless at the same time, that was me.

And I would have continued with the LRSD teams if it hadn't
been for one night. That was a dark night on the Mexican border. I was the lead now, taking my LRSD team in. The top
half of them were in civilian clothes, the lower half in tactical.
I checked my compass and looked up at the moon as my teammates got into a wedge formation. We set up our antennas for
long-frequency shots back to headquarters. I had become the
eyes and ears for the Border Patrol as well as the military.

We were working with Joint Task Force Six out of Fort Bliss,
Texas, on Counter-Drug missions. But I was also with Border
Patrol officers that night, trying to gain what we called *atmospherics*: in other words, what was going on in the area. So I was
there when the patrol stopped a suspicious van. I was prepared to
find drugs, but that was not what I saw when an officer opened
the van's rear doors.

The sight inside stopped me, burning into my brain. There
were stacks of humans. One on top of the other. Mothers holding children. The stench of feces and urine. A sense of hopelessness and fear. It wasn't drug smuggling, it was human trafficking.
This van of innocent women and children were going to be
sold into slavery.

As I stood there, a different kind of energy came over me.
The fire that had been burning inside me started to change into

something else. Something tighter, hotter, and more intense. During high school it had been my hate for oppression. Now that hate was turning into rage.

That night I couldn't get the sight of those captive people out of my mind. Was this how I and my family had looked to those Russian supply-boat rescuers seventeen years ago? I would never know. But one thing I did know. From here on, if I could help captives anywhere in the world I found them, I would.

After that, I rotated out of this JTF-6 mission. Everything I had learned before now was propelling me—reminding me of an ancient teaching. Not from *The Book of Five Rings* but from one of the texts that book had led me to, by Hagakure, also known as *The Book of the Samurai*.

"Although it stands to reason that a samurai should be mindful of the Way of the Samurai, it would seem that we are all negligent. Consequently, if someone were to ask, 'What is the true meaning of the Way of Samurai?' the person who would be able to answer promptly is rare. This is because it has not been established in one's mind beforehand. From this, one's unmindfulness of the Way can be known."

They had been just words to me before. Now they were a call to action. I was ready. It was time. Now I was reminded of why I started my journey as a warrior in the first place. My mindfulness would be known. It was now time to free the oppressed.

# 10

It had all led up to this. I felt like everything I had suffered, everything I had learned, everything I had done all led up to this: the Special Forces.

I had on my uniform. It was starched; my boots, spit-shined. I was a proud young soldier. More than that. At this time of my career, I was a young Long Range Reconnaissance Team Leader—one who was looking down at an old pamphlet, navigating through the stairways of an old barracks in the Special Forces building.

I opened the door to the recruiting station, which was filled with Special Forces recruiters, all typing away. I stepped up to the nearest desk and handed over my packet.

"Last four?" the recruiter asked.

I wrote down the last four numbers of my Social Security number, then my name and present unit. The recruiter motioned me to have a seat. I sat. I waited. And I waited. You wait until they're ready to talk to you. That much I knew. Apparently, they weren't ready.

So, I kept waiting. As I did, I noticed how these Special Forces recruiters would glance at me as they typed. I could see how they were already sizing me up, judging me. I could just imagine what they were thinking. I didn't look like most of the men they saw coming in here. The fact of the matter was back then in the Special Forces, there were very few Asians that made the cut to the A-Teams.

"Sergeant Lam." I looked over to see a recruiter in an office doorway.

"Yes, Sergeant," I answered him.

"Come on in," he said.

It was an office like so many others in the military. There was an old recruiting poster showing a Green Beret and a commando dagger. The poster read "This says more about you than you can say about yourself."

The recruiter was a former team guy from 7th Special Forces Group. By the look on his face and the badges on his uniform, you could tell he had been in a few gunfights.

"Hand me your packet," he instructed.

He scanned through my record, making sure I had the proper Armed Services Vocational Aptitude Battery scores—commonly known as ASVAB. These scores are what the military grades your intellect with. Special Forces weren't just looking for good soldiers, they were looking for smart ones. Even the minimum score had to be high just to be considered here.

"One hundred and thirty," the recruiter said as he flipped through my packet. "That's almost maximum GT score."

GT was General Technical, or general knowledge. One-ten is the necessary minimum.

"You're smart," he commented. As I smiled, he added, "Or not," and went back to check on my physical-training scores. The mind games had begun.

I had scored a three hundred on the Army PT Test at that time. That was the best possible score you could achieve. I was really fit. As far as I was concerned, scoring three hundred was actually not that hard. At least not for me. But a lot of soldiers struggled with it. It was always important to me to uphold the Army standards to the best of my abilities.

The recruiter closed my files, now understanding that I

wanted to go to the top percent of the US Army. He looked me up and down. He saw that my posture and uniform were straight and sharp. He saw pride on my face.

"So," he said, "what do you want to do in the Special Forces?"

I was ready for the question. "I want to be a weapons sergeant," I answered immediately.

"Well," he snorted, "good luck with that."

I wasn't going to let that comment lie. "Why is that, Sergeant?" I asked.

"Well, you have a really high GT score," he answered, "so they're going to put you as a medic or something that requires intellect. So just be prepared, man. It's going to be hard, but good luck."

"Thank you, Sergeant."

I left, secure in the knowledge that I had prequalified for the US Army Special Forces Assessment and Selection. It was what I had always wanted. It was what I had been preparing for since I was sixteen. So I did what I always did: I ran.

I ran through the Special Forces training grounds, on the side of the highways, and through the backwoods of North Carolina, where I used to run as a child. But now, I was twenty years old and running differently. Thanks to all the training, I was running at different speeds, navigating, always with a heavy backpack.

But Special Forces assessment selection waits for no man. It came faster than I thought it would. On a cold, wet February morning in 1997 the bus came to take me to Camp Mackall, North Carolina—and into foothills of pine needles, dirt trail roads, and thick, muddy swamps. That was where the Special Forces did their training.

Instructors called out a list of candidates who were coming from different units all around the United States for this particular class. First, they crammed us like cattle into the bus, then all but dumped our duffel bags and rucksacks on top of us.

Even so, it was quiet during the trip, each trainee deep in their own thoughts.

Through the heavy, cold morning fog, I could barely make out the wooden post on the side of the road that read *Special Forces Training Grounds*. As the vehicle screeched to a halt, the instructors started yelling.

"Get off my fucking bus!"

We double-timed it off their fucking bus, but even though we were running fast, we made it just before our duffel bags were thrown after us. And the instructors just kept barking.

"Get off my fucking bus, now!"

"Drop your gear right in front of you!"

"Line up in formation!"

Guys were falling over each other, some stepping on top of others' backs, trying to get into formation, all while dragging their duffel bags—hoping that it *was* their duffel bag and they hadn't grabbed someone else's.

"Open up your duffel bags," the instructors told us. "Open up your rucksacks. Dump all your contents out into the ground."

It was muddy, wet ground on that cold foggy February morning. Didn't matter. The instructors went through it like threshers, looking for any contraband. They were going to make damn sure that we weren't sneaking in anything that could enhance our performance during assessment and selection.

Very quickly what clothes had been clean were no longer clean. They were now accessorized with mud, dirt, debris, sawdust, and anything else the instructors kicked into our gear.

Suddenly, there was another instructor on a podium shouting about different types of gear, telling us, "Once I call it, pack it!"

After the instructors searched through, and announced, every one of our belongings, we were ordered to move into our living quarters. I immediately realized these were World War II–era barracks—cold and drafty—with bunk beds throughout. Students were running around, dropping their gear and trying to get it all in order. But then the instructors started calling all of us back out again.

Then we were in front of the barracks, looking up at them on a podium. I took a second to glance around. There must have been at least two hundred candidates there. The instructors told us to get in formation, then started announcing the count.

One by one they quickly called out our roster numbers. I watched, waited, and listened as the candidates beside me got theirs, one after another, getting closer and closer to me.

One one one, one one two, one one three, and then me. One one four.

I wrote it down immediately. One one four. I sewed it on to my uniform later that night. 1, 1, 4.

I was no longer a human being. I was a number. This number. Number one-one-four. Then the training truly started. Ironically, considering they had just reduced us to numbers, the first part of that training was called Individual Week.

We had to conduct strenuous physical training starting at zero-five—five o'clock in the morning. We were to assemble in our Battle Dress Uniforms, which were camouflage fatigues, with combat boots on. We were supplied with dummy weapons that weighed the same as the real weapons because they were lead on the inside, rubberized on the outside. Everything, all the equipment, whether it was a magazine clip, a claymore mine, or an antitank weapon, weighed exactly the same as the real thing.

And everything we were given had to be identified with our roster number. It had to be sewn on all our uniforms, marked on our rucksacks, and taped on our weapons. That way, just in case any part of you was lost or left behind, they knew where to go and how to track you down.

Already I could tell what separated Special Forces from all the previous training I had graduated from. I could tell from the planning. These were a different breed of instructors. They were clearly smarter in the way they tore candidates down and sought to put them back together again.

That first day set the tone. In an area away from the barracks they brought out, and set up, a whiteboard.

"Men," an instructor standing in front of it said, "this whiteboard can change within fifteen minutes. That means that anytime it does change, you must react within fifteen minutes. If it was to read *Formation within fifteen minutes*, the whole company must react and get out here with the proper equipment, the proper uniform, and the proper combat load, as designated on this whiteboard."

At the time, it seemed really simple. But if you thought about it for more than fifteen minutes, you'd realize what a nightmare it was going to be. Except you wouldn't be able to sleep long enough to have a nightmare because the board could change at the first second after any given fifteen minutes passed.

So within two days, we were losing our freaking minds, and our bodies were breaking because all we wanted to do was sleep, but we couldn't sleep because that whiteboard could change at any time of the day or night.

It was all about mind games. And this was just one of many mind games perfected over forty-five years since the Special Forces had been formed.

As we packed up our rucks, they gave us instructions. Each squad was broken down into certain key individuals. They were the designated leaders picked out of the class, depending on their positions within the United States Army. The senior noncommissioned officers were ordered to take accountability for all the other students.

A new mind game had started.

"All right, men. So, what we're going to do is we're going to learn nighttime navigation. So, what we're going to do is you're going to walk from point A to point B. This is called dead reckoning. Very basic, simple navigation."

We had a lensatic compass back then. And basically, you read and plotted off the map, converted grid to magnetic azimuth, locked in the lensatic compass, and you got dead reckoning. That meant you wouldn't steer off that line. So if there were bushes in front of you, you went through those bushes. If there was a river, you went through that river. What you didn't do was deviate from that line.

I was soon chest-deep in water, crossing a swamp with my compass and a full combat load, a rucksack, and a weighted rubber weapon, heading through the backwoods in the training grounds of the Special Forces.

They taught us how to plan attack points to a pinpoint location. They taught us how to run, utilizing and paralleling roads. They taught us how to understand ground temperature and how that translated to high and low ground.

Ultimately, they taught me how to understand terrain and how that influenced the compass, the unit, and the individual on a Special Forces A-Team.

The Navigation Phase took a week. Long movements, extremely long routes, under heavy combat load. Sixty-five-pound rucks, weighted-down rubber weapons, simulated ammo weight on your gear, and water. Water became very important, and was soon another thing that weighed us down too.

During Individual Week we'd had to take all our physical-training tests again. Two-mile run. Five-mile run. Eighteen-mile run. Everything timed. The standard twenty-one pull-ups. If you couldn't pass that in full combat load, you're a no-go.

It was long, grueling hours of physical training during the day, followed by long, grueling hours of classroom academics at night. Each day, instructions were given to each student, and only once. We had to study and perform tasks to the teachers' exacting standard. They were looking for the individual who could be trained quickly.

It was never easy, but it wasn't supposed to be. I finally finished that week in the pitch-black of night and dropped my ruck at the final checkpoint.

"Roster number?" I heard.

"One, one, four," I immediately answered.

"Load your ruck, get in the back of the truck."

I followed orders and felt the way I had felt every day. Aching. All over. Every day the navigation got longer. Every day the movements got harder. It was designed to break our bodies and put the miles marched directly on our shoulders. Because the real pain was still to come.

As an instructor called out to me, I was in the back of the truck, moving my canteen from my mouth to over my head. I peered into the night and could see the shapes of other candidates as they reached the checkpoint. One after another they climbed in after me. In the pitch-black I could barely make out the roster numbers on the white strips on their shirts. Soon the truck was full.

An instructor closed it up. "Take them back," he called to the driver. "Take them back to camp."

If anybody thought that was it for the night, they were wrong. As soon as we off-loaded, we heard another instructor.

"All right, men, you got fifteen minutes. Throw your rucks back in the barracks and grab your notebooks. Meet us in the classroom in fifteen minutes."

Fifteen minutes. Special Forces training was all about fifteen minutes. That was almost an impossible amount of time to do what we were constantly ordered to do. *Almost* being the optimal word. Because Special Forces was about finding the ones who could always beat the almost impossible.

All of us ran back to the barracks, dropped our rucks, tried to clean up as much and as fast as possible, then grabbed our notebooks and ran back to get into formation just in time for the class leader to march us into the classroom. Once there, we stood by our desks at attention. That's when the instructor came in.

"Take a seat," he said. As we complied, he turned toward the leader. "Is everyone here?"

"Yes, Sergeant."

"All right," he said. "Men, at this time, you see the piece of paper in front of you. What I need you to do is I need you to geographically draw the continents of the world. Then I need you to divide those continents into countries and start labeling them. You have thirty minutes."

I could practically hear almost everybody in the classroom think the same thing I was thinking.

*Fuck.*

I had been trained for a lot of things in the military, but not world geography. So I went to what I knew: Asia, starting with Vietnam. I drew that and tried branching out from there. I quickly realized that I didn't know as much as I thought—especially when it came to the Middle East, Africa, and South America.

But I kept drawing until I hit a mental roadblock. Only then did I glance around, and saw some students were falling asleep while still trying to draw. Only then did the creeping exhaustion start to reach me too, and I suddenly realized how hot it was.

They had purposely turned up the heat. It was ninety degrees in there.

Then I noticed the instructors stood silently in the shadows all around the room, staring at every student. And as each one passed out or fell asleep, the nearest instructor made note of his roster number.

As I turned my sweating, drooping head back to my map, I heard inside my brain, *I think this is it.* But then I heard two words outside my head.

"Pencils down!"

My pencil dropped out of one hand as I wiped my eyes with the other.

"Drink water, men."

We didn't have to be told twice.

The norm had become a full physical-training day followed by academics. As always, they were looking for guys who were smart and had the ability to push through pain and suffering.

It was not about if we knew the continents, it was about how hard we tried to follow their orders.

"All right, men. There's a piece of paper in front of you. All right, this time you got one hour. One hour. You need to write down why the fuck you want to go into the Special Forces. Good luck."

They hadn't turned down the heat. It felt hotter than ever in there. And just to help, they started playing classical music. And it wasn't the loud, stirring stuff either. They might as well have started playing lullabies.

Looking down, sweat dripping off my face, my spirit powered me. Why did I want to go into the Special Forces? As I thought of my childhood self drifting out into the ocean off Malaysia, the words started flowing through me.

To fight oppression. To fight suppression. Hopelessness. Geno-cide. Racism. It was a promise I'd made to humanity as a child. It was a promise I'd made to myself. It was to find a strength that I didn't have. It was a journey to discover that strength.

As the heat pressed down on me and the sweat dripped off me, I wrote while other candidates fell asleep around me.

To free the oppressed...

"Pencils down!"

I sat up.

"On your feet."

I stood. Tired, yes. Unsteady, no.

"Get the fuck out of my class."

Lining up in formation, we moved back to the barracks.

"You know the drill," the class leader told us.

As we walked off, the instructors gathered up each one of our papers. They were going to correct our grammar. They were going to critique the way we constructed our paragraphs and how we wrote. They were going to study the narrative. They were looking for intelligence and purpose.

We were looking for sleep. But when we got back to the barracks, we heard the worst thing we could.

Achoo!

*Oh shit. Oh fuck.*

We all knew what that sound meant. If one guy got sick in these cold, drafty old barracks, with all our immune systems weaker, everybody got sick.

The only thing we could do was what our mothers told us: wash your hands. I washed my hands a lot. I washed my nose a lot. But in the end, the guy across from me got sick. Then the guy next to me and then, of course, I did. All the hand- and face-washing in the world won't help if germ drops got into your eyes, nose, or mouth.

Did they delay the training and bring in a squad of medics? What do you think? No, almost immediately afterward, I was staring down at a map.

"All right," said an instructor, "you're going to look at an identifiable point on the ground, then you're going to take your compass and shoot an azimuth to that terrain feature to get a back azimuth. Then you're only to look for another identifiable point on the ground and get a back azimuth from that point." He wasn't done. "At the intersection point is where you can pinpoint yourself on the ground. If you don't know where you are on the ground, you look at two points on the ground and convert it into a grid intersection. That's where you are. Do you understand?"

Now, imagine hearing that with a wicked head cold.

*What? On the ground? What?*

"Do you understand all that?" I asked the candidate next to me.

"Oh yeah," he said. "That shit's easy."

It didn't matter if I believed him or not, because I didn't understand it. On top of that, I felt a fever coming on.

"All right, men," the instructor immediately droned on, "if you don't understand that, what you're going to do is you're going to parallel this road and then, from the road, you're going to pick an intersection, and from there you're going to take a re-azimuth to pick your attack point. Do you understand?"

*Huh?*

Getting sick did not help, because at this point in the Special Forces training it was not about basic land navigation anymore. These were advanced-level land navigation skills, and they were teaching us at a hundred miles an hour. Like the flu going around the barracks, you either catch it or you don't. Only the material was a lot harder to catch. That was part of the selection assessment. They were looking for guys who were able to catch on to things quickly.

But at that point, I was barely making it. Through my viral fog, I tried to plot my reintersection on the map. Giving up the practical exercises, I plotted with a ruler and an azimuth and a compass—changing magnetic to grid on a map, while coughing, as well as dozing in and out.

I looked at my compass like it was a black widow spider. I twisted and turned it, trying to make heads or tails of the instructions.

*Fuck, I don't even know where I am*, I thought. *Quit.*

Thankfully, even though it was a cold February, lightning cracked outside, distracting me from my thoughts. A second later, lightning actually flashed through the door and all the lights went out. We were plunged into complete darkness.

"On your feet!" I heard.

All of us immediately stood, hearing the rumbling of all the moving cadets as our boots hit the ground. Only more lightning strikes let me see the shapes of my fellow classmates.

A second after that, the lights came back on. Standing there, in front of us, in front of me, was my uncle.

My uncle. In combat fatigues. Wearing his Special Forces Green Beret. Now a full bird Colonel. My uncle looked across the candidates. I was just one of them now.

"What's the count, Sergeant?" he asked.

"Four hundred eighty men, sir."

The appearance of my uncle meant that we were now going into Team Week.

Team Week was the Green Berets' brutal variation on the Navy SEALs' Hell Week. The previous attempts to break our bodies and minds were minor inconveniences compared to Team Week. Here they weren't going after your body or mind, they were going after you. Team Week was designed, developed, and perfected to break a human being. You can never train hard enough to prepare for Team Week.

It was about to start, and I was sick as a dog and wanted to quit. Then my uncle looked across us all, but it seemed as if he was speaking directly to me.

"Walk or die, men," he said. "You fucking walk or you die."

You could hear a pin drop in that room filled with almost five hundred men.

"You know," he continued, breaking the thick silence, "in World War II in the Philippines, Americans and Filipino rebels—a guerrilla force—were fighting against the Japanese, when General MacArthur issued an order to retreat. These Americans and Filipinos were captured, then forced into what is now known as the Bataan Death March. They said that if one man dropped beyond one arm's length from the next man, the Japanese would pull him aside and bayonet him where he stood. So you walk or you fucking die, men."

He was saying it to the class, but his words went into my brain like a laser-sighted missile. I don't know if the universe brought him here at this point, in a flash of lightning, to yank me out of my flu-induced self-pity, but I didn't, and don't, care.

I was going to walk. Or I was going to die.

# 11

I walked, but barely, because it was Team Week.

"Oh shit, fuckin' A, this is heavy."

Now we had to move full-sized telephone poles that could weigh over a thousand pounds. And we had to move them with forty-five-pound steel poles that were lashed together across our backpacks.

The telephone pole was laid on top of these steel rods, and as my teammates balanced one side, I balanced the other. That meant at least three hundred pounds per man—a man who also had to carry full combat load weapons, all at a pretty rough pace.

My jungle boots, well worn-in by this time, dug into the soft earth in the foothills of the Special Forces training ground. A makeshift map was given to each of us. Our job was to move these telephone poles, which stood in for weapons of mass destruction, to an unknown point, as fast as we could.

Two instructors per team were evaluating every movement of every man. If you couldn't lash the telephone poles, if you didn't understand how to quickly organize your team and solve the riddle of how to turn a bunch of steel rods into a telephone-pole carrier, then move them quickly and effectively by organizing and leading your team, the instructors would make note of that.

They would also note your skill, or lack of it, in navigating these simulated weapons of mass destruction through an unknown area of foothills while also creating and maintaining a forward- and rear-security system—complete with a rest plan so you and your teammates wouldn't collapse.

Doing all that within an unknown deadline could break a man mentally and physically. But what else was new? That was their job. Our job was not to break.

As we moved, I could see the team leader, the students, and the candidates all being graded by instructors who were dogging on them like pit bulls.

"What the fuck are you thinking?" one instructor barked at the team leader.

"Sergeant?"

"What the fuck are you thinking? Why are you moving through here? Isn't there a better route? Did you do your reconnaissance?"

In the Special Forces, it's not about fucking around like in Army games. It's about intelligence.

"What I'm asking you, candidate, is did you do a map check?"

"No, Sergeant."

"That's what you're telling me? You're telling me that you're walking around blindly?"

"Yes, Sergeant."

"You're fucking dead," the instructor told the hapless team leader. "Sit down."

Before the team leader could even follow that order, the instructor had already turned to blindly pick another candidate—a candidate who was just turning around himself.

"Step off the stack," the instructor snapped at him. "You're the team leader now. You move these weapons of mass destruction as fast as you can to this designated point. Do you understand?"

"Yes, Sergeant!"

We started moving again, at an even faster pace.

Quitting was an everyday thing. Quitting could happen at any time. Quitting came for the weak ones, the strong ones, even the ones I thought were exceptionally fit. I eventually found that they could be the first to quit: they had the bodies for it but not the minds, and without the mind, it didn't matter how ripped you were.

As we continued to move the telephone pole, I felt something next to me. I looked over at a teammate. The look on his face said it all. I had felt him giving up before he even acknowledged it. But he acknowledged it now.

"Can't do it anymore, dude," he muttered. "I can't do it anymore, man. I'm out."

When he stepped off, I could barely hold on, as another teammate collapsed trying to balance the weight of that quitter. Somehow, we kept going. That was the name of the game for us nonquitters.

Quitting happened all the time, like at night when everybody else was sleeping. They would slowly pack their bags, walk through the dark, quietly open the door, and disappear into the night. Quitting wasn't reserved for physical training either. It could happen in the classrooms too.

"You fail one more test, you're out. You understand?"

I had looked over at the classmate as the instructor gave him this warning. His body was strong, but his mind was struggling. That night I saw him pack up his bags in the dark and walk out of the barracks.

But no matter what time or where you quit—day, night, during training, academics, or meals—the instructors made sure everybody knew it. And they'd do it the same humiliating way every time. The camp loudspeakers would come on, and we'd hear the same five singsong words.

"Another one bites the dust!" Lyrics from the rock group Queen.

As always, it was about mind games compounded by our lack of sleep and food. But to me, the biggest mind game of all was the whiteboard.

I remember hearing a classmate running through the rocks

outside the barracks while I was half-asleep in my bunk. The rocks he was kicking up got louder and faster, then he yanked open the doors.

"Fucking formation in ten fucking minutes!" he shouted. "Get all your shit! Fifty-five-pound rucks!"

All of us were up and scrambling until I heard one say, "Fifty-five-pound rucks? You sure?"

He wasn't. That was another problem the whiteboard had. On it was written all the instructions: what uniform to wear, what combat load to bring, how heavy the rucks, even the weight of the canteen water. Everything.

He had seen the formation order, but he had not memorized or thought to write down the rest of it. The candidate shut his mouth, spun, and ran back out. Was the whiteboard right outside? No, of course not. He had to run as far as a football player to the end zone, memorize the instructions, then get back to us, as we're scrambling, packing up our gear, doing the best we could to prepare for whatever the board actually had written on it.

"Sixty," he gasped, out of breath. "Sixty-five-pound rucks!"

We loaded up the correct weight. There was a scale on the outside of each barracks—far away from the board. It was suspended by a military rope and had a hook on it. We put our rucksacks on the hook and waited for it to show us the weight. And that's how the instructors would measure your rucksack and your combat load and your gear. Each instructor tested each student. Every formation, every training, every obstacle.

I remember standing in formation on the second day of Team Week. It was three in the morning. It was cold and wet. We had just finished carrying those telephone poles, as well as our combat-loaded rucksacks, through unknown distances in the foothills and swamps of North Carolina.

Already the class had thinned out. A great many had quit. The barracks behind us were shrouded in fog as an instructor stepped up to the podium. He didn't speak at first. Instead, he made a sound like a man about to feed the starving.

"Mm-hmm," he said. "Well, I'll tell you what, men. I got some freshly baked doughnuts right inside my barracks, and they're super warm and toasty. Who wants to go into my barracks and get warm and toasty with some doughnuts?"

There seemed to be a nearly imperceptible chill going through the remaining candidates. Even so, no one moved as the instructor slowly raised a steaming cup of coffee to his lips. Then his tone changed from a happy clown enticing children to an executioner.

"Just fucking quit," he said. "That's it."

He took a gulp of coffee, then sniffed the air. He looked at us like we were lambs for the slaughter.

"Who wants my doughnuts?" he wickedly drawled.

Then he jumped off the podium, and another instructor took his place.

"Well," the second instructor said as if it was the most logical thing in the world, "if nobody wants his doughnuts, then what you're going to do is ruck up. Put on your fucking rucksacks and follow the chem lights."

Non-military might know them as glow sticks. They marked the trail of our next mind game. Sometimes they marked a four-mile walk, sometimes eight or twelve miles or more. Ultimately, it didn't matter. We walked or died. Or quit.

"Line up, move out."

I started moving but heard rucksacks dropping behind me.

"Roster number one one one?" I heard.

"I quit," was his answer, immediately followed by a familiar tune.

"Another one bites the dust!"

Smelling the coffee and the doughnuts, I moved into the darkness and the rain. That was just day two, but already my mind started rebelling.

*Quit*, it said.

*Just follow the chem lights*, I silently replied.

I did, and they led me around the parking lot—right back into our barracks. It was always a mind game. Especially to a tired and hungry mind. Thankfully, unlike one one one, I lived to survive day three.

"Roster number one one four. Do you understand the task?"

"Yes, Sergeant!" I answered, looking down at another rudimentary map.

"You have twenty minutes. Do you understand, one one four?"

"Yes, Sergeant!"

"Your time starts now."

Clicking his watch, he walked away. I ran back to the team. We looked down at two downed pilots made from bags of wet sand. And these pilots were five hundred pounds each. Then there were forty-five–pound metal poles and lashings. I had twenty minutes to come up with a plan on how to best move these thousand pounds of Mr. Heavies to point B—and I was being evaluated every second.

But, by then, I knew it was all about teamwork. It wasn't about one individual. I knew the strengths and weaknesses of each member of the team, and I let them do what they did best. They responded with great work.

"Hey, man, we can do this," one said. "We can make an X bar, lash the pilot to it..."

"And then," said another, "we can load it on the back of our rucksacks..."

"And then we can do any shift change as we're moving, because the poles will allow enough for two guys to get underneath them..."

"Got it?" I asked them.

"Got it. Smart plan."

"Then, let's do it, men. Let's do it."

Beyond hunger and exhaustion, the thing I kept in mind was that these candidates came from the top of the United States

Army. They were the best. And we were there to work together to help one another get passed through selection. The instructors were waiting for this. They were waiting for teamwork. And fuck doughnuts, we were ready to give them teamwork.

We started moving through the foothills, but all too soon the weight was dragging us down.

"Guys are dropping back, man," one of my teammates told me. "What are we going to do?"

"Just hold what you got," I told him. "Let's wait."

An instructor pounced on the seeming pause. "Candidate one one four, what are you doing?"

"I'm waiting for my team—"

"Negative," he interrupted. "Negative, one one four. If they're unable to keep up, you leave them, you understand?"

I looked carefully at the instructor. "Yes, Sergeant," I said, but no, I didn't understand. You never, ever left a teammate. Never.

"What are we waiting on? Move!"

So I started moving, but I also changed my pace. It looked purposeful, but it was intentionally slower. The bullhorns started blowing. The harassment started up.

"And what are we doing here? What are we doing here?" the instructors barked as they thumbed the siren on their megaphones into my ears. But their assaults on me had given the rest of my team just enough time to catch up.

"What are we doing here?" one instructor all but yelled in my face. But then his tone became quiet and deadly serious. "You are to move the men," he said, seething. "You are not to slow down to facilitate somebody quitting. Do you understand?"

"Yes, Sergeant!"

I couldn't fool these superiors, who had seen it all in their years of training candidates, but I could do what I thought was right. Quickly looking around, I assessed the team, and reorganized quickly.

"All right, move!"

We started moving, just as I saw the instructor nearest me grinning. As we kept moving, we made good time. We got to point B and dropped the apparatus.

"One one four," the instructor called to me. "Come over here." He pulled me aside. He wasn't grinning anymore. "What the fuck is your problem?"

"Nothing, Sergeant!"

"We're here to assess the men," he said into my face. "We're not here to carry the men. You understand me, one one four?" He didn't let me answer. Instead, he told me something I've never forgotten. "You carry the men here, those men will get you killed in combat." He stepped back. "We're assessing the team, so let us do our fucking job. Quit carrying the fucking men."

"Yes—"

"Get out of my fucking face."

Team Week continued with academics at night, only ending when we were well and truly exhausted in mind and body. But even our sleep wasn't free.

"All right, men, all together now, we're going to sing 'Ballad of the Green Berets'!"

It was two o'clock in the morning, and now they were seriously trying to drain us with a sing-along to Staff Sergeant Barry Sadler's 1966 chart-topper.

"Fighting soldiers from the sky..." the instructors led us with maniacal grins on their faces, "Fearless men who jump and die..."

Naturally, they had turned up the heat in the barracks. Even struggling out of our exhausted stupor, some candidates still passed out from the strain. And all the while, instructors who weren't singing stood in the shadows, assessing everyone and everything.

The next day we were pushing a jeep that only had three wheels up a hill, slipping and sliding through dirt and mud.

Guys were falling back. Guys were quitting. And once a guy quit, the team still had to get the damn jeep up the hill, trying immediately to pick up the slack.

Instructors silently weeded out the quitters, always watching as the exercise got harder and harder. These were not like the Ranger instructors who got up in your face and yelled. These instructors were deathly quiet. They didn't need to yell. They just needed to weed out the ones who wouldn't make it up that hill.

Twenty-one days later, standing in a classroom were eighty-eight men and me. Eighty-nine remaining from the four hundred and eighty original candidates. I had a stress fracture, I was broken, I was done—but I was also selected, so then I was on a bus back to Fort Bragg, North Carolina. I was going home to wait for the Special Forces qualification course start date.

You think it was all done once I survived Team Week? Oh no. Once you pass Special Forces assessment selection, you have to attend the longest pipeline of military training in Special Operations Command, which is the Green Beret pipeline. Back in 1997, the course was broken down into three phases.

The first phase was patrol phase, which was broken down into raids and ambushes for a twelve-man A-Team. Within that group, Special Forces guys had to be able to infiltrate behind enemy lines, train rebels to be able to either overthrow an existing government, like in El Salvador, or suppress a rebel force, like in the war in Iraq. So that was what they were training us for.

All too soon I was back at Fort McCall and the Special Forces training ground. For this phase, we stayed in the field. No more drafty barracks for us. They made us pitch tents into a bivouac site. And if we didn't have tents, we had ponchos, and we had to make a lean-to into a survival tent, and that's where we lived off our rucksacks for a month.

And that month was filled with reconnaissance, ambushes, and quick hit-and-run-style raids. We would contain and isolate an objective. During reconnaissance missions we would cloverleaf around the objective to offer different vantage points, gather intelligence, develop a course of action on the basis of our intelligence, then conduct a strategic hit off that intelligence, utilizing the training and tactics we had been taught.

And all these tactics came from hard-fought experiences in Panama, El Salvador, Vietnam, and every conflict since America began. But the basis for all the development, the foundation on which all the strategies were built, came from Native Americans. At their heart, these were their tactics—going all the way back to simply feeling, listening, and even smelling the ground to track a moving force.

We used a lot of Native training techniques that settlers saw in the French and Indian War. Even after more than two hundred years these techniques are still being utilized on the battlefield today because they work. That is also why the Special Forces patch is in the shape of an arrowhead that points straight up. That symbolizes unconventional warfare in the military.

As I patrolled the foothills of Camp Mackall, I smelled the pine needles once again. I felt the vibrations of the earth through my boots. I saw that the fog was lifting. I heard the birds singing. I could even hear them flying. By then, we were so thoroughly trained that we became part of the environment. We could smell, hear, and feel everything. And we used it to set up an ambush.

Human Intelligence told us a rebel force was moving supplies down a simulated road. We had fifteen minutes before reinforcements came. Fifteen minutes to hit with speed and violence, grab any intelligence and supplies, and then retreat back into the woods, undetected.

Each of the twelve in the A-Team did their job with precision. Machine guns fired. Pyrotechnics exploded. Green Berets surfaced, wiping out every enemy moving through the kill zone. We opened doors, grabbed laptops and maps, then started digging through the dead no matter where they fell, taking anything we could find—anything that could gain us intelligence. Weapons were thrown into a pile, explosives thrown right on top of it, like clockwork.

Seven minutes in, we were moving off-target to the release point. The team leader counted off the men as we set up the V-shape perimeter, got into formation, and loaded up our rucks. The team moved quietly through the shadows and blended back into the woods.

At this phase of the Special Forces pipeline, students were trained to operate at the basic level as a twelve-man, hit-and-run team, trained in patrols and small-unit tactics.

After a month of such training—sleeping underneath a poncho in the woods—I was back on a bus to Fort Bragg. I cannot tell you how nice it was to take a shower, eat an unhurried meal, and get more than one hour of sleep a night, but I knew I had to appreciate it fast, because phase two of Special Forces training was about to start.

Phase two was about individual specialty. You had a team leader, which was an officer position. You had a team sergeant, which was a senior noncommissioned officer position, and the most experienced senior position on the team. You had a highly skilled Army warrant officer. And then there were demolitions, combat medics, a communication sergeant, and a weapons sergeant. And within each one of those skill sets were two guys— a junior who learned from a senior.

I was training to be a weapons specialist. That meant I had to learn about every weapon there was. I had to be able to quickly assemble and function with every one of them. I had to be the expert on small-unit tactics, be able to understand strategy, utilize different weapons no matter where, and have the ability to understand the effectiveness of each weapon within specific terrain and political infrastructure.

When you knew weapons at that level, you had to be able to hard-stop tanks and utilize antitank weapons, as well as know the tactics that were proven in different environments to funnel the tanks into your land mine. You had to be able to understand how to shoot down a moving rotary-wing aircraft.

If you were out there as a team member, you had to understand how to call in artillery and naval fire. It was not just about being able to pull a gun: you had to be able to use that gun as effectively as possible, all the way up to being able to drop a kinetic strike—another name for a lethal air option—onto your enemy.

So to start, I had to learn how to work a basic weapon system. And in phase two of the Special Forces Qualification Course, you had a lot of instructors that would tell it like it is.

"You understand what that is?" I heard Scully's angry voice yell at me.

"Sergeant," I answered calmly, "it's a 1911 A1." I knew that because my stepfather had me take one apart in 1981.

Then the sergeant in question held up a Browning high-powered pistol, then a Magnum, and an M9, one after another. He had a whole table of them. After identifying them, I looked down onto hundreds more guns that I had to memorize.

The weapon qualification course is the shortest one of all of the others, but is still the longest pipeline within Special Operations Command. The regiment invests a lot of time and money into training a soldier to be able to work proficiently in small numbers that are forward-deployed into hostile areas with little to no support.

Weapons training is usually run by veterans. My veteran was Scully. Quite a character. On this hot, humid Fort Bragg range, he worked me over. As I looked up, trying to plot a mortar position on a spinning grid, Scully looked at me with one of his eyes in his hand. He started, slowly, knowingly, polishing his glass eye.

"Why are you taking so long, chink?"

"Sir?"

"Shouldn't take that fucking long. Plot the damn thing, then drop the fucking mortar round in there! By the time you do it, everybody will be fucking dead. Plot the fucking thing faster!"

"Yes, sir!" I said as he put his prosthetic eye back into its socket and walked off with a limp.

Scully was a Special Forces legend. Back in Vietnam, the Viet Cong tried to overrun his camp. Scully kept them away with his 60 mm mortar and his ability to effectively put fire where it was needed. He paid with one eye and one leg's mobility. But here he was, a retired Green Beret, teaching future Green Berets like me.

"Well, damn, I worked all day for this, but all your guys would be dead. You need to plot faster, man, faster!"

As I adjusted the dial, he got on a loudspeaker.

"Elevation..." he moaned miserably, "elevation!"

I quickly adjusted, learning how to be an effective foreign observer and call in an accurate mortar strike. But no matter how quickly I adjusted, it wasn't fast enough for him. His calls of *elevation* became softer and softer. Soon I could hear him drop the microphone. I still waited for his instructions—even though he had fallen asleep.

That was Scully for you. But he seemed to get better as I got better. I doubt that was a coincidence.

Special Forces training was long, but we had the weekends off. Even so, I was always training, because in phase two we had to get our bodies even stronger for the legendary phase three.

Unconventional warfare.

I heard the commercial aircraft propeller spinning as I stood on the tarmac of a rustic airfield in a rural North Carolina town. The night was pitch-black. My face was camouflaged up. I was in full combat gear, carrying eighty-five pounds of combat equipment. Guns, antitank weapons, claymores.

I took a look at my team as a country boy came out from the airfield shed.

"This is the team?" he asked in his Southern twang. He counted twelve men. "Okay," he said, "load 'em up!"

We made our way to this aircraft, which looked like an overgrown crop duster. We packed and hooked up to the cable line inside.

The aircraft took off into the night and flew toward a mocked-up town, whose inhabitants had been paid by the United States Army to act as foreign nationals. Everybody in this town spoke the same foreign language as dictated by the storyline. Our mission was to enter this mock country by means of airborne infiltration and link up with a resistance force. Then we were to conduct an over-the-border crossing either by foot or by vehicle. We were supposed to link up with the leader of the resistance, then advise, assist, and train the resistance force to overthrow the country that had been corrupted by Communist supporters.

"Rob," I asked one of my teammates, "you good?"

"Yeah, man," he replied, "I'm good."

The plane dropped through the darkness. Even the clouds below us looked pitch-black. Standing up wasn't easy. So we took a knee, sitting on our backpacks, until the red light came on.

"Hook up."

The Jumpmaster checked the door, looked out, and placed his hand as a reference point from the aircraft to the ground. Then he looked back.

"Shift aircraft right," he called to the pilot.

The aircraft shifted and then leveled out. The Jumpmaster came back to check his outstretched palm—again as a reference for the ground marking.

"On point," he said. "Stand by..."

It was my last chance to bitch, so I took it. *I got so much shit on me*, I complained in my head. *It's so hot!*

Then the green light came on.

*Fuck it*, I immediately thought, ignoring the heat and the weight. *Time to free the oppressed...*

Each team member went to the door and disappeared into the night. The parachutes opened, one after another. As we descended, we tried to stack as much and as decently as we could. I took my machine gun out, looked down, and checked around. I lowered the front release of my rucksack, dropping my gear just as I combat-rolled into a parachute landing fall so as not to injure myself.

Under the cover of darkness, we wrapped up our parachutes, then moved to the assembly area to dig a hole into which we dropped them. We then camouflaged the hole and started moving toward the designated point where we were supposed to make contact with the resistance.

We came to an intersection, where teammates set out left and right for security at the juncture. We scanned our sector. We prepped the fire-support position and checked our watches. It was time.

A vehicle approached, and a man jumped out and looked around. Then he took a stick, placed it against a tree and kicked and broke it. That was the predetermined signal for the A-Teams to make contact.

The team leader slung his weapon and put both hands over his head as he approached the rebel leader. The rebel leader turned toward him, guns drawn. The leader spoke softly.

"Americans."

The rebel leader looked around, trying to spot the rest of us. We were not so easy to spot.

"How many?" he asked in broken English.

"Twelve," the team leader answered. "With gear."

A truck pulled up, its bed filled with hay. The rebel leader and the truck drivers moved some of the hay so we could fit ourselves, and our gear, inside. Then they pushed and laid the hay atop us before starting to move us into the country of... well, let's call it Troy.

Yes, it's that time. I've progressed so far in my tales of training that now the Official Secrets Act is coming into play again. Because a lot of this training is classified, I'll tell you what I can.

Anyway, we moved into the country of Troy, then we had to do what's called an over-the-border crossing because, in reality, they could not just drive these vehicles across the boundaries. The truck stopped eighteen miles from the border.

"This is as far as I could take you boys," said the rebel leader. "Good luck." He pointed at the countryside. "That area is mined." He pointed at the road and some trails. "That area is heavily patrolled." He pointed at a swamp. "That is the area I recommend."

Of course he did. It was the worst area to traverse. Because not only were there enemy soldiers and police, dogs were in play here. If the police found us, we'd be put in jail. Dogs would bark, alerting their owners, and they'd report us. Dogs, on their own, might do worse. That was part of the game. And the role players in this town were being paid by the United States Army to catch us.

As we moved quietly through the foothills of Troy, we played it for real, because all too soon it would be, and our lives depended on what we learned. So we moved through the farmlands and the swamplands. We patrolled. We used countertracking techniques. And all the while, instructors remained quietly in the background, observing and assessing our every action.

It started to rain, but that didn't help those candidates who were already exhausted by the days of little sleep and less food. I saw some of their heads droop, their half-closed eyes staring at the ground, their guns lowering. But thankfully they didn't drop. We trudged on, staying as quiet and invisible as possible.

Soon it was two o'clock in the morning. We were still in the woods, but there was a radio tower looming overhead. The team leader locked eyes with us.

"A-Team," he whispered, "you understand?"

"Yeah, got it."

"We're going to move to the primary objective," he said.

We had to place explosives on this radio tower, while setting up an assault position to support that action. Anytime you want to take out a country, you take out their ability to communicate first. And that was what we were doing. There was a guerrilla force to train, advise, and assist in taking out a corrupt dictator in the country of Troy, and this was how we started.

"Okay," the leader said, "you understand the mission. Once you move, we're going to be in place first. So once we lock down left- and right-side security of this road, nothing gets in and nothing gets out without us knowing. I got you covered. Move!"

The command was given through our individual radios. We quickly moved to the base of the radio tower. There, our demolitions teammate carefully studied the geometry of the structure and the ground it stood on. Then he quietly and quickly placed C-4 where it needed to be in order to twist, bend, and break metal as well as concrete.

"Set."

We pulled back to the darkness. Immediately, three instructors stepped out of the shadows to examine if the student had properly placed the right amount of explosives needed to defeat the tower. He had: the mission was considered a success. In the Special Forces, everything was conducted at the most detailed level possible.

We were given more missions, which we completed. We continued to both train and assist rebel forces in taking down dictators, crooked politicians, and corrupt law enforcement until it culminated in my graduation from unconventional warfare training.

Was I done yet? No, I was not. Now it was on to SERE training: Survival Escape Resistance Evasion. This course was developed the hard way, by Colonel Nick Rowe, a Special Forces officer who had been captured in 1963 Vietnam. He was one of only thirty-four American prisoners of war to escape. In 1971 he wrote the book *Five Years to Freedom*. In 1981, he designed and built the Special Forces resistance program based on his experiences.

SERE is still very classified in terms of the tactics of evasion and resistance they teach, but what I can tell you is that they trained me in wartime behavior. In other words, if I was to get caught and become a prisoner of war, I had to understand the Geneva convention and how best to hold on to the secrecy of the mission while being interrogated.

And, of course, *interrogated* is a nice way of putting it. Ultimately, what I was being taught was how to bear physical suffering and pain through physical suffering and pain. Back in 1997, they could hit you, among other things.

But first, they taught me how to survive off the land, how to navigate without a compass, and how to evade. Much of this is not for public consumption, but I can tell you that one of my strongest memories was of the Tunnel.

As I reached it in the Fort Bragg training grounds, I looked down its long, dark length. It was eleven o'clock in the morning on a crystal clear, beautiful day, but it was pitch-black down in the Tunnel.

There were rungs along one side, so I used them to lower myself into it. Turns out that the Tunnel was the entry into a bunch of cramped mazes. I looked around to get my bearings, but mostly all I could perceive was the sound of boots echoing in the darkness.

I looked up, and my eyes had adjusted enough that I could tell I was underground. As I crawled on my hands and knees, I entered another part of the thing so black, so dark, and so cold that my fingers started freezing over. From there, the hole got tighter. The pipe kept getting narrower. I stretched my arms and started crawling.

*Survival, escape.*

But this training was more than just physical suffering and pain. It was, of course, mental suffering and pain as well. The infamous mind games were back with a vengeance. The Tunnel was specifically and effectively designed to psychologically unsettle candidates. And it was working. I couldn't shake the growing gnawing feeling that I was buried underground, crawling for my life.

I didn't let it stop me. I pushed my feet. I pulled with my fingernails. I forced myself through this squeezing pipe until, finally, I came out the other side. The Special Forces program was designed to find weakness. No matter how strong I thought I was, everyone had a weakness, and the instructors were there to find and exploit it.

I was out of the Tunnel, but then came survival training. We learned how to enter a swamp by fashioning a walking stick and poking the wet, foliage-matted ground in a certain pattern. If you did it right, you'd hear a dinking noise, then you would be able to stick your hands into the swamp and pull out a snapping turtle. Those things were huge and dangerous and could bite your fingers off. Therefore, we were taught the proper way to catch them.

They taught us a lot of these Native traditions, like how to track and catch wildlife, make fire, and purify water. Given my background, I was grateful to benefit from the teachings of these sorely used Natives.

After that came evasion training. I ran for my life in my military uniform and boots through the backwoods with dogs howling all around me. I ran up foothills, passing teams who were barely making it. I ran, ran, ran as instructors fanned out to find us. But that was not all. Everyone in the area had been told that they'd get paid for each Special Forces student they found.

It was a big game to them. Guys came out on horses, with dogs. People showed up with their truck's flatbed filled with family ready to hunt—all just to catch a running Special Forces student like me. So I ran through the foothills, falling, getting back up, trying to check my bearings, jumping into the swamp, backtracking, hopping on a log, and whatever else I needed to do to stay free.

It was an extremely effective education. Not just the running but also the starving. There's just so many wild onions you could find, and just so much nutrition you could get boiling pine needles. Why onions and pine needles? Because I couldn't catch shit in North Carolina. Squirrels were jumping around all my traps as I sat there, feeling stupid and hungry.

Those damn squirrels were some seriously good students. So good that I went up to the paved paths and looked for roadkill. I heard some lucky candidates managed to find a dead raccoon, possum, and even a deer. But not me. Nothing. So I ate a lot of wild onions and drank a lot of pine-needle tea. In other words, I starved for ten days.

The evasion exercise ended when we made it to linkup after two hundred and forty hours of running. A role player pulled up at the linkup location in a white van. Bona fides were exchanged, and then they hooded me, before throwing me in the back of the van. The van was full of hooded students and all of us waited for what came next.

What came next was resistance time. We pulled up to a checkpoint, explosions happened, and a rebel force appeared to drag me to a prison camp. I was hog-tied to a chair with a cloth over my face. As they slapped me through the cloth, I could just make out the shadows of my interrogators. I heard my teammates yelling their Social Security number as they got hit. Finally, the cloth was yanked off my head.

"Who are you," one asked in a thick accent, "and why are you in my country?"

"My name is Sergeant—" I got hit. Hard. So hard my chair fell over, taking me with it.

There were more questions and more hitting, until I was dragged back to a cramped cell. Then it just kept repeating. Interrogation. Starvation. Interrogation. Over and over again.

It was twenty degrees or lower that February night as they

shoved me back into my cell. It was so small I had to curl up into a ball. Couldn't even stretch out. As I shivered in the cold rain that covered the ground, I found out that each cell had a hidden speaker. Through it they played the sound of a baby crying. For hours. It never stopped.

Very soon I started to understand the psychological effects of that. But it didn't stop there. Just in case you could ignore the crying baby, every fifteen minutes a guard forced you to drink a bowl of water through the cage door. He didn't leave until you drank that water. If you refused, he'd drag you out and beat you until you did.

Every fifteen minutes. To the second. So I drank the water.

Suddenly, in comparison to this fifteen-minute deadline, the whiteboard seemed kind.

I was shivering in the cell, the baby was crying, and water was being forced down my throat. Even if you're exhausted enough to lose consciousness, peeing yourself would probably wake you—especially since the cell's floor is sloped so that the urine flowed back onto you. Of course, then it started to smell even worse.

Hours of this, and then, finally, there was a new sound. The sound of other candidates.

"I fucking quit!"

That was always immediately followed by the sound of their cells opening, and their piss-soaked bodies being dragged out. Ironically, that only made some candidates want to quit more.

If you made it through the night, you could look forward to manual labor in the prison yard.

"Get into formation, you stinking dogs."

At that point, the description was all too accurate.

Even though we knew it was still a training course, we were wet, tired, and beaten. Was anything worth this? Some of us who were almost broken may not have thought so. Still, I got into formation with other surviving Special Forces students when I was ordered to. Then, as if on cue, it started raining. Cold rain.

"You're going to salute my flag every single day for the rest of your life," our head captor announced. "You understand? You are nothing but scum. Now, you scum, turn around and salute my flag."

We turned around. It was the American flag.

You know, that might not mean anything to a lot of people reading this. But when you're broken in mind and body, and you're wet and hungry, and they bring you to a point of suffering where you think your own country has forgotten about you, to then turn around and see the American flag waving in the sky made all the difference. I had been broken, but now I was not.

All I felt was patriotism. True patriotism, flooding into me, deeper than on any other day in my life.

Good thing, too. It prepared me for all that came next.

# 12

"French."

"Sergeant?"

"French," the instructor repeated. "That's what you learn. French. For First Group. Good luck."

I was both surprised and pleased. Pleased, because the Special Forces Regiment is broken down into groups. Each group has its own areas of responsibility. First Group was formed for contingency operations on the continent of Asia. Third group was for Africa. Fifth group was the Middle East and all the stans: Pakistan, Afghanistan, Kurdistan, and the rest. Seventh Group was responsible for operations in Central and South America. Tenth was there for Europe and Eastern Europe.

Over the years and wars, things could get kind of mixed up, but in 1997, that's how everything was aligned. And assignments came complete with four months of language school. Mine was French, so you might think I was assigned to Tenth Group. But no. My assignment was with First, but there are so many difficult Asian languages that French, which many Asians use, was a good compromise.

Like I said, things might seem a bit mixed up, but I wasn't looking this gift horse in the mouth. First Group was really hard to get because, in the Special Forces world, that was considered the icing on the cake assignment, and they didn't give that to

any old guy off the street. Because of a shortage of Green Berets, especially Pacific Theater Green Berets, I was given Okinawa as my first assignment, and that was very rare.

But first I had to graduate the French course. Not only did
I pass that, but I also started taking general college courses to
fulfill the promise I made to my mother. That was important to
me. So once again, I left North Carolina and twenty-two hours
later, touchdown in Okinawa, Japan. It looked, smelled, and felt
different, because this was the home of Bushido.

I waited for my bags amid crowds of Japanese travelers, while
many more US Army guys poured off the aircraft behind me.
I breathed in the new atmosphere and filled my eyes with the
sight of all the others whose eyes and skin were more similar to
mine, until someone with an unmistakable Army aura showed
up in my peripheral vision.

"You fucking Tu?" he said more than asked. He had the Army
mouth and attitude as well.

"Yes."

"Get your shit," he said flatly before I even finished the word.
"Let's go."

He didn't offer to help. In fact, without waiting to make sure
I had all my shit, he started walking away—fast.

I did my best to keep up and was doing okay until we reached
the airport doors. Then the humidity hit me. If I had been wearing glasses they would have fogged up. Instead, my eyes were
filled with images of palm trees and my nostrils were filled with
sea breeze.

I managed to catch up with him at the parking lot, then made
my next smart move. Whether it was jet lag or not, I went directly to what would have been the passenger side of the car if
we had still been in America.

"You going to fucking drive?" he snapped.

In Japan, like the UK, the passenger seat is on the left. I was
blocking the driver's side.

"N-no," I stammered, quickly correcting my mistake.

"You know I'm here to pick you up," he informed me as I went. "My name is—"

Let's call him TD. TD was the explosives expert on the team that I was slotted to go to. I soon found out that he was a highly trained Senior Green Beret with a wealth of knowledge. But on that first day, he was a cocky jerk.

"Fuck you looking at?" he snapped as I got to the correct side of the car.

"Nothing," I muttered, hoping he wouldn't think I was calling him nothing. He easily could have indulged the classic senior-officer maneuver of taking whatever the junior said literally, but I guess he had gotten tired of waiting for me.

"All right," he said. "I'll drop you off at the barracks. You do whatever you gotta do to in-process, then I'll see you at the box tomorrow."

"The Box" was a nickname they gave the First Group compound.

Very limited instructions. Very Green Berets-ish.

True to his word, he dropped me off at the barracks, and true to his manner, he drove off almost before I got my shit out of the car. I quickly signed in and moved into my room. I spent the rest of the day getting accustomed to my new surroundings. The next morning, at 0500, I showed up at First Group compound, boots spit-polished, uniform sharp and starched, looking every inch the prime, prepped soldier.

Nobody was there.

So I waited.

Occasionally a team guy would show up. Not a First Group guy, but a team guy. I could always tell a team guy because they don't really wear Army-issue uniforms. They wore half-civilian, half-military outfits. They're the rogue guys, the ones that the higher command always seek to control because, at the team level, they're always the first to fight. And our higher command loves the team guys because they understand that's where the team came from. Army Rules team guys always push it.

"You know somebody, dude?" I heard.

I looked over to see a team guy, who looked back at me like I was a particularly interesting Asian insect that had somehow gotten inside.

"Um," I said, "I was told to report to this team."

"Oh," he replied. "Yeah. They're out doing a jungle run this morning. Come back at nine."

I was tempted to just stay there for hours more, just in case he was playing a joke, but decided to take the time to wear off any leftover jet lag. I came back at zero nine, still spit-shined and starched, the very picture of a proud Green Beret. I stood by the door and waited as the first guy came into the team room.

"Hi," I said, "my name is—"

The first guy walked by me without a glance or word, went through the door, and closed it behind him.

The next team guy came in shortly after that.

"Hey, my name is—"

Same thing happened.

It was nine in the morning on the Special Forces compound in Okinawa, and, with the sun up, I realized why the compound was nicknamed The Box. The box was hot. And humid. The team rooms were old rooms dating back to 1957, and the creation of the First Special Forces Group in Okinawa. These were old barracks. These were old offices. And the box was like a sauna.

As I stood there, sweat was literally dripping off me. I could barely breathe.

The front door opened again.

"Hi! My name is—"

He walked past me, went through, and closed the door behind him.

I lost three of the four hours I saved by not standing there from zero five to zero nine by standing in the rising heat from zero nine to noon. But at twelve hundred hours the other door finally opened, and the whole team walked out.

"My name is Tu Lam," I said. "I was told to report."

Nobody turned to me. They just walked out the front door. Maybe going to lunch. All I knew was that I wasn't going to follow them. I was told to report here, so I was going to stay there until they acknowledged me—whether I could barely breathe or not.

The team came back I don't know how long later.

"Hey, guys. My name is Tu. Sergeant Major told me—"

Again they walked through the door and slammed it behind them.

More hours passed in the box. The team-room door opened and closed all day, but as the time wore on, at least some teammates actually looked at me as they passed. Finally, near the end of the day, TD poked his head out.

"We're ready to see you."

The Tu Lam they saw was no longer spit-shined and starched, he was now soaked in sweat.

The team that was waiting for him was in a gauntlet formation. So sure enough, I had to walk down a line of abuse.

"What the fuck you looking at?" I kept hearing that as I passed each guy.

Finally, I arrived at the team's intelligence sergeant, who was second man to the team sergeant.

He didn't say "What the fuck you looking at?" He stared at me with something between a scowl and a sneer, then said four words.

"We don't trust Charlie."

There it was.

Now, in Special Forces, Charlie is the team's explosives expert. But I was not assigned as that. So for now, after coming all this way, and waiting in the box sauna all day, I gave them the benefit of the doubt and replied as a Green Beret.

"Oh," I said in my best there-must-be-a-mistake tone, "I'm Bravo."

Bravo is the weapons expert on a team. Delta is the combat medic. Echo is the communications expert. So I was a Bravo. But according to them, not today.

"You're a fucking Charlie," one maintained.

Charlie in here was supposed to be the explosives expert, but Charlie in Vietnam had been the enemy. That was the nickname American Vietnam War soldiers had for the Viet Cong. And how did most of them know who the enemy was? Because they looked like me.

These were my teammates, so I continued giving them the benefit of the doubt. They weren't racist fucks, I decided, they were cautious warriors trying to push my buttons—trying to test me.

I stood there, maintaining my best Bravo composure until, finally, our team sergeant stepped up. Let's call him Pete. Pete was full of positive energy—a happy, almost hippie kind of energy.

"What's up, Tu?" he said like none of this—the waiting, the gauntlet, the labeling—had happened. "What's up, dude? How's it going?"

He was the highest-ranking enlisted guy on the team, so he was knowingly resetting the tone after all the abuse. I knew his rep. He had been part of the Grenada invasion, so he had been a Grenada-era Ranger. He was a Green Beret. He was a combat diver. He was an explosives expert. He was an assaulter. He was a sniper. He was everything.

"Good," I told him.

"Well, welcome to the team," he told me. "We don't have a desk for you, so tomorrow what you're going to do is you're going to hang out, and you're just going to kind of clean the team room."

Well, they obviously didn't know my rep if they thought I would take offense at that. After my upbringing, cleaning team rooms was something I knew how to do damn well.

"Okay, Sergeant," I replied.

Couldn't be sure if I had taken him by surprise, but he echoed me.

"Okay," he said. "Well, cool. Nice to meet you. Welcome to the team." Then they headed out, but just before he left he turned back and delivered the kicker. "Oh, by the way, we got PT to-morrow morning."

PT was also something I could do, but I should've known that, while the location could change, the mind games never did.

The next day PT started zero five with a run, but the thing was, it was a Pete-reprogrammed run. He rerouted it because he knew how the sun would rise on the island. My big clue was the instruction that no sunglasses were to be worn except by senior members of the team.

Sure enough, the sun was always in my eyes. The whole five miles. Followed by a swim. For me the swim was a reward for the sunburn.

My childhood had been filled with near-death experiences. My body may have recovered, but my subconscious never forgot. No matter how fast and far I ran, I always wound up where I started. The chem lights always brought me back to the barracks.

But when I swam, the sense of freedom was like nothing else. Even when I nearly died in the Indonesian Sea off the coast of the refugee camp, I remember being okay with it. I've heard that when you drown, just before the end there's a feeling of com-plete freedom. That's the way I felt when I swam.

But not everybody on the team felt that way. I found out that I was one of two new recruits on the team. The other? Let's call him Ian. Ian was a very athletic man, but he and I were treated like problems by the team. They were always evaluating us, al-ways trying to make us quit. As new guys, they wanted to know if we were worth their time.

So, as a new team guy who had worked so hard to become a team guy, my mantra was Shut Up and Learn. One of my fa-vorite experiences in those early days was sitting in a Zodiac as we were moving away from Okinawa. I'm looking at Ian, who's trying to put on his fins and mask as the raft rocked and rolled in the choppy surf.

Pete was looking back at us, acting like we were about to spend the day surfing.

"It's a beautiful day, dude," he said with a big smile, while giving me the *rock on* hand sign. He told us all about the history of the island and how beautiful it was, until we got to a spot where I could barely make it out in the distance.

Then the cool hippie guy went commando. He grabbed our fins and hurled them into the sea.

"Swim back, bitches," he sneered, before sending us into the surf.

Again, he didn't seem to know my rep. At that point, I was an amphibious reconnaissance guy. I had been part of the LRSD team. I knew how to swim.

But Ian really didn't. So they got the Zodiacs going around him in circles, creating high chops, to the point where he could hardly stay above water. But for me, I knew how to study and penetrate the water, so I was able to fin without a problem. I passed the test for that day, but I knew I would have to keep at it.

Every morning we did physical training. We did hand-to-hand combat. We ran the beaches. Weapons training was every week—from light and small arms to heavy weapons. There was cross-training in combat trauma with our Special Forces medics. There was communications training, up to and including building jungle antennas.

We patrolled through the jungles as a team. Ruck runs happened every week, where we would go in full combat gear and load-bearing equipment with a gun, a map, and a compass. And we would run as a team through the jungles. Our team was fit. Our team was hungry.

Since becoming a Green Beret, I had been sleeping on pallets in the back of a C-130, or swinging from a hammock in the jungle, or lying on a cold cement floor in an abandoned old rat-infested hangar next to a pallet of ammo and demolitions. Or I pulled guard duty all night. Because I was a young Green

Beret, I was stuck on most guard duties, but I didn't mind. In fact, I loved it. I loved my life.

What wasn't there to like? I was driving on dirt trails or mud roads, with a pistol on my pelvis and a book bag on my back. No, I never forgot my promise to my mother to graduate college. I typed term papers in grass huts. I drove to internet cafés to take midterm exams because there was no broadband internet: it was dial-up back then.

Eventually I got it down to a regular schedule. I would get up at around three thirty in the morning, make coffee to wake myself up, and start studying for college. That would go to five thirty, when I would start my Green Beret day. Physical training went to eight. I had roughly an hour to shower and eat and then report to work, which usually consisted of either prepping for missions or being on a mission. If I had a lunch break, I would study. And then I would continue to train in the Special Forces and do whatever anyone required me to do after work.

Then came my first mission: Laos. Actually, it was just one of my first missions. My actual first mission was to go to Camp Zama in Japan and take the six-day Equal Opportunity Leaders Course, then turn around and go to truck-driving school. I had to go to every school that nobody else wanted to go to because I was the new guy. Still, I graduated with honors in one, and at the top of my class in the other. But Laos was my first major mission where I was a teacher, not a student.

Soon, I heard the roar of UA60 rotors as we flew over the Indochinese Peninsula and the only landlocked country in Southeast Asia. This was the same kind of helicopter that was used during the Vietnam War. And there I was, a twenty-one-year-old Green Beret looking down, trying to see through the triple canopy of the tree tops to the jungle floor.

All I heard was the booming *thump, thump, thump* of the helicopter blades as we made our way over the rivers—deeper and deeper into a seemingly prehistoric landscape. Finally, I spotted the village, complete with a small landing zone.

I looked from the vegetation below back up to the pilot. He was smiling at me. He was a real character, practically a Laos cowboy. Like many from the Phonsavan area, which had a distinct cowboy culture, he wore an old Stetson and I could tell that he'd been through it all and learned from it and didn't care what anybody thought. By the way he swooped down and landed with perfect precision, I knew he had earned his reputation.

I unshackled, picked up my packs, then threw off my weapons and equipment as a civilian male in his twenties ran up. He was wearing half-military and half-civilian clothes, augmented by some god-awful jewelry. Even then (as you might have noticed), as a Green Beret I was always analyzing everything.

He yelled over the helicopter engine. "Hello, hello, Sergeant! My name is Habu!"

"Hi," I said back.

"I am your linguist," he yelled. Habu tried to grab my bags, only to discover it wasn't that easy for a linguist to haul Special Forces equipment. He barely made it out of the landing zone as I plucked my weapons case from his weak grasp.

"It's all right," I said. "I got it from here."

"Oh, okay," he said with a sigh, deciding it was probably better to stick with what he did best. I needed a good interpreter more than a bad baggage handler.

As we moved down a very primitive dirt road leading from the LZ, we neared a fence of tall grass that surrounded the village. Appearing from it was a bunch of kids who came to see the helicopter land.

One particularly bold girl, around nine or ten years old, broke free of the others and ran toward me. I could tell from her expression and energy that she, like me, was curious about everything.

She said something to me in her native language, and I looked over to my linguist. He smiled and said something back to her, which she immediately replied to.

"What is she saying?" I asked as I pulled out some candy and handed it to her.

Before he could answer, the little girl pulled my hand down. I took a knee as she quietly said something else while giving the candy back to me.

I turned my head to call to him, but Habu was already there, leaning down over my shoulder. He said something more to the girl, who replied again.

"Do you have a pencil, sir?" he asked me. "A pen, maybe?"

I did, so I pulled it out of my pocket and handed it to the little girl. From her expression you would think I had just given her the keys to the kingdom. A smile lit up her face, she took the pen from my hand, then kissed me on the cheek. After that, she ran back to her friends and proudly showed off her new treasure.

Seeing the village behind her reminded me that I was here for more than gift-giving. There were bandits all around this area. But even that wasn't my primary mission. I stood and, without another word, led Habu to the village.

The main reason I was there was that, during the Vietnam War, we had left hundreds of thousands of land mines all over the jungle floor and in the rice paddies. I was there to see how best we could correct that.

The Special Forces were not just about going in and training a guerrilla or foreign internal-defense force. It was also about building rapport. Having gone through my childhood and my training, I felt that if we were able to get into these areas and help each other out as human beings, that was what freeing the oppressed was truly about.

As I walked around the village, I looked at the machine-gun positions. I looked at the security posture. With Habu's help, I interviewed local villagers to employ human intelligence to better understand the situation.

Lunchtime came quickly. But even then, I was intent on

learning more. As I pored over map data, I noticed the linguist looking at me. After a while it became distracting. Putting down my military plotter and grid coordinates, I turned toward him.

"What is it, Habu?" I asked. "Why are you looking at me like this?"

"Sir," he said with humility, "do you know what you did this morning? For the little girl?"

I put down the map. "Did I do something to offend?" I asked.

"No, sir," he told me. "You gave the girl an education." That got him my full attention. He went on. "They don't have schools. They don't have pens or pencils. So in a very real sense, you gave her hope, sir. Thank you."

My mind instantly went back to my own childhood. It reminded me of what my mother had said on my first day of school.

"No matter what happens," she had told me, "if you have education, you'll never be oppressed."

The power of a pen. The power of a tool to better yourself. Such an amazing thing. It's a key to education, a key to knowledge, and a key to a better life. It can lead to a deeper understanding of yourself. It certainly led to my better understanding of these villagers.

Maybe I had given that little girl the keys to the kingdom after all. But I wasn't going to leave it at that.

I went directly to our Special Forces communications sergeant. Let's call him Tom. Tom was like any Green Beret I knew: full of humanity and compassion.

"Tom," I said. "Cross trace-back communications to headquarters in Okinawa requesting more support." Then I explained what I had in mind.

That day grew into a month. After our Special Forces support team arrived, we found, located, and marked land mines. But that's not all we did. We trained the Indigenous force to also find and mark these land mines, then disarm them as safely as possible.

We taught them how to utilize terrain in order to find and mark the mines. We taught them how to probe with sticks without setting the explosives off. We even taught the children how to find, identify, mark them, and disarm them.

We did that every day for a month. Training, advising, assisting—all without a single injury. And almost every day I couldn't help thinking of what Lao Tzu, the author of the *Tao Te Ching* and founder of Taoism, said.

*If you give a hungry man a fish, you feed him for a day. But if you teach him how to fish, you feed him for a lifetime.*

Did we leave it at that? No, we didn't leave it at that. With Lao's quote echoing in my mind, our demolitions team found a nearby waterway, where they solved the mathematical problem of putting in enough explosives to reroute the river so the village had running water.

After that, pens and pencils were delivered to all the children. Then, to give them someplace to use them, a makeshift school was built.

Only when that was done did I consider my first major mission a success. Many more were to follow. First Group was soon rotating all over Asia, completing all kinds of missions I can't tell you about. Singapore, Korea, the Philippines six times, Thailand more than a dozen times, and more.

My life was full of fire, but still I could feel even more growing inside me. I had been drilling for war for years, and now I really wanted to taste it. If I didn't, and soon, I wasn't sure what would happen. Luckily, a special, controllable war came to me.

# 13

I had started my martial arts journey at the age of eight. Now, thirteen years later, I was a Green Beret, trying to graduate college, but at that same time I was always a student of Budo and Bushido. So when I found myself in Japan—the essence, if not the birthplace, of this art—naturally I doubled down on my martial arts studies.

My weak point back then was ground fighting. I was more of a stand-up fighter. I did years of just ground, submission fighting—because I was seeing the growing success of Brazilian jujitsu in the States, and here I was in Japan learning the pure form of Japanese jujitsu, which is where Brazilian jujitsu came from. The Gracie family, who were to Brazilian jujitsu what Bruce Lee was to American kung fu, extracted the teachings of Japanese jujitsu, which dated back to 710 CE, and made it their own.

Jujitsu is a form that is used to disarm an opponent in close-quarters combat. It's used to get leverage and angles to disarm them of their weapons. But my understanding of martial arts at that time was basic, and I knew that wouldn't do. At the same time, the Ultimate Fighting Championship, the UFC, was getting very popular. I could see a true divide developing in the martial arts world. They, like me, didn't want to just learn, they wanted to fight.

One night, I was driving to get my weekly groceries at a store near a Marine base. Usually I did that during the day, but I wanted to free up time the next morning to go scuba diving. I loved diving in the morning because the beautiful coral reefs in Okinawa were infused with daylight. Very glorious. Very Zen.

I was in a beat-up four-wheel-drive van that had cost me five hundred bucks. It looked like the Scooby-Doo "Mystery Machine" van, except it was all rusted up and stank of salt water and cockroach killer, because these big island roaches would nest in the van and hatch eggs in the spring. So I had to toss in a bug bomb every few months.

It was sunset as I neared the base, which was on my left. But as I approached I saw a sign in the distance on my right. It was all lit up, and there were cars parked all around it. I looked closer. It read *Toughman*.

I turned right and parked. And, as I sat there, I could feel the fire inside me get even hotter. I got out and walked right in. There were all these Marines screaming and drinking, and I'm like, *What is going on?*

Breaking through the crowd, I saw a boxing ring. And inside the ring there's these guys fighting it out, wearing open-hand gloves. I'm looking around like it's a party, and this one barrel-chested Marine in uniform must have seen the hunger in my eyes, because he got my attention.

"What is this?" I asked above the yelling crowd.

He started to say *Toughman*, but I cut him off.

"How can I get in there?"

He answered, "You have to be active duty and you have to get your commander's approval."

I turned around and left. The next week I was back, ready to go in my shorts and Special Forces T-shirt. I had a Torii Station Okinawa 1st Special Forces Group insignia on my chest. I was so proud, right?

The same barrel-chested Marine looked down, his expression losing its incredulity and said, "Army, huh?"

I said, "Yeah, Army."

He goes, "You know what Army means, right?"

"No," I replied. "What does it mean?"

"Army," he told me. "Ain't Ready to be Marine Yet."

"Wow, that's amazing," I deadpanned. "When's my fight?"

By that time, he was ready to see me eat the floor, so as my fight was getting arranged I was getting ready. It must have looked as if I was just stretching, but inside I felt the fire raging.

To this day I cannot completely explain the rage I was feeling. For years I had been moving through Special Forces training classes and facing live fire, close-quarters combat, demolitions. But it wasn't enough for the rage inside me. Apparently, I wanted to do more than help out. I wanted to lash out. After all I had been through, I needed to lash out. My inner rage wanted this.

A moment later, it had this. The fight was on.

First, the referee went into the ring. Then a big Marine came in. I remember thinking *He's a tall fella.* He was tall, all right, with a long reach. It might have looked like I was just standing there, waiting to go on, but I was studying his range. I was looking at his stance, his attitude, his moves. It looked like he had done cardio…lots of cardio.

As I approached the ring, I could feel my rage surge. It was going through my muscles, going through my mind, going through my spirit. I could feel my blood pumping through me. I could feel it all as I entered the ring.

It was true rage, but one that hadn't been tested yet. It was something different than the hate I felt in me during all those years of oppression.

I pushed the hate back and let the rage grow. At this point, I was a twenty-three-year-old Green Beret looking at this big Marine. He looked down at me. He laughed. Then he turned his back.

Fine. I knew Marine training. It was very directional. Had no pivot point. *Very powerful in one direction*, I thought. *Yeah, let's see.*

I was one hundred ninety-five pounds at that point. Lean for so much rage. I didn't understand how to completely control it, but I could channel it.

The referee pulled us in.

"Ready?" I asked the Marine.

"Yeah, I'm ready," he snarled. "You ready?"

I just looked at the ref. The ref did his job. The fight started.

As the Marine charged, he extended his long arm like I thought he would. I knew he had range on me. He was a typical Western-style boxer, who extended his jabs to find my distance. As I moved, he extended his long range again from a distance, a pattern that was now established, then confirmed when he extended his fist toward me again.

So I entered at an angle and hit him with a right intercepting fist. Basic move. Nothing fancy, just speed and strength. The Marine went down.

It had taken seven seconds.

The referee called it. I won. I stood there processing how easy this win had been.

Then the guy who had met me at the door came into the ring. Apparently, he was the enlisted rank in charge, and he said to me, "What do you have to say to the crowd?"

The fight did not surprise me, but that question did. All my life, nobody had ever asked me if I had anything to say. So now, I just stood there, staring at the screaming crowd. All through my life, people hadn't understood that I was actually shy. I seemed sure of myself, but having grown up being bullied and spit on, I had very low self-esteem.

Turns out my host was a good promoter. He hardly paused before asking me another question.

"What branch of service are you?"

I immediately, almost automatically, replied. "United States Army."

That did it. It seemed as if every Marine in the place started baying for my blood.

From that night on, there was a long line waiting for me to eat the floor. And betting on me to kiss canvas. But as the Toughman fight nights continued every week, sometimes more than once a week, I continued to fight—and defeat—Marines.

I was impressed because there was no shortage of opponents for months. Almost none of my Special Forces teammates knew what I was doing in my free time. The commander who gave me the approval knew, but the only other guy I told was the medic on my team. Let's call him Steve. Like me, he was a young Green Beret, but unlike me, he was an educated man who spoke several languages.

"Please don't tell anybody about this," I begged him. "Just patch me up when I'm fucked up, okay?"

"We shouldn't be doing this," he warned me. "We're going to get in really big trouble, you know."

My answer? "Shut up, Steve." That became our running joke: him giving me wise and caring counsel, then me rejecting it.

But he had my back and did what he did very well. He was a great friend. Before every fight he would wrap me up, and after every fight, he would patch me up if needed.

From then on, outside First Group, fighting was all I knew. And money. I made good money out of it. I was making more than I'd ever made before. It was around a thousand dollars a fight, and a thousand dollars every Friday night was really big for me. I would take my teammates out when we had the time. As you might imagine, Special Op guys didn't just work hard. We played hard. The rest of my winnings I would spend on martial arts and scuba gear.

So I kept winning and rising in the rankings, until I was getting used to it. But one night, in the Toughman locker room after another win, I heard something I had never heard before. It was just shoes walking on the concrete floor, but unlike any shoes I had ever heard. It was like when I heard the Fayetteville school bully's mother's high heels coming toward the principal's office all those years ago. I knew then that those shoes were different, and now, I knew these were different too.

As they approached, I could tell they were city shoes, expensive shoes, and coming closer, through the darkness of the hall into the light of the changing room was an older, well-dressed Japanese man. He looked at me, then spoke with a deep, guttural voice right out of a samurai movie.

"My name is Misumi," he said. "I like the way you fight to light your spirit."

Steve stared at him while cutting my gloves off. When Steve was done, I threw the gloves into the corner.

"What do you want, young Green Beret?" Misumi asked. "I'd like to see you fight more. Would you like to fight?"

"I'll fight anybody," I answered truthfully.

Misumi smiled and offered me a small rectangle of expensive stationery. "Here's my card," he said.

I took it, my sweaty hand smearing it. The writing was Japanese.

"I own a school forty-five minutes away from this location," he said. "It is my school. I teach hard-form karate there. I bring in fighters from Thailand to teach, and I set up fights." He let that sink in before delivering the capper. "You want to make money?" he asked softly from his gut. There was no mistaking that he wasn't talking about Toughman money. "You come see me."

I took the card and threw it on the bench in front of him. "It's not about the money," I told him.

That didn't faze him. In fact, it seemed to please him. "You want to fight?" he answered. "Or do you want to see how good you are? Either way, come see me."

Then he walked out of the room and into the darkness—the sound of his expensive, different, city shoes growing fainter, then silent.

Steve and I looked at each other, clearly thinking the same thing. *What the fuck was that about?*

I thought about it all that night and the next day. That night I was sitting outside a club next door to a US Air Force base. Steve was inside with multiple women. I saw the Japanese bad boys with their orange hair driving around on their motorcycles. Drunken Marines were walking past me. I could smell vomit, alcohol, and cigarettes, not necessarily in that order. But the only thing I could think about was if I was going to go on fighting.

When I woke up the next morning, there was something different inside me. I looked and acted the same, but I could tell there was something different in my spirit.

I walked from my quarters to my van. It was a beautiful morning in Okinawa. Palm trees swayed in the air as I threw my diving gear in the back and got ready to go to my favorite scuba spot.

Not many people went there, but I knew it well. It had an old Japanese stone pagoda on a beach path I had stumbled upon. I drove my van down the tropical road as far as I could, then I strapped on my tanks, scuba gear, fins, and goggles. I had my scuba shorts on and my shirt off.

The sun hadn't come up yet, so I entered the water in the darkness. Turning on my diving light, I saw the coral reef glow as if a master artist had just painted it.

When I surfaced, so did the sun. I came back to the beach, dropped my gear, and sat in meditation.

The water. The wind. The palm trees. The earth. Heaven. Pain. Fire.

I got up and drove to Misumi's school. As the sun rose further, so did the volume of the music in my van.

The neighborhood of Misumi's school had big buildings but small parking spaces. It was hard to find a place for my van downtown. Finally, after multiple turns and repositioning, I wedged into a spot. But then there was hardly enough room to open my door. I had to suck in my stomach to get out.

As I held Misumi's business card, I looked up at all these buildings and started walking through the concrete maze until I finally heard a sound I recognized.

The sound of "kiai!"

The sound of "oss!"

The sound of punching. The sound of stomping. The sound of power.

I had studied for many years, so I knew the energy that drew me closer to this dojo. Finally, I was there and put my head in. And there he was. Misumi, in full *gi*. Two *dan* black belt, red stripe.

As I stood there, Misumi was saying something in Japanese. When he finished, all his students, one by one, bowed out of the dojo. As they did, he looked at the ground, going into a form of meditation. As the last student bowed out, Misumi looked up at me in the doorway. He smiled, clapped his hands twice, and spoke.

"I knew you would come."

Taking off my shoes, I bowed into the dojo, but within five steps of Misumi, I went to both knees and bowed to the master.

"So," he said, "you want to fight?"

I said yes.

Misumi sat there, evaluating me. He looked me up and down, trying to see if I was a worthwhile investment.

"So you want to fight?" he repeated in a tone that was flatter and with an expression that was blank.

"Yes," I repeated. "I'll fight anybody."

That, apparently, was the right answer because I saw something change in his face. I recognized the expression from some of my previous opponents. I could practically hear him thinking *Let's see how good you actually are before I invest in you.*

He apparently thought that when I said I'd fight anybody, he'd also heard *anytime, anywhere,* because he laughed quietly before he stood up smoothly.

"Follow me" he instructed, then started out of the dojo.

I followed his lead. I bowed out and walked behind him.

He paused on the street, then looked back at me. "The traffic is very heavy at this time, you know," he said.

"Oh yes, I know," I said in agreement. I was already well aware of the crazy, congested Okinawa traffic.

"Follow me," he repeated as he got into his Mercedes, one with the windows blacked out. Apparently, he didn't mean into the back seat of his ride, because the door closed in my face. I squeezed back into my van.

His style of Mercedes was a rare thing in Okinawa—very rare on a tropical island. The style of most Okinawan drivers was practical, not flashy. There was a difference between mainland Japan and Okinawa. Everywhere I went in Okinawa, residents always told me that.

I had to let that observation process in the back of my mind in order to concentrate on following his Mercedes. He drove like he owned the road. It seemed that the rest of the surging traffic got out of his way. I, however, in my rusted-out Mystery Machine, was not so lucky. I did my best dodging and weaving, and thankfully managed to keep him in sight until, finally, he stopped.

I pulled myself out and looked up to see what appeared to be a high-school gymnasium but detailed with Okinawan touches like red roof tiles and limestone walls built to withstand typhoons. My attention shifted to Misumi who was walking up to my roach-infested van.

"Bring your gear," he instructed. "Enter through the side of the building."

*Oh, it's going to be like that, huh?*

I pulled out my Brazilian jujitsu double-stitched collar *gi*, wrapped with its blue, four-striped belt. Moving toward the doors, the heat hit me. It was not just hot, it was Okinawa hot. Tropical heat. Looking down at my smartwatch, I saw that it predicted a hundred and five degree heat index. With humidity.

I heard derisive laughter as I entered the building. There was a group of Okinawan boys already in there, rolling around, stretching out. They were roughly my age, some younger. The majority looked like they were in college. None of them were reacting to the heat. I guessed they were used to it.

"You can get dressed," Misumi said, "and we'll meet you back here."

I found the changing room quickly and threw on my *gi*. Even that left me nearly breathless. The heat and humidity were crushing me like a fist. By the time I came out, my *gi* was nearly drenched in sweat.

One of the Okinawan bully boys rolled over to me. Like a monkey. He looked at me with pity, said something in Japanese to the others, and they all had a good, snide laugh. Then he stared pointedly at me.

"Hi," I said. "My name is—"

He did not want to hear my name. Not yet. He just wanted to continue making fun of me. He said something else to the others, which they, naturally, found hilarious.

Finally, he broke free of the Japanese language.

"What's your name?" he asked me in broken English. Okay, now he was willing to hear my name.

"My name is Tu," I said quietly, preparing for whatever insulting stinger he was preparing.

"Where you from?"

"America."

"No, No. Where you born?"

"Vietnam."

That was cause for more sarcastic, clearly derisive Japanese directed at his friends. Again, they laughed knowingly.

Despite the heat and humidity, I felt a chill spreading out from my spine. I was a soldier. I had heard the stories of the Japanese who had teamed with the so-called master race to spread across Asia and slaughter millions just a few decades before. He reminded me of them. He was almost a caricature of the sadistic ones who wanted to humiliate any other Asian. He wanted to find the biggest insult he could by reminding me who I was and where I came from—two things they looked down upon, even spat at.

That's when Misumi reappeared. He looked at me evenly. "Well," he said, "we have to see your ground game."

It almost sounded like a death warrant. The others certainly reacted to it as such. Instantly all the windows shut. The gymnasium became a sauna.

The ground cleared; the students lined up to one side. The boss bully who had mocked me remained. He was my opponent.

"Are you ready?" he taunted, looking at me like a sadistic clown, shifting left and right like a monkey. "Are you ready... boy?"

*Boy? Okay. We'll see.*

"Ready?" Misumi asked me.

"Yes," I said.

"We will begin at the standing position," Misumi told us both. "Fight."

I moved left. I could see Monkey Boy judging the distance, his eyes scanning. I could practically see him thinking. It was obvious he knew Japanese jujitsu. But he didn't know Brazilian, and he didn't know me.

He dropped his base like a wrestler. Keeping his eyes on me, he shot in, grabbed one of my legs, and tried to suck me back.

I fell into an open-guard position. I feinted to the right, getting my knees in, getting leverage, and pulling him over.

I went for a scissor sweep. Basic move. He had a weak base. Grabbing the back of his head, I drove my knee into his stomach, then completed a side-mount position. I had control.

*Boy, huh?*

I dropped back into a low-mount position. I began to put my shoulders under his throat, bending his neck. Bending his jaw, I could hear it start to crack.

As he tried to get out, I moved back into a side-mount position, kneeing him right in the stomach.

*You invaded and just wiped out millions, right?*

So I just kept coming and moving into an alternate side-mount position, putting my other knee into his stomach, riding him like a surfer rode a wave. Basic Brazilian jujitsu move to force submission.

He quickly pulled up, grabbed my leg, and tried to kick out. I knew that if this move was executed effectively, he'd blow out my knee. So I spun, knowing that this boy did not care if he hurt me or not. In fact, I was now sure he was here to hurt me.

Too bad *his* ground game wasn't that great. I got back into a side mount, in prep for a full-mount position, and all too soon, a clock choke.

No, he didn't know Brazilian style, and he sure as hell didn't know me. My technique worked fine. I was soon choking him out—literally. He didn't tap out, so it was lights out for him.

The Okinawans yelled as if they had bet their life savings on him. I slowly got up. I could have looked at the yelling men. I could have looked at Misumi. Instead, I just stared at my once-sneering opponent, who just lay there.

Suddenly the heat, the effort, and the emotion dropped on me. I could feel bile rising in my throat. My vision blurred. What looked like black smoke began clouding my view of my fallen opponent. Then, apparently, I collapsed.

The next thing I remember was looking up at Misumi, who was bending over me.

"Oh, that was good," he said. "Are you ready for the next opponent?"

Ready? I was barely breathing.

"Yeah," I muttered as I dragged myself up. "I'll fight anybody."

I moved into the start position, barely even able to hold my weight up. I looked at the next opponent. It didn't take a psychic to read his face. I had beaten his boss bully. I had collapsed. He clearly wanted to make me pay as quickly and completely as possible.

I don't remember if Misumi said *Fight* this time. All I knew was that my second opponent quickly shot in for another one-legged takedown. Been there, countered that on opponent number one, so I just got back into a side mount. Then got back into a side-sweep position and executed the move easily. But this time I didn't have any gas left, so I just lay on top of him.

They say that submission in Brazilian jujitsu is just if you're able to get control of these positions. If you put your weight on top of your opponent, you're taking their breath so you can actually rest. So I'm resting on this guy while he's yelling. I didn't understand what he was saying, but a third Okinawan translated.

"This guy is fat," my opponent was yelling.

Oh, rude. Nice excuse too, for letting an exhausted, overheated Vietnamese rest on top of you. But I wasn't thinking that then. I was remembering that we were just recently deployed to Thailand and I was eating a lot of their food. So, yeah, I had gained ten pounds before I fought this guy.

So while he was right, it was still rude, so finally I got into a side-mount position and used the choke hold again.

And again, almost the same things happened. He didn't tap out, and I kept up the pressure until he couldn't. The only difference this time was that I didn't get up, then collapse. This time I just lay there. I couldn't even get up.

It may read like it was easy for me to win in this oven, but it wasn't. I just lay there, hoping they'd let me take a nap, but I knew they wouldn't.

Sure enough, I heard Misumi get up. I heard, because I was too tired to even turn my head to attempt to look at him. I could tell it was him by the sound of his footsteps. He walked over to where I could see his toes out the corner of my eyes. He bent down to my level.

"Are you ready for the third opponent?" he asked quietly.

I was too tired to try to hear any emotion in the words. And at that point, I didn't care whether he was being sarcastic, sardonic, or even concerned.

"I'll fight anybody," I think I said, not caring if he could hear my words or not.

This time I crawled to the start position. My third opponent rose, then almost did a combat roll right into the starting point.

Again, Misumi might have said *Start* or *Go* or *Fight*, but I don't remember hearing it. All I knew was that, unlike my second opponent, my third had been watching and learning. Rather than do what the other two had tried, he did what I had done. He got into a side-mount position, and now he laid his weight on top of me.

I could barely breathe. I could barely move. I could barely think. But if I had been able to, I might have predicted what happened next. Because my first impression of these racist bullies was accurate. They looked down on other Asians. They looked down on every *gaijin* outsider. It wasn't enough to defeat me. They instinctively wanted to humiliate me.

So opponent number three got greedy. My training and Brazilian jujitsu instincts took over, no matter how tired he thought I was. I was able to sweep him, and then, suddenly, I was back in control. Now I laid my fat, Thai-fed, exhausted Vietnamese butt on top of him. To literally rub it in, I pressed my chest to his face, smothering him. Or maybe I collapsed on him, I don't know. What I did know was that I had superior weight.

Again, he learned from his two predecessors. He didn't join them in unconsciousness. He tapped out.

Suddenly the steaming gym was filled with the sound of two hands clapping. Misumi applauded me even though I could barely move. In fact, I wished number three hadn't tapped out so I could've used him as a Japanese body pillow.

"Very good," Misumi chuckled. "Very good."

The three student stooges quickly bowed out, leaving us alone in the oven. I lay there and replied to the man.

"Very brave," I corrected him, "in this fucking sauna."

I could barely take off my sweat-soaked *gi*. I dragged my

gear bag and almost collapsed again on the way out. I did collapse on the grass once I got out and could breathe some slightly cooler air.

I correctly diagnosed heat exhaustion. The same kind as when I'd had to punch myself in the face at the Rangers school. But this time it was almost life-threatening. I reached for my phone and dialed my mercy number.

"Steve," I gasped. "Come fucking get me."

I didn't see Misumi again that day, but it didn't matter because, in the year following, I saw him plenty at the events he scheduled for me. And every event proved to be a lesson for me as I prepared and observed. The fights continued, as did my winning and prize money. But as much as I loved it, they were not my priority.

My military career was. I continued to take Special Forces training. At that point, I went from a combat search-and-rescue team into a highly trained counterterrorist capability within the Special Forces. And you had to be able to go through and pass specialized training in order to get there.

I never wanted that route. I came from an amphibious reconnaissance team. The way it usually goes is that you naturally gravitate to a route within Special Forces with whatever you were really strong at. The company generally tries to put you into that role to make sure that you succeed. Well, because I was strong in communications and in reconnaissance, I had that intellectual thing that the teams were looking for.

But I wanted to be a combat diver. I was on a combat search-and-rescue team that was right next door to a combat diving team. Those underwater guys have to go through prescuba and graduate combat diving school in Key West, Florida.

That's what I wanted to do, even though it was hard to even qualify for Combat Dive School. How hard? They tie your hands behind your back, then tie your legs, and you have to swim three hundred meters. You have to do breath-holding techniques. You have to be able to tie and untie knots underwater. There's a lot of very demanding physical training. But I wanted that.

So in between fighting, training in martial arts, and going to college, I also studied to be a combat diver. I learned by watching the combat diving team I idolized, and I soon knew the process required to move from my present position to combat diver. To feel free all the time seemed like heaven.

So that meant when the pool was closed at night, I was that guy who climbed the fence and went swimming in the dark. I was the guy who was holding his breath for minutes and tying knots underwater while everybody else was enjoying their time off.

I did that for months. There was a high washout rate for combat diving. Even in Special Forces teams, everyone thought it was extremely hard to pass diving preschool.

Day after day, week after week, I was tying knots underwater at night. You had to tie five different knots underwater, one after another, be able to bob your body, then swim through the night with your hands and feet bound. I practiced and practiced until I felt I could do it in my sleep.

When the time came to qualify, I was sure I was ready. I was highly fit. I felt really good. I was winning every fight. I was swimming, bound hand and foot, every night. I never felt better. Nothing could stop me.

Except me and my fighting fire.

It started as just another rotation into Malaysia. We did a lot of jungle warfare training there while working with the Commando Force. In Malaysian martial arts, they liked to introduce hard bone to soft tissue areas. That means if you're throwing a punch, they'll use their elbows to block it. In that situation, bones can break really easy.

I was loading supplies in an old, abandoned hangar that was filled with rusted shelving units, when this Malaysian commando came in. He had been practicing his martial arts form, and I wanted to understand it. So there we were, two commandos facing off. He started to explain it to me, but my fire got wild.

I pushed him, and I remember he reacted with his defense. Then I laughed, moved his hand, and tapped his face.

He went, "Ooo" and got into a commando stance. I slapped his hand and smacked his face again, showing him that my martial arts were better than his. He immediately pushed me back and set himself.

I threw a Muy Thai kick with my right leg. He checked it with his knee.

My ankle immediately shattered.

I dropped back. My ankle couldn't hold my weight. I dropped down. I couldn't move. I screamed.

The Malaysian commando quickly ran out and got my friend Steve, who ran in and started yelling.

"Dude! What happened? All you had to do was load the supplies!"

And now I'm acting all innocent. "Dude, I don't know…"

I spent the afternoon at Kuala Lumpur Hospital. They x-rayed my ankle. A Malaysian doctor came in.

"Well," he said, "it looks like it's a fracture."

Long story short: six months in a cast.

The combat diving test was going to happen within a month after this. Yeah, I could swim with my wrists and ankles tied, but I couldn't do it right, or for long, with a cast on my leg.

So there I was, in this commando camp, with a shattered ankle. Couldn't stand, couldn't fight, couldn't be a combat diver.

My dream was gone. My shattered ankle shattered my world.

# 14

The thing about dreams is that they may disappear one night, but they can come back. And the thing about being shattered is that everything I had survived since I decided on a life of military service had been designed to break me. And everything I had learned before that—from Bruce Lee, Miyamoto Musashi, and my teammates—had taught me that I could survive. I had learned how to carry on. I learned how not to be shattered.

It's just that sometimes I forgot.

So as always, I sucked it up and carried on. I was rotated back to Okinawa. I was on crutches and walking around in my uniform and a big cast. As I watched in frustration, the prescuba combat diving school started—the class I should have been in. But all I could do was stand there with my fractured ankle, brokenhearted—but not broken.

Life was not going to stop for any Green Beret, leg cast or no leg cast, so I continued to do everything I could. One day I was ordered to go to Hansen's Range, which was a close-quarters combat house, and drop demolitions off to the Black Ninja.

I knew of these guys. They were Special Forces members who had their own higher-level security clearance, a clearance I didn't have yet. Fine. I drove two hours to make it to that training camp. It wasn't easy. I went to this remote base, and then from there I had to drive down a dirt road through jungle canopy to finally get to a shoot house. That was where the Marine Force Recon guys were. That's where the specialized Special Forces guys trained in close-quarters combat.

And there I was, not even with the right security clearance. It didn't matter to me: orders were orders. I was told to drop demolitions off, so I was going to do just that. I jumped out with my cast and hobbled around, struggling to load the demolitions onto their training table.

As I did I kept hearing *bing, bing, bing, bing.*

I didn't know exactly what that was, but I had a sneaking suspicion, so I hobbled some more and looked around until I came upon an Asian guy popping steel. An Asian guy?

The "bing bing bing bing" was him running and gunning. Shooting from the hip, shooting from a vehicle, shooting one hand, shooting incredibly fast, and I'm like, "oh my God."

I didn't know what else to do, so I just stood there, amazed, as he shot, reloaded, shot again, and kept doing it, seemingly all day. I had never seen a guy and a gun move that fast.

Finally, he turned and looked at me.

"Hi," I said, "my name is Tu Lam. I just dropped off the demolitions, and they're right there."

He said, "Come over here."

So I went over there. There was no name on his uniform. He looked at mine with my name and all my badges, and he said, "Lama?"

"Excuse me?"

"Lam?" he said, getting it right the second time.

"Yeah."

"Ah!" he exclaimed with a smile. "My name is Nguyen, and I'm Vietnamese too."

*Not just Asian. Vietnamese.*

"Ah, great," I told him honestly. "The demolitions are right over there, and—"

He interrupted me again. "Come over here," he repeated. I

approached again, closer this time. "How long have you been here?" he asked.

"Three years."

"What happened to your ankle?"

"I broke it. Fighting."

He shook that information off. "Why don't you go and try out for the selection training coming up?" he said.

"When is that?" I immediately asked.

"Two weeks," he said. "You've got to pass the shooting school, and you have to go to North Carolina. It's high-intensity shooting all day long. You going to be okay with your cast?"

"Yeah," I instantly told him. "I'll be okay. I'll see you there."

I drove back to base, happier than I had been since my fibula fracture. *Two weeks, two weeks!* I slapped my cast, telling my ankle "You better heal!"

I got back and parked, then went hobbling into my team compound and announced, "I'm going to training in two weeks!"

And they were like, "You're not going to do that."

"Why not?"

"Because if you get in, then you're not going to be on this team anymore."

I hobbled miserably away on my crutches. My Sergeant Major, an African American badass, saw me. He was one of the few Special Forces African Americans. The majority were white Americans, of course. Asians and African Americans were few and far between, but today, in short order, I had communed with two of them—one enthusiastic and helpful, the other not so much.

"What the fuck are you standing there for, Tu?" my Sergeant Major said.

I snapped into parade-rest position.

"Step into my office," he ordered. Once we got in there, he went on. "What the fuck? What are you doing?"

I closed the door and stood at parade rest trying to balance on my cast in front of him.

"What the fuck are you doing?" he repeated. "Just sit down."

I sat down and immediately started in. "Sergeant Major, I want to tell you that there's a selection in two weeks—"

"You ain't fucking going to that," he interrupted. "If you go to that, you'll go to that specialized company and I'll lose you."

"Yeah," I said, "but Sergeant Major, that training is in two weeks."

"Did you hear what I just said to you? Get the fuck out of my office. You're not going."

I remained at parade rest.

"Get out," he demanded.

So finally, I got out, then went down the hallway. At first, I didn't know what to do. But "at first" usually doesn't last long for me. I thought about it for a few seconds, then hauled my cast down to the compound's secret company area, where you need special clearance just to get in. But just like encroaching on the Black Ninja's training ground, that didn't bother me either.

I faced a metal door with a lock on it, and above that was a camera. I started banging on the door. Then I heard a click. Like an unlatching of a lock.

The door didn't open, so I banged on it again. And again there was that click. I thought about it for less than a second, then banged on the door a third time…and heard the click. I may not have been bothered by security clearances, but no one ever called me intuitive.

I was about to bang on the door a fourth time when I heard a voice coming from the speaker beside the camera.

"It's fucking unlocked, dumbass. Just come in!"

Responding to clicks was not my specialty, but following orders was. I went in, and there was another Sergeant Major standing there. A Caucasian one. He was in charge of the unit I'd work with if I made it through selection training. I remember he had a Colt 1911 on his desk. He was sipping coffee as he looked at me.

"Who the fuck are you?"

"Sergeant Major, my name is Tu Lam, and I heard you guys are having tryouts in two weeks."

"Get the fuck out of my office," he responded. "Who the fuck do you think you are? You don't just come here whenever you want. We ask you if you want to come here. You understand me?"

"Yes, sorry, Sergeant Major," I said, almost tripping on the way out.

I thought that was it, so I just went on with my recovery and responsibilities. I was hobbling to work a few days later and heard someone yelling at me.

"Two weeks! See you there!"

Incredibly, it was Nguyen.

"They won't let me go," I blurted back at him.

"What do you mean?"

"I have a cast, and my team told me they don't want to lose me."

He went, "Huh..." then nodded. "See you in two weeks," he said before leaving.

Tung M. Nguyen made it happen. The Distinguished Pistol Shot Badge recipient and future Small Arms Championship winner saw to it that my orders came through, and in two weeks I was in the northern training area of Okinawa on a shooting range with a garbage bag wrapped around my cast.

It was pissing rain, and I was training on close-combat tactics with a pistol. I was learning how to get tight on a shot group. I was learning mechanics of speed with a gun and how to use a rifle at the speed they needed me at.

All these drills, all these movements, were timed. It was a pass or fail event. All of it had to be done with speed and precision and accuracy. You didn't hit the accuracy, you lost. You didn't hit the speed, you lost.

Garbage bag-wrapped cast or not, I didn't lose.

It culminated with what was called an urban stress test. This took place on a simulated cityscape on a shooting range where you had to shoot high, shoot low, jump over walls, and crawl under stuff. You had to maneuver through center-fed and corner-fed rooms, hallways, and collapsed sectors. And each second, your every movement was being judged and evaluated. If you didn't understand the tactics, you're a no-go.

So there I was, shooting on a flat range, understanding tactics, and learning these movements—with my leg in a garbage bag. We were closing up training on a Friday night, and the sergeant in charge pulled me aside.

"Hey, Tu," he said, "you're doing good on accuracy, but we're concerned about your cast. Are you going to be able to move and shoot? Because you're going to have to be able to move and shoot next week. Everything's timed on this. And if you don't pass the time, you fail the course. Are you okay with your cast?"

"Yeah," I answered. "I'm perfectly fine with my cast. In fact, my cast is coming off this weekend. The doctor said I'm ready to go."

"Well," he replied, "that's good. I'll see you Monday."

"Yeah," I answered. "See you Monday."

I got in my van and faced the truth. The truth was this cast was supposed to be on for the next four weeks.

I drove to the first hardware store I could find, bought a hacksaw, and drove back to my barracks. Soon it was Sunday night and I sat there contemplating the hacksaw and my cast.

As far as I was concerned, I had no choice. I needed to get my stabilizing muscles ready, so I broke the cast. When screeching pain didn't immediately rip through my body, I thought *Oh my God, I'm fine, I'm fine.*

It was weird because the leg felt unusually light. What wasn't that weird is that it also felt totally off balance. On the whole side, no muscle was moving right, and I didn't know what to do. My right foot was numb. Actually, everything was numb. I had no muscle stability. How could I pass the stress test?

I started doing drills but kept falling over because I had no stability. Still, I was intent on passing that stress test so I took the adhesive tape they used to seal up the sides of helicopters during the Vietnam War and wrapped my ankles. I remember booting myself on the morning of the stress test and wrapping up the boot too.

Stress-test time came. I stood there. In the rain.

The instructor looked at me.

"Shooter," he announced. "On line."

I stood on my castless, wrapped, numb ankle.

"Load and make ready."

I loaded my pistol. I loaded my shotgun. I loaded my long gun.

"Shooter, ready."

He was looking at me.

For the first shooting event you had to sprint fifteen yards, engage two rounds in the chest and one round in the head of your targets, then transition to this barricade and pop the steel barrier while wearing a chemical-, biological-, and radiological-protective mask.

"Shooter, ready...move!"

So I ran. I remember sliding. I slid so much that I almost fell, but I stabilized and shot two rounds in the target's chest and managed to put the third round in the head before I actually fell.

"Go."

Transition. Mask ready. They were throwing smoke. Masking up now, blowing out the air, looking. Coming up with my gun. Moving to the training apparatus. Popping steel through the smoke.

"Go."

All right. I moved to urban phase. We loaded up in a van to the staging area. For this one, I was running with four different instructors. These instructors—when entering a house and you're part of the stack—were going to move with speed, and you have to master speed. You have to collapse your sector, your responsibility. You have to kill all threats, and you have to eliminate all in your area. I stood there with an instructor.

"Stand by," the instructor said.

Charge set on a door, door blew, flash-bang, four guys entered at speeds I couldn't even process. I came in as the last guy, popping rounds in my designated areas as the instructor evaluated me.

Sequence of a flash-bang, sequence of a shotgun, sequence of how to collapse your sector of fire. All shots are accounted for. Everything was evaluated. Everything was processed.

Last event.

I had to jump over this barricade. I had to move through this trail. I had to urban-climb these ropes. I had to get through this window. I had to engage with my pistol. And I had to transition to a rifle.

As I stood there, the rain stopped. The tropical moisture was sucking the air out of me. Heat. I saw steam rising from the jungle floor.

Five hundred yards to the first barrier where I could engage, five hundred yards farther I had to jump over a low wall.

"Shooters, ready!"

I looked over at the instructors. "Shooters ready," I said.

"Stand by."

The go buzzer sounded.

I ran, I slid, I shot. I remember my foot going numb. It didn't matter at that point. Grabbed a rope. The rope was wet. Didn't matter. Pulled. I could not lock my legs because of my broken ankle. Fuck it. I used all my upper body strength, all the way up, drew my pistol, shot where I needed to shoot. Engage, move.

And I made my time. As I stood there, as the smoke cleared, as the last steel target dropped, I knew I had made my time.

"Show and make clear!" The instructor looked at me. "Show and make clear!"

I dropped my mags, pulled the bolt back as a round ejected, cleared my weapon.

"Clear, Sergeant."

"Move off line, candidate… Good job."

So broken ankle or no broken ankle, I made it. And the cast never went back on after that. Two weeks later I was in training for a position I can't talk about. But I can talk about my ongoing Toughman and underground fighting career.

I was still addicted to the fire energy that those fights fed. And it satisfied me like nothing else when I was able to inflict pain on other fighters who were there for the same reason I was.

Free the oppressed, defeat the opponent.

Even as a highly skilled individual I was still fighting Toughman matches. But I rationalized that it was helpful, more along the lines of Budo Strategies. The Special Forces allowed me to manipulate terrain and environment toward my enemy, whether it was in the field or in the ring.

As my ankle continued to heal, I trained and practiced my martial arts every day—adapting and compensating. The ankle was my worst injury, but it wasn't my only one. My martial arts evolved around my injuries, and you had a lot of injuries in Special Forces. We were doing jungle runs through mountainous terrain in boots, running through the jungles while navigating, and a lot more.

When my legs were injured, I would go and roll around on the mat. When I hurt my neck, I would go into Muy Thai. Maybe I'd do more jujitsu if my hips hurt or go more into kicking if my shoulders ached. I would change throughout the week, depending on what pain I could endure.

I could also endure more than Toughman and underground fights. I had started scheduling sanctioned matches—anything I could get my hands on or fists into. Toughman matches were not enough for me anymore. I wanted to fight no-holds-barred. I wanted something like a street fight. No rules. There were obviously some rules, since we didn't fight to the death. Still, it was satisfyingly brutal.

I fought everyone and everywhere I could. Whatever country I was deployed to, I found sanctioned or sport fights. I was doing very well, and people were also making a lot of money off me. I had a great record, so Misumi thought I was ready to take on the most important, most famous, and most daunting match of my career.

Budokan fight night in Okinawa.

# 15

Nippon Budokan is probably the most famous arena in Tokyo. But it was also the name of a huge indoor stadium in Naha, Okinawa, as well. In fact, the word *budokan* literally translates to *martial arts hall*.

In any city, the Budokan was where the up-and-comers went. Not only did they accept me, I qualified for the main fight card. But with Budokan, there was no keeping my fight career secret anymore. This was the big time. Anybody in the fight game and all the fans attended that match. Thousands of people went there, including military Special Forces. So I knew the jig was up. But it seemed that the people who could have made trouble for me were fight fans, so there was hardly a peep.

Besides, now I had gone through top-secret training at Fort Bragg. Budokan was set up while I was successfully completing the course. Now that I was part of this new military team, I was required to make myself available for assignments at any time. We had to have weapons and equipment ready to push in and operate in any area we were sent if there was a hostage situation or embassy threat.

I was part of all that when I got word of my Budokan opponent. It would be the champion of the famed Pancrase Hybrid Wrestling promotion in Japan. The organizers wanted a champion to come in to shut me down because I was an up-and-coming *gaijin*. Gaijin meant any kind of outsider. But I was a two-hundred-and-ten-pound outsider at that point, full of rage and fire and power and endurance.

So I prepared myself. I swam for miles, then ran under the water carrying a huge boulder in my arms. I did Special Forces training during the day, then hand-to-hand combat at night. It might sound exhausting, but I was exhilarated. I'd never felt better. The fire inside me was volcanic.

One month out, I was in the top fighting shape of my life. I remember having dinner at a new soba noodle place on a side street near Torii station. The soba chef was making light conversation with me as I sat underneath the overhang of a *yatai*. It was at that moment I was contacted and told to return to base.

I bowed to the Japanese noodle chef, paid my bill, and, within a few hours I was on a plane flying over Asia. We didn't know where we were going yet, but the gun trucks and vehicles were loaded. I was in my uniform, gearing up my kit on the back of a C-130, getting intelligence.

Hostage situation.

We touched down around eight hours later. The C-130 dropped its ramps. Bundles got pushed, commandos came out, and we loaded into a bus and were taken to a hangar under the cover of darkness. The partner commando force was all around us, guys we'd trained with for years. Total security. Quickly, we unloaded the bus. Secretly, we put on our gear.

Other trucks had explosives and demolitions. Commandos and cops were shutting down the roads. We entered an old, abandoned hangar.

I got off the bus—now a twenty-four-year-old Green Beret. I was part of counterterrorism, highly trained in intelligence and direct-action operations. I was the guy who came in, kicked open doors, and conducted close-quarters combat. I was part of high-risk operations, hostage rescue, direct action. But now, I, and everyone on the team, waited.

I looked across the bay and saw snipers. The intelligence was that hostages had been taken to a soccer stadium. Where in the stadium we couldn't pinpoint yet. The snipers immediately went to work with Malaysian commando forces to contain and isolate, then report back intelligence in order for guys like me to prep and plan for direct-action assault.

I started pulling weapons and equipment—laying out the demolitions because we might need to blow doors. I pulled bolt cutters and quickie saws in case we needed to cut through chain-link fences. Like surgeons, we were laying out our instruments.

I studied the intelligence coming in. Because it was a stadium, our ladder packets were added in case we needed to scale high walls. Reports of a metal front door were confirmed, so we had to adjust the charges we would use.

As more intelligence came in, we kept changing the plan in order to maximize its value and ensure mission success by fine-tuning our equipment.

And we kept doing that, and doing that, and doing that, for three weeks.

Three weeks later, I was sitting on the edge of a fold-up Army cot, looking at the rats scurrying all around the hangar—when they weren't eating the demolitions that we had prepared twenty-one days before.

Intelligence was still coming in, and the snipers were still remaining ready. We just hadn't met the trigger for the commander to send us in yet.

Three weeks.

The only tub we had was this old dip bath made from a worn cement block. The water was cold and green from algae. No showers, no running water. We shit outside.

Our bodies were rotting away.

I pulled out a little portable DVD player. I flicked it open and hit Play.

Steve said, "What are you doing?"

"You know," I told him, "they're sending in a prizefighter from mainland Japan."

"What do you mean?"

I said, "Look, I got a DVD of him, and I'm studying his movements."

Steve took a look. "He's a big boy, Tu."

"Yeah," I replied. "So am I."

"Yeah," he echoed. "It'll be a good fight. You sure you're ready?"

"Yeah, I'm ready," I told him. But in that hangar, it sounded a bit hollow.

As my team slept, I kept watching the DVD, covering the little screen with a blanket so as not to disturb them, and studied the movements of my Budokan opponent. Then I had to take a shit.

I went past the green pond area, because the shitter was way out there. We practically had to go into the jungle to get to it. Luckily I had my equipment on me.

*Luckily* because as I was about to use the facilities, my alarm went off.

*Holy crap.* Literally. Nothing like an alarm to aid your digestion.

Trigger was met. It was an emergency assault. They were moving the hostages, and we had to stop them. Commander gave us the "Green Light," and there I was running toward the hangar. I remember almost tripping, and I only had on my T-shirt and fatigues—my uniform top was back in the hangar. But I didn't have time for that now. I had to get onto the helicopter. Its blades were already spinning.

I remember grabbing my equipment and throwing it over my shoulder. I couldn't even buckle them down. I threw on my helmet and couldn't buckle that down either. I loaded onto the helicopter just as it took off. Only once I was onboard did I load everything up and buckle everything down.

As we came into the stadium, the helicopter flared as we

kicked ropes. We fast-roped down and moved to our designated point, where I had to plant explosive charges.

The only other thing I can tell you is that we blew the door, went in, and took out the threat. The company saved the hostages. Mission complete. Evaluation: success. We inventoried our weapons the next day, loaded up, and flew back to Okinawa.

But the thing was it wasn't the action that became the problem. Turned out, it was the inaction that got us. We had stayed in that hangar for so long, that, once the job was done, a lot of us started getting sick—including me. I was vomiting, had a temperature of more than a hundred degrees, and wicked diarrhea. I now weighed in at a hundred and ninety pounds.

Budokan was in three days.

My endurance was gone. If I threw a jab, it took everything out of me.

The next seventy-two hours were just a blur. I remember there was a lot of bed and a lot of latrine. My body ached. Even my spine hurt.

But Budokan fight night waited for no man.

I could barely get dressed, walk downstairs, or drive to my team room. But I did. I managed to open my team room and sat down. I thought about the fight that was going to happen later that night.

Digging through my backpack, I pulled out an IV bag. I hooked it above me, ran a line to my vein, stuck it in, and tried to hydrate myself. Then I tried to meditate as the intravenous fluid flowed. I tried to concentrate, to harmonize my mind and body.

But it was all just a blur.

Suddenly it was later, and I was wrapping my hands with Steve in the dressing room. Budokan, the sweet science. I could hear the growing crowds outside. It was different now. The sounds were different. This was war.

I could feel the stadium's energy. It was no longer a little fight in a bar or an overheated gym. As Steve taped my hands, I could feel the energy, yes, but I could also feel the weakness in my body. Everything hurt down to the bone.

I heard Steve talking as if he were at the end of a long hallway.

"Look at me, dude," he said. "Look at me. You can't fight like this. You're going to fucking die. You can't fight like this."

As usual, I was reasonable and understanding. "Shut up, Steve," I muttered.

Then Misumi came into the dressing room. "You cannot fight like this," he said in his deep, guttural voice.

But even he couldn't sway me. The only thing that came to my mind at that point were the words of my uncle. The words he told me when I was a bullied, frightened child.

*Do you want to be a fucking commando today?*

I looked at Misumi and said, "I *am* fighting like this."

I put on the gloves and stood. Steve faced me.

"Let me see what you got," he said, raising his hands for me to punch them. "One, two, one two."

I punched his right palm, then his left. I repeated the move twice, going as fast and hard as I could. Then I ran to the bathroom.

Diarrhea, vomiting. Not necessarily in that order.

"You got five minutes," I heard.

We headed to the staging area. As I walked down a long hallway, the arena opened up around me. Thousands were there. Somewhere among them were my teammates and commanders. Like I said, there was no hiding it now. They knew I was there. It was a big fight.

As I looked upon this entryway into the arena, I could feel even more energy. The roar. The war.

But I knew I was weak and depleted. The smoke and lights that slammed into my face as I stepped into the entry didn't help. Nor did the blaring music that assailed my ears. Japanese and Americans all around me were screaming.

As I came out into the eye of the energy, the rage pounded through my blood. As I came into the ring, the fire erupted through my body.

As I was shaking my gloves, loosening my hands, the lights went out. Seconds later, lights and smoke appeared opposite me. And here came this good-looking Japanese guy with beautiful hair and a huge body.

He was sauntering out, enjoying his stardom as champion of Japan. People were screaming as he passed, and as he got closer to me, he didn't get any smaller. He entered the ring, looked at me, and laughed.

*What is this?* I thought, full of rage, full of fire, full of disease.

The referee stood up. "Are you ready?" he asked as the crowd screamed even louder. We nodded. And then, "Go."

The champion attacked full force, with a Pancrase-style open hand. I checked the strike and hit him full in the face. Blood splashed from his nose and mouth. But when I hit him, I hit him so hard that it took too much energy out of me.

He grabbed my leg, trying to take me down to the ground. But I had a good base. So I whaled on him with my elbows against the side of his head, and his ear busted. I could see it, so I came around to try locking his neck.

If I torqued it too much I could break it. But I knew if I went slow, I could get a good angle on him. So there I was, torquing his neck, but as I did he lifted me up, then slammed me down to the mat.

That was fine. I was skilled. I grabbed his hip and moved my legs so he would have to fight in between my legs in basic jujitsu style. He rose up. Bad move for him. I got into a scissor and tried to sweep him. Couldn't do it. Too heavy of a base.

I had never felt that before. It was really easy for me to flip everybody else. Not him. I tried again. Still too heavy of a base. I looked over. He was sitting too far back. I didn't have the leverage. I needed to bump him up. So I came underneath and bumped him up over me and, as I did, he rose up and gave me a fast, powerful shot to the face.

Hard. Very hard.

Second shot. I moved and his hand hit the mat. Third shot, I grabbed his arm, trying to climb up it, but he had the leverage and came back down with his elbow. His elbow also hit me right in the face.

Boom! I saw stars.

But just like me back at my first underground match, he didn't stop there. He hit me again, and again, and again, and again, and again, and again.

The referee grabbed him and looked down at my bloody face.

"Are you okay?" he asked.

"No, not okay," I managed to answer, "but I'm going to fight."

So he pushed away, and the champion continued to whale on me.

Thankfully, after the first few face hammers, I really didn't feel pain anymore. It was like my head was being buried alive under falling anvils. I just kept getting slammed farther and farther into the mat as it got darker and darker. Still, I never went out.

Finally, from what I was later told, Steve threw in the towel.

I had never lost a fight. Now I had, and just because a friend didn't want me to be beaten to death. I lay there on the mat, looking up at the lights on the ceiling, blood coming down the side of my cheek, face, nose... My jaw felt like it had popped off my skull.

But all I could think was *defeat*.

Then I could see the champion towering above, looking down at me. I could hear the crowd cheering. Slowly, I tried to get up as my blood dripped down. I couldn't do it. I fell back to the mat.

My team rushed into the ring and pulled me out. They helped me into the back. They got me into our dressing room. They told me everything was okay as they wiped the blood away.

Even then, all I could think about, all I could feel, was defeat. I had never been defeated. And I never wanted to feel that way again.

Silly me. Defeat was not done with me yet.

# 16

Even an ass-whupping was not going to keep me down. In fact, it inspired me. I continued my career kicking in doors throughout Asia and seeking more missions in more countries than ever before. I had fully recovered from my illness and beatdown and was back to being fit, able, and ready to go, so I ran and swam deeper into what I did best.

At that point, I was twenty-four years old and deployed throughout Asia to work and train with other host-nation commando forces. We would cross-train with all these nations' premier counterterrorist units for a variety of reasons. One reason was to get knowledge.

The Special Forces work through rapport-building, combined with and through intelligence-gathering. I also held a higher security clearance, so we're back to what I can legally tell you.

First stop, South Korea.

In the vernacular of the team, we were on a flat range, shooting MP5s. I was closing in from a submachine gun, transitioning to my pistol, front-sight focus, trigger press, and the round exits through the tempo of a target. We were doing a bilateral hit with the Korean team in a training scenario. But not just any Korean team.

The Korean 707 was South Korea's premier counterterrorist team. The unit was formed after the 1972 Munich massacre where Israeli athletes were slaughtered by Palestinian terrorists at the Summer Olympics. That forced the South Korean government to create a counterterrorist unit in time for the 1988 Summer Olympics, which were held in South Korea.

That's who we were running with. Moving in their tiger-stripe camouflage outfits next to me, a 707 Operator compressed his MP5 as I shot—always two rounds to the chest, one to the head.

*Pop, pop, pop.*

As I moved around, I also compressed my MP5 in harmony with the 707.

*Pop, pop, pop.*

As one of them rounded the corner, I checked his opposing threat.

"Clear."

Two rounds to the chest through the door as I saw the threat. It went dark.

I could hear the teams move. As I turned around, I engaged a threat, two rounds through the head. The teams disappeared.

I heard *pop, pop, pop.*

As I entered quickly, white lights came on, then went off. As I went along on a sweep of my sector, I could see the 707 move through—two holes through the chest of a target, one through the head.

*Pop, pop, pop.*

Then it was quiet.

"Clear."

The lights came back on. We had gone through a training simulator maze in the 707 compound.

A month later, we were training with the Thai counterterrorist commando force. I was upside down. Literally. My body was suspended, inverted, as I placed explosives on a window. I was totally a spider-man as commandos floated next to me. Their team set explosives at the other windows.

"All team set?" their Commander asked quietly. "Bravo team set?"

"I have control," our Commander replied.

Five, four, three, two...

Snipers took a shot through the window as I pulled my charges. The window exploded. Commandos roped in through the opening.

Spidering down, I transitioned, pulled the slack from my rope through my rappel harness, drew my pistol, checked the area, went to the door, and pulled security as my number-two man stacked at the door. As we quickly engaged threats, we entered and moved to our points of domination. *Pop, pop.* As we collapsed our sector of fire, *pop, pop.* Clear!

He gave me the door. I entered. He followed, then number three and four entered, collapsed sector in the center, and interlocked the kill zone. Clear!

A week later, touch down in Guam.

The C-130 ramp dropped as I was cranking in the back of a gun truck. I adjusted my night vision and saw my teammates looking at me on the ramp as they prepped their dirt bikes and adjusted their own night vision. As the ramp dropped, two dirt bikes emerged under cover of darkness. Land Rovers came out next.

I was on the gun truck moving down. We were all on an airstrip moving to a target site. I could see the dirt bikes and my teammates running down the dirt trail roads, heading for the main avenue of approach as they were sweeping sectors and intersections with their guns and infrared lasers. As I rolled through, I could hear that we were on final approach.

"I have control," I heard the Commander say. "Stand by."

As the vehicles were turning into the village I could also hear the countdown.

"Five, four, three..."

Then snipers, who had already free-fallen in two days before to give us intelligence, snapped their targets as the force entered. We all placed explosives, collapsed our sectors, and neutralized the threat.

One month later, Singapore, working with their premier counterterrorist force on close-quarters tactics for linear targets. We cross-trained on tactics and developed new ones by working with our partnered forces.

We did jungle raids, ambushes, and much more all over Asia, working with the best counterterrorist groups. Kept kicking in doors, employing explosives, completing reconnaissance. Malaysia six times, the Philippines six times, Thailand thirteen times. We were deployed roughly eight months out of the year, for multiple years.

Is it any wonder it all became a blur to me? I was living in villages, living in the jungle, running with the Indigenous populations, learning ancient primitive practices, shifting from country to country multiple times, training with every commando force, and gaining knowledge from some of the best in the world. At that point, the world was my teacher.

So, of course, it wasn't enough for me. Enough for a commando, maybe. Not enough for a rōnin. I had to find martial arts matches to fight in on the side. I'd fight anybody who wanted to fight me, because I was aware of The Way. The way of the Tiger. The way of Tao. The way of Dharma. The way of rōnin. By any name, it was energy I couldn't describe.

So, if I was in the Philippines I would learn and fight their traditional martial art, Arnis, also known as Kali or Eskrima. If I was in Malaysia I would definitely learn and fight the Southeast Asian martial arts known as Silat, because there was no way I wanted to break another ankle, or anything else. And if I was in Thailand I would fight Muy Thai. It was never hard to find matches there: Muy Thai was a national pastime.

So while most of my teammates enjoyed Bangkok, I made

the fateful decision to find a fight. It wasn't hard. Soon I was standing in the center of a ring in a tent as a Thai fighter raised his hands, and his legs moved like he was an animal marking his territory.

At that point, I knew he would either push-kick me or he'd roundhouse-kick my thigh. I didn't want to set it up where I would respond in kind with a roundhouse or push kick. So my plan was, as he roundhouse-kicked me, I would either eat it or step into it, pass the energy, and show him what a Western-style right hand was.

Well, that might have been my plan, but his first kick happened so fast I couldn't register it. Same with the second kick.

*Huh? How? Okay. All right. Let's go.*

I gave him some feigned confusion. That made him cocky. With the third kick, he started snapping his hip into it, creating a pattern before the kick. Mistake. So I came in and he… well, I introduced him to what a Western-style right hand was. And it leveled him out.

But I tell you, I couldn't walk out of that ring. My legs were bleeding. Thankfully, as always, Steve was there with his healing knowledge.

"I told you, dude," he said while he stanched the blood. "Why can't we just go somewhere and, you know, just *be*? Like, why do you have to fight?"

As always, my reply was calm, assured, and well-reasoned. "Shut up, Steve." But I said it with an honest, appreciative smile—like I always did.

You never know who's in the audience of a Muy Thai fight. Some of them could be those very same commandos you were fighting alongside earlier that day. Some could be martial arts fighters themselves.

One of them was definitely a certain Sergeant Major Name-Redacted, of my next assigned unit. He went to a friend who was watching the match and said he wanted to contact me about that next assignment.

Little did I know where that would lead me, and little did I care. I had my groove back, and nothing was going to stop me now.

Except an invitation to my brother's wedding.

# 17

"I can't go."

"What do you mean you can't go?" my stepfather asked.

"I really don't have time," I told him. "I'm in training, and those days are long. There's a lot of window-breaching, and a lot of other stuff going on. And me being the new guy, I can't just suddenly break away. I can't go to training and then, you know, just leave for personal reasons."

My stepfather could have argued. Instead, he simply said eight more words.

"It's your brother. You need to be there."

I tried to think of a way to argue with that. When I couldn't, I begrudgingly said, "Well, when is it?"

"This weekend."

Ah, I got him. "But I haven't got a plane ticket—"

"Don't worry. I already have a ticket for you."

Game, set, and match.

Truth was I didn't want to go. I didn't want to be reminded how happy he and the bridal party were, while I had given up on love. I had done a lot of partying over the years, but whatever relationships I'd had never worked out. That wasn't surprising. Special Forces training took total commitment. You had to put yourself, your team, your goal, and your country first.

Beyond that, I hadn't lied to my stepfather. I was already cer-

tified and trained through the schoolhouse and had run with
the teams for at least a year. And now we were doing a team
training on how to utilize new Petzl harnesses to effectively get
into windows on an explosives breach.

But that's not what I told my stepfather.

"Well, I'll tell you what," I said. "I don't know if I can make
it, but I'll try. I promise you that. I'll try."

That's where we left it. Like I said, I really didn't want to go.
Not because I didn't love my brother. I did. It was because I
was self-consumed at that time of my life. I was always trying
to educate myself—to constantly learn more. Trying to seek the
best training in order to be the best. My life was about fire, not
family. And I meant to keep it that way.

At 0800 hours the next day, my team sergeant yelled for us
to load and make ready.

My team sergeant, who we'll call Greg, had a lot of experience in counterterrorist operations. He had been an Airborne
Ranger, now he was a 1st Special Forces Group Operator and
team sergeant. Greg was highly respected in the company, and
he had a wealth of knowledge—having cross-trained and helped
stand up some of the most lethal Counter Terrorist units in
Southeast Asia.

"Stack up," Greg yelled to us.

We followed orders, stacking up at the breach point of the
door.

"I have control."

Five, four, three, two, one.

The door blew into shrapnel as we entered, collapsing our
sector of fire and neutralizing the threat. Over and over that day
we breached windows with charges. The precision and teamwork needed to perform at this level was a lot to take in. With
each live-fire exercise, Greg continued to refine our team movements in close-quarters battle. Until he said something I didn't
want to hear.

"All right, boys, we're going to call training early today."

I immediately checked my watch, subconsciously hoping that it was later than I thought. It wasn't. Four o'clock in the afternoon. My flight to the wedding was at eight.

"Hey, Greg," I called over with seeming nonchalance. "Is there anything else I can do?"

"No," he said, "just call it a day." I started to turn, only to hear him toss me a crumb of hope. "Steve's going down to Myrtle Beach. You should go with him."

Myrtle Beach. What a great place! Especially for team guys. And after a life of oppression, both being and freeing, I was always ready to party when the time was right. Sadly, the time wasn't right just then. I knew the correct thing to do was to attend the wedding, so that's what I did.

My airport marathon started. I dropped off my gear, showered up, ran out the door, raced to the airport, and sped through the security checks. Finally, I made it to the plane that would take me to Ohio, where the bride's family lived. I started the flight mentally bellyaching.

*I don't even know why I'm going. I have so much to do.*

Really, I didn't, but I tried to convince myself I did. But as the plane descended through Ohio skies, I faced it. I didn't want to believe that love was possible for me anymore. When you dedicate your life to so much fire, you really can't know what love is. Because you see so much hate and violence, maybe you don't want to know. Just staying alive took so much time and concentration that there really wasn't room for anything that could distract or weaken me.

And maybe I didn't want to be reminded of how happy my brother was either.

As I disembarked, I was mentally armed to grin and bear it.

My brother and stepfather picked me up at the airport and drove me to the house. There's so much to do to prepare for a wedding—especially a traditional Asian American one—that they immediately went to take care of other things. Alone in the front yard, I hoisted my duffel bag and headed for the door.

I really wanted to see my mother. I wanted to share with her what I had experienced in Malaysia. I had been the team leader training with Malaysian commandos in jungle warfare. At first, I had felt sorry for myself because it was wet all the time and there were leeches everywhere. But I had gotten over that quickly and plunged into the thick of it. Concentrating on effective tracking, I saw a break in the vegetation in front of me. I got down on my hands and knees and poked my head through.

A Malayan tiger looked back.

There was an endless fight-or-flight second—or, more accurately, an attack-and-eat-me second. But then my own tiger energy calmed me. After all, I had been born within the hour of the tiger in the Year of the Tiger. It told me that there was a reason I was here and a reason I was seeing the tiger on this day.

As that endless second ended, the magnificent animal the Malayans called *harimau* simply looked away from me and went back into the jungle.

In Chinese mythology, the dragon is the strongest in the spiritual world, but the tiger is the strongest in both the spiritual and physical world and can easily move between them. My mother, who was also born in the Year of the Tiger, was uniquely qualified to understand why I saw that tiger in that jungle and why it didn't eat me. She and I were both tigers—fearless, curious, always getting into trouble, and not always making the right decisions but hopefully learning in the end.

I knocked or rang the doorbell or something: I can't remember which, because, after the door opened, I forgot everything else—even my mother and the tiger.

Because the sister of the bride, the future Ruthie Lam, stood there.

Flash, bang, boom.

Unless you've experienced something similar, this is going

to sound like total BS, but I'm incredibly happy to say it wasn't. We looked at each other, and my mind, body, and even soul felt a connection I had never felt before.

I think she felt it too, or at least she felt something, because she immediately slammed the door in my face.

I didn't care. The image of her stayed in my mind as I blinked. Usually a mental image would fade, but this time it grew stronger.

I reopened the door to see her moving quickly to the next room. I did not take offense. I guessed that she had slammed the door and retreated because she had been surprised by, and shared, the same feeling I had. Even now, as she moved into the next room, her energy was welcoming.

I watched her, thinking, *What a beautiful, beautiful human being.*

I had never believed in love at first sight. Now I did. I tried to deny it, but I couldn't. I had never felt anything like this before. I had never been so present in a moment.

Team life is so fast-paced that, as I've said, it can become a blur. This was both the opposite and the bookend to that period of my life. This moment was in sharp focus. I had never cared so much. I had never wanted to get to know somebody so much. And, until she writes her own book, I think it's safe to say that, on the basis of how we looked at and acted around each other, she felt about me the way I felt about her.

My life with Ruthie was never a blur, although the rest of that visit was. I vaguely remember my brother getting married, but I remember distinctly how Ruthie and I became part of each other's lives that day.

After the wedding, as much as we didn't want to, we had to be apart—her back to college, and me back to training. I had to prep for major missions. I returned to Okinawa, while Ruthie was still studying at Ohio State. They say long-distance relationships don't work. Happily, we were the exception. Being in Special Forces is extremely hard, but it had taught me steadfastness. Being raised in her Asian family was very strict, but she remained steadfast in her love for me.

Finally she got permission from her parents to come and visit me in Japan. We both knew that her visit would mark a new, important stage in our relationship. And I knew the day she was scheduled to arrive would be a day I would never forget.

The day she was scheduled to arrive was September 11, 2001.

# 18

That day I got my workout in, made sure my apartment was in order, then finally managed to relax in my barracks as I waited for her flight to touch down. To fill the time, I sat down and turned on the TV.

I saw the first plane crash into the Twin Towers.

Then the second.

My teammates rushed into the room, and we watched as the planes crashed, again and again and again.

It was at this time we were contacted and told the same thing. *Stand by and be ready.*

Radio silence was quickly imposed and stayed that way for twenty-four hours. For me, Ruthie was in the twilight zone for a day—as I was for her.

I can tell you my heart was racing for those twenty-four hours. Like so many, I was unable to sleep. My heart ached as I kept watching those planes plow into the towers. My soul burned as I watched the towers collapse. I could feel the fire rage inside of me as I watched those innocent people die.

Twenty-four hours later, Ruthie finally called and was able to tell me she was okay. Our love only got stronger, because we had felt what it was like to be without each other. Our love did not diminish, especially since we both knew what I then had to do.

Training continued as the situation continued to develop. President George W. Bush declared a war on terror, and the world changed. So we did too. Our training, our equipment, our gear, everything, started ramping up. We knew that we were going to go to war in Special Operations. We just didn't know where or when.

Then orders started dropping for the Global War on Terror. Multiple areas. Multiple continents. Multiple war zones.

First Group were a contingent force for anywhere in Asia, so it made sense that our main zone was the Philippines. Our primary concern was the Jihadist militant group Abu Sayyaf and their affiliation with al-Qaeda. So we were prepping all our equipment for jungle warfare.

At the same time, I was maintaining my relationship with Ruthie—trying to downplay everything that was going on, without outright lying. She was in her early twenties and intent on her college work, so that was a blessing.

Leaving her to her studies, I was deployed to the Philippines a few times to start prepping our collaboration with their national counterterrorist unit, which we had helped set up. Under the Philippines' President Arroyo and the State Department, we worked out their counterterrorist-strike capability. The first Special Forces Group had trained them for more than a year and a half prior to 9/11, so after 9/11, we had a counterterrorist force in place that we could do bilateral operations with.

Despite the developing situation, things remained relatively constant for me. In addition to doing productive work, I was in love, and Ruthie was truly the balance to my fire. I looked at her like I looked at no other person in my life. The only woman that I loved as much was my mother. I see the strength that both Ruthie and my mother had. Both were very determined and very driven in life. The thing was, no matter how many things Ruthie had going on in her life, and it was always a lot, she always managed to put me first.

After a while, she again got permission to join me in Okinawa.

This time she made it to Japan without delay or incident, and all the time we spent together only further cemented our bond. But eventually she had to return to school, while I continued to travel around Asia as the Global War on Terror continued.

Eventually, my allotted time in Okinawa came to an end and, by Army rules, I had to be rotated to another station. To both my and my new love's appreciation, my next stop was the first Special Forces Group in Fort Lewis, Washington. Now, instead of being almost six thousand miles apart, we were just over two thousand, with no oceans in between. That's practically next door for two people in love. In fact, even before I reported for duty, I visited Ruthie. And she gave up everything to move to Washington with me.

So there we were, two young kids in an old college car packed to the brim, driving cross-country. And in those twenty-three hundred miles, we got to know each other even better. We visited the Grand Canyon on our journey west. We looked at the stars and we looked in each other's eyes. I had a tough time deciding which were more beautiful, but, ultimately, Ruthie won.

For the first time, I was truly in love. I had never felt so fulfilled.

We moved into a small, one-bedroom apartment in Washington State. It was all we could afford. Enlisted guys don't make much, and Ruthie wasn't working yet. But once we settled in, it didn't take long for her to find a job. All too soon, she was working as a receptionist at a fitness center during the day and continuing her college studies at night. In short order, we added a Westie Terrier named Stitch to our team. We were so happy and so in love.

She lived in our one-bedroom apartment, went to work at four a.m., then went to night school, but always took care of the home and me—while I continued to rotate through and train in different countries. Our first year did not go by in a blur. I remembered and loved every second of it.

But there was still a war going on around us. Teams were dying. One was taken out in Zamboanga by a motorcycle bomb. Others from helicopters crashes. All teams were in conflict areas, and anything could happen at any moment. From all my training and experience, I knew one thing for sure: love lasts forever, but people don't.

So soon after our first year together, Ruthie and I were sitting in my parked jeep. It was quiet, the interior illuminated by the glow of parking-lot lights. I looked over at her, then took her hand.

"Would you marry me?" I asked quietly. Maybe too quietly.

She looked up. "What did you say?"

"Would you marry me?" I repeated, a little louder.

She grabbed my hand in return, took only a few endless moments to kiss me, then answered.

"Yes, yes, yes, yes."

Four times. I counted them.

We married as soon as we could in a small chapel outside Fort Lewis, Washington. We also did it as quietly as possible— because in our culture, it's dishonorable to get married secretly. The Vietnamese custom is to have big weddings full of rules and traditions. Just ask my brother.

We avoided all that because I not only wanted to marry Ruthie but I felt I needed to make sure she was taken care of in case something happened to me. By military rules, that would only occur if she was my wife.

Now she was, and I couldn't have been happier, and, in a way, more relieved because I knew me. I was not going to stop training, learning, and taking on more opportunities to free the oppressed.

She knew that too, and we made the most of our time together as my training continued—and the day for my deployment back to the Philippines came closer.

Pallets were packed. Guns were zeroed. I understood ballistics, data, and charts. I had collected all our equipment and gear. I checked everything.

"Ready?" I was asked.

"Set," I answered.

Every day up until then, Ruthie would bring lunch to an old chapel right across the street from the Special Forces Group compound. The area was covered in pine trees. It was always wet in Washington State, so moss had overgrown the old chapel's roof.

Every day I would join her to try a new dish that I'd love. But this was our last day before I deployed again.

"I made you egg rolls today," she said.

"I love your egg rolls," I answered truthfully. They were as good, or even better, than my mother made.

We ate underneath the shade of a wet pine tree, then said our goodbyes.

And that became normal for her during the next twenty-three years. Like the popular Green Beret song by Sergeant Barry Sadler says, "Back at home, a young wife waits." It was always Ruthie who held everything together while her warrior went to fight.

And it was also Ruthie who eventually had to care for the monster who ultimately came back.

"You got everything?"

"Sir?"

"Stop calling me *sir*." Again he insisted I call him by his name.

"Yes, Blaze, I got everything."

Blaze was my team leader. On every Special Forces A-Team, there's a team leader: he's the highest-ranking officer there and rarely does he want to be called something other than *sir*.

"Well," Blaze said, "Paul's around the corner, so make sure you give him the list so we can turn in the weapons."

"Yes, sir!"

"Blaze," he corrected me again as I ran out into the team room to find let's-call-him Paul.

Every team room had a television that was always playing the news. The Green Berets were always looking for what the next target might be. As I walked by I could hear President Bush again addressing the nation about the War on Terror.

It was a global pursuit, so, as we surmised on 9/11, every Special Forces Group was going to be busy in every region on every continent. But that day the President made it clear that we were going to strike Afghanistan first.

And as he said "Some of you may not come home," I could feel the fire rage inside me. Ruthie was now almost seven thousand miles away, so the fire had turned into an inferno. This is what I had waited for—how the universe had prepared me to experience the teachings of Bushido in this lifetime.

*A warrior is worthless unless he rises above others and stands strong in the midst of a storm...*

"Tu!" Paul interrupted my recollection of samurai Yamamoto Tsunetomo's words. "You got my weapons list?"

I handed it to him. "Here you go."

Soon after, we were flying over Basilan Island in the Southern Philippines. I took off my headset, checked my gear, and looked at the teams as they rolled and folded up their sleeping mattresses, hammocks, and cots. The C-130 ramp finally dropped, and we were instantly hit by a wave of heat and humidity. It was like stepping into the mouth of a hair dryer set on High.

Basilan Island had a reputation for crawling with Abu Sayyaf bandits who were affiliated with and funded by the Muslim extremist group al-Qaeda. This group wanted an independent state, so it sought to take this area from any other religion by extortion, beheadings, bombings, rape, enslavement, and mass murder.

That was why we were there.

"Tu."

"What you got, Paul?"

"Go link up with the LRC, make sure they have all their

weapons and equipment. We're going to move into the jungle tonight."

"Got it."

The Light Reaction Company, aka the LRC, and later the Light Reaction Regiment, were the best the Philippines had to offer when it came to counterterrorist direct-action operations. And they were trained and equipped by us. In fact, as soon as I showed up in their camp, they acted like I was a superstar.

"Sergeant, Sergeant!" one cried, trying to bear-hug me.

"Get off!" I barked. "You got all the gear? You got all the equipment?"

"Yes, Sergeant," the man said enthusiastically.

They hadn't seen me in more than six months. Like I said, we were role models to them. We'd freed them from their oppressors. We'd educated and trained them. And now we were going to move into the southern Philippines and work with them to help contain and isolate the extremists.

Working and training with the Filipinos was amazing. We were able to get more Green Berets in, gather intelligence, and plan special missions. At the same time we were in an old, abandoned, rat-infested hospital which was called Camp Masaisai— a local word that describes a wave movement made by water. Bruce Lee's "be water my friend," was never far from my mind. There we were able to continue training these commandos and raise their level of tactics and close-quarters combat.

This had been a real hospital where many people had been saved and lost, but we were there as a bilateral Filipino and American commando force. So we put up fake walls and doors for explosives-breaching training, maze navigation, shooting, and fast-roping into the windows.

By day, we learned Kali extreme knife-fighting from them while training them how to protect presidents, diplomats, generals, and any other VIPs who might need it. By night, we practiced raids by running through the jungle using only night

vision. We were getting to know each other in our weapons capabilities because we were prepping to take direct action against
Abu Sayyaf.

And all the while, I slept in the jungle, studied in grass huts,
took time to find internet cafés so I could take my college
exams, and, of course, checked in with my wonderful wife as
often as possible.

Finally, after months of this, the order came that I needed to
learn cliff assaults in preparation for possible deployment to Afghanistan. To do that, I was sent to India. Naturally I expected
it to be steaming hot. I was wrong. Very wrong.

"Oh fuck, it's cold."

I was at nineteen thousand feet on a snow-covered mountain in the union territory Jammu and Kashmir—at the border
of Pakistan, India, and China—a place where they say heaven
touches earth. If that was true, heaven was frozen. I was waiting for the moment when the sun crested over the mountain
peaks—just to give me some sense of warmth.

We had just finished our latest cliff assault during the five
weeks of mountain-warfare training. Even though it was fucking
cold, my body was drenched in sweat because we had climbed
all night. And we had climbed all night because we had to get
into this position on the cliff in time for the dawn breaking because that was when we could provide a support-by-fire position for our assault team. That was what training in cliff assaults
consisted of.

It was cold, my body was shivering, and it felt like the earth
itself was sucking the life out of my soul.

*How did I get here?* I thought.

A month before, a six-man Special Forces Operational De-
tachment Alpha, which included me, prepared to cross-train
with Indian commandos. To accomplish this, we had to take, of
all things, a commercial flight into New Delhi. After that, try-

ing to go unnoticed despite our packs, we had to take a taxi to the bus station.

There we loaded up onto a bus straight out of *Slumdog Millionaire*. The old, aromatic vehicle was crammed with Indian locals carrying wooden crates filled with chickens. There were even goats on this freaking bus. Piles of luggage were everywhere. People were eating rich, spicy food. Kids were climbing on top of each other. We just tried to stay inconspicuous.

We drove farther and farther until we had finally made it to a commando-training ground. There, a single Indian commando came out. He checked our names, looked over the bus, went in, and threw all our gear off. Some commando behavior never changed, no matter what country they were in.

That night we had linked up with more Indian commandos. The next morning we started our mountain-assault training, using proven tactics that had been passed down since World War II. Despite our somewhat unusual journey to get to them, we were learning these tactics with the best in the world.

How did I know they were the best? One clue was that, while I was young, well-disciplined, fit, and uninjured then, I had a hard time keeping up with even the smallest of these Indian commandos. They were used to working at this elevation. I was not. But that wasn't the only reason.

Their body frames, the way they moved, and the loads they could carry all reminded me of the Nepalese Gurkhas who were made of solid muscle and quiet determination. These were elite tactic soldiers. They knew how to silence their movements. They understood how to move up and hold high ground. We trained with them day in and day out, from four in the morning until ten at night.

But not on the weekends. On weekends the rest of my team just wanted to relax. They wanted to sleep in. They were drained. But for a young samurai, no, that is not the way. So I grabbed one of the local Indian commandos and said five words.

"Take me to the temples."

It was arranged. The commando drove me up makeshift roads, winding higher and higher around a mountain. As he tried to prevent us from plummeting to our deaths, I spotted mountain goats jumping up and down in the hazy fog. We got so high up that we literally drove through clouds.

Finally, he pulled up to a huge, gated wall. The Indian commando said something I believe was *Tibetan*.

In a warrior, there's always a relationship with spirituality. No matter where I went in the world, monks, spiritual teachers, and healers were always drawn to warriors. Perhaps warriors needed the most guidance.

As the gates opened, the Indian commando drove through the clouds. I couldn't see even five feet in front of me. Finally the vehicle stopped at the red doors of an old temple. The architecture was beautiful. There were Tibetan, Chinese, Indian, and other influences. This ancient temple had been there—where heaven touched earth—for two thousand years.

The temple door opened a crack, the Indian commando spoke to someone, then motioned for me to enter. I started to, but the Indian commando did not follow. I turned to him.

"How long, Sergeant?" he asked. When I pondered his question, he explained. "I must guard the door. How long?"

"Give me an hour."

The door closed, blocking him from my sight. I was left in the company of a combination doorman, host, and translator. He led me past candles which illuminated walls covered with ancient writings, as well as paintings of Buddha, monks, and dragons. I smelled incense.

I was directed to a corner to watch Tibetan monks meditating. I sat there as the monks started to hum *om* as one tapped a golden singing prayer bowl. The deep, reverberating, soothing sound it made, and the energy they all created, vibrated to the core of my being.

Although I had spirituality, I wasn't a religious man back

then. I never gave much credence to what I guess you could call man-made religions. My life was a journey to find out what my true religion was.

The Tibetan monks then went into another meditation of mindfulness and reflection on life and death. I could see they were disciplined in their teachings and their diet. I could see they were ready to accept and share gratitude. But looking back on it now, I can tell you I wasn't ready. I wasn't ready at that time to understand what any of it meant. But I wanted to learn. I wanted to know.

So I sat with a monk and thought about what to ask him. Immediately memories of being left for dead when I was three years old appeared. With the linguist there, there was one thing I decided on.

"Why is the world so cruel?"

The man interpreted this with the passion I had given it. But the monk simply took the linguist's hand and smiled kindly. Then he turned his caring face toward me and touched my hand.

I don't know if I was fully present that day, but even so, when he touched me, something felt different. Better. The feeling was even stronger than when that Indonesian monk gave me that orange all those years ago, after we were finally rescued from the fishing boat.

Then the Tibetan monk rose with me and, through the linguist, asked me to go out with him behind the temple. As we did, as if on cue, the sun crested over the fog, and it started to clear. But not for me.

The monk picked up a stick and went into an old courtyard, where he drew a circle on the ground. Then he grabbed two small sacks that had obviously been there for a long time. He calmly, kindly, spoke to the linguist, and then the linguist told me what he said.

"He sat here for many years thinking. Every time he had a bad thought, he would cast a black stone into this circle on the ground. If he had a good thought, he would toss in a white one."

The monk looked at me and smiled, then the linguist kept translating what he had said.

"For many, many years, all he did was cast black stones into this circle on the ground. Looking around him, being present at a moment, being aware of what his thoughts were, he cast these black stones onto the ground. Then, finally, one day, the first white one was cast."

The linguist looked at me and said, "Now all the stones are white."

The monk smiled. There was not a shred of artifice in it, or him.

Standing there, looking down at this circle, my soul cried. But my eyes did not. I can't describe the healing energy I felt. But I can tell you I still wasn't ready to accept it. I had too much fire, too much anger.

I went back to training for another week. The Indian commandos patrolled with us through high elevation and taught us to understand reconnaissance in a high-desert environment. But on the weekends, I returned to the temple to visit the monk.

On my final visit, we were sitting on the edge of a river. It was beautiful, but I was still not willing to enjoy it. I looked at the monk. He was smiling, so grateful for life. I was right next to him, stone-faced, so full of pain. I turned to him and asked what so many had asked for so long.

"What is the meaning of life?"

His answer was immediate. By this time he was speaking calm, quiet, accented English.

"Who are you?" he asked back.

"Who am I?"

"Who are you?" he repeated.

"*Who am I?*" I said, getting frustrated. "I'm asking you the meaning of life."

He was unfazed by my reaction. "Well," he said, "you don't know the meaning of life unless first you know who you are. Life is a journey."

I gave the monk my full attention.

"You see, what you seek is already here. Life is but the hand that's submerged in a flowing river—a gift from heaven to earth now melted down in this flowing body of energy. You seek to grab this water. Unattainable. The hand grows numb from the temperature. The current moves the hand and rocks and sand. Remove the hand. Wipe it dry. Did that moment not last for eternity?"

Hearing the river flow and watching that beautiful mountain landscape, I felt his words sink in...then disappear like a seed in thick mud.

I had gotten what I came for, but I was too sour to accept its sweetness. The answer, it turns out, was useless to a man who was not ready, willing, or able to appreciate or understand it.

And then, as if in a blink of the monk's eye, I was rotated back to the Philippines. At that point, it seemed especially dark in the triple-canopy jungle of Zamboanga. But that was the night where it all changed for me again.

The night-vision technology was not as developed at the time, so I could barely make out the Filipino commandos. Even so, I carefully watched and listened to the jungle.

We were about to do an ambush to cut off a resupply—prepared to interrogate the living and search the dead. We became part of the jungle, letting the dark and dampness swallow us.

I waited. And waited, and waited.

Finally, I looked down at my watch.

*Bad intelligence*, I thought resignedly. That happened a lot. There would not be a truck to ambush tonight. Not here. I mentally shrugged. Chalk it up to another training exercise. I alerted the commandos, and we all headed back to camp.

"Tu," I heard once I settled in.

"Oh," I grunted at the teammate coming into my grass hut. "Hey, I'm trying to read this history book. I got a term paper next week. What do you want?"

He didn't blink. The team was used to me by now. "You got an email, dude."

The supply truck not showing up hadn't surprised me. This did. We were in the middle of nowhere. Hell, we were in the middle of the middle of nowhere. No communications out here. The email bringer would've had to hook up satellite communications in order to hook up another line to even retrieve this email.

The history book went down. I got up and followed him to his hut. We stared at his fuzzy comm screen as data trickled down like jungle damp.

"Dude, why is it so slow?" I complained, covering my curiosity and concern. For someone, anyone, to contact me here probably meant something big...or something bad.

The man sniffed, concentrating on his job. "Dude," he complained back at me, "we're pumping all this data through—"

"I don't care," I interrupted as the message finally took shape. I leaned closer to the screen.

*Packet accepted,* I read.

*Return to headquarters.*

I straightened and spoke to the man's back. "They're telling me to return to headquarters?" I wanted to make sure I got it right.

"Yeah," he confirmed. "It just came through on comms. You got to return back to headquarters, dude."

"All right," I said, heading back to my hut without even a thank-you. "Later, bro."

I packed up my rucksack, loaded up my weapon, took an azimuth to a designated intersection, then walked down a road, scanning the sector for any enemy.

*I offset five hundred meters from the road intersection on an Overwatch position. Observing the dirt road...*

A jeep picked me up and drove me to headquarters, which was also a grass hut in the jungle, only bigger and better, with running water and a secure-communications phone line where I could get the email corroborated.

*Packet accepted. Picking you up in the Philippines. Need to coordinate time, date, try out.*

The email signature was the name of the man who had reached out to a friend to contact me after that Muy Thai fight all those months ago. He had come through with an offer to put me in for a special, prime position.

Packet accepted.

Soon I was looking down a dirt road as a dilapidated airplane flew in through the cover of the triple-canopy jungle. The foliage scattered all around the plane. The wings dropped sickeningly low. If it shifted too far left, it would crash. If it shifted too far right, it would crash.

It didn't crash. The plane landed perfectly. Good deal.

"Load up your gear," the old pilot, who looked like he had become part of his plane, said with a thick accent.

He flew me into Manila. The next day I was back in Fort Bragg, North Carolina.

# 19

"Congratulations," let's-call-him Doug said as he handed me a valor award. "That's badass. You're fired."

In 2004 I had moved from a Special Forces Direct Action role and went through eight months of very rigorous technical and reconnaissance training to start working one of the highest-classified assignments. How classified? Even the name of my unit was secret.

I had a dream assignment. Originally, I was supposed to teach combatives while being rotated into overseas conflicts. I got to go around America and train with different martial arts instructors and, in between, go overseas to do combat rotations—driving, gunning, and supporting the operators.

But then, after about a year, we got in a huge gunfight—an eight-hour, very dangerous, close-quarters gunfight. I was on a tactical vehicle. They were shooting at me. I was shooting back. I survived, we won, and I thought nothing more of it until I heard that I was put in for a valor award.

When it arrived, I was called into the Selection and Training Command Sergeant Major's office, where I reported to the guy we're calling Doug, and he congratulated, then fired me.

"What?" I said to him.

"Yeah, you're fired," he repeated. "You're in a Sergeant-Major position, which is an E-9 position, and you're only E-7, so you need to go somewhere else."

Red tape was universal. My security clearance and role was not quite high enough for the rule-makers. I stared for a second.

*Let me get this straight. If I hadn't won that valor award, none of this would've come to your attention?*

That was the kind of thing I thought but didn't say. Instead, I said, "Well, where do I go?"

"I don't give a fuck," Doug immediately replied. "Go find yourself a job, or I'll find one for you."

I didn't want him to find anything for me, so I walked down the hall to the reconnaissance wing. As you can probably tell by now, I had a special affinity for reconnaissance, whether on land, sea, or air. I applied for it, went through their hiring process, then went through their training—which took six months.

During that time I was learning even more advanced communications techniques. It was different from what I had been doing as a Green Beret. Now I would employ technology against the enemy. It was like changing from a sledgehammer to a laser scalpel. For me, it was truly about learning the art of war.

It, too, was a great assignment, made all the more potent when the reality of the situation was brought home to me in a deeply personal way. I was rotated into Iraq where I had gotten to work directly with my mentor, SFC Tung Nguyen.

I idolized Tung. He was the one who supported me when others just wanted to keep me on a combat search-and-rescue team. He saw a skill in me that nobody else did. He believed in me. It was because of him and the opportunities he gave me that I ran with the crisis-response force in Okinawa and was allowed to cross-train all over Asia.

And there we were, at the same level. It was a dream come true. It was a good time.

It didn't last. One night I was continuing my work back in my room when I was contacted and told to report to headquarters. I immediately ran over and went to the squadron commander.

"Sir?"

"Hey, Tu," he said quietly. "You mind stepping outside?"

*Oh fuck. That can't be good.* "Yes, sir."

The Sergeant Major opened the door, then closed it behind me and put his hand on my shoulder.

"Hey," he said, "we just got word that your friend, Tung Nguyen—"

As soon as he said the name, my heart sank. *No. Let my fear be wrong.*

"Yes, sir?"

"He's in critical condition over in Baghdad Hospital. The team asked if you would go see him."

Tung, at that point, was running as a sniper with the 3rd Special Forces Group. The Task Force Commander, the Sergeant Major, and I reported to Baghdad Hospital, where I was able to enter the room where Tung was.

It was quiet on that morning except for the humming and pumping of the machines that were attached all over him. Tung was on his back, eyes closed. He was unresponsive, surrounded by his team.

One of his teammates came up to me.

"Hey, Tu. The machines are keeping him alive, man. Say what you need to say."

As I stood there, standing by the bedside of the man I idolized, I thought about the previous time I had seen him. It was just a few days before as I had been going over some reconnaissance on a house we were thinking of targeting.

He'd appeared in my doorway to bring me a cup of coffee. After all this time and everything he had accomplished, he would still think of the other guy first. Looking down at my notebook, I had the imagery of the target building. I kept studying the terrain and the exposed areas as I gratefully accepted the cup of coffee he had brought me.

"What do you think, Tu?" he had asked me.

"Oh man," I had answered, "I think it's a bad house. And, you know, we should be careful."

We both knew the enemy was starting to understand that we were going after specific things. They had started to understand certain patterns and how they were being found, fixed, and finished. The enemy was adapting. And that was what brought me to this hospital room.

Say what I needed to say? I couldn't say anything. The wind had gone out of me. I had no words. I just stood there, looking down at my friend. No words.

Yes, I just stood there with the team as we cried.

Twenty-four hours later 3rd Group was told to pick up Tung's body so they could escort it back to Fort Bragg, North Carolina. I was honored to join them on a Black Hawk flight over Baghdad to the airfield of the task force. Waiting there to pay their respects were some of the bravest, most capable, most effective, and most elite warriors in the world.

And then, again, they asked if I would say a few words before they shipped his body back home.

I looked down on my brother Tung. He was wrapped in a body bag. It was partly unzipped so we could see his peaceful face.

I glanced around for just a moment. It was a warm, windy, summer night in Baghdad. I stood on the open field next to Tung Nguyen's body, in the company of SAS commandos, Airborne Rangers, Special Forces Crisis Response Operators, and National level Intelligence Operatives—some of the world's most heroic men.

My heart was beating hard in my chest. That gave me all the inspiration I needed. So I spoke from my heart.

"You know," I said, looking down at him, "Tung came from Vietnam. He escaped on an overloaded wooden fishing boat, like hundreds of thousands of other refugees—including me. And like Tung, I knew oppression. And I know what it means to lose. But even so, he chose to go back and free the oppressed. God bless him."

I looked to the others and used the Latin Special Forces motto.

"*De oppresso liber.* Say your words of peace and honor as we return Tung's body to his wife and family. *De oppresso liber.*"

My lasting memory of that night was looking at him for the final time and saying my final words to him.

"Safe passage, my friend."

# 20

I kept running, trying to ignore the loss and the pain, not knowing that a certain classified troop was looking for someone with a unique capability at that stage of the war. They needed a technical-reconnaissance capability because we couldn't just kick in doors in areas other than declared war zones. Army rules of engagement, support, and everything else changed when we were outside of a war zone.

So now I was asked to be that technical-reconnaissance capability. My last post had been one of the top, and this was one notch higher—maybe two. It was the assignment every special-operations guy wanted to try. If they assigned you to this, they were saying they were depending on you to be the best.

So, on a cool fall morning in North Carolina some time later, I was driving a Jeep Wrangler through the backwoods maze on the edge of Fort Bragg. I could smell the pine needles as I pulled up to the home of Special Operations and the unit's front gate.

"Good morning, Tu," said the security guard. He'd been working there for five years now. He knew every unit member.

"Good morning. How are you?"

"Oh good, man, good." He badged me in. "So you guys have a great day."

As I drove through the compound, I thought about this experience. I'd been working there for three years now, running with the top unit the Army had to offer. Most of them came from a Ranger or Special Forces background. I parked, grabbed my bag, drained my coffee, and carried all the books I needed. I walked through the compound and badged in again.

"Good morning, Tu," said another security guard.

"Good morning, sir."

I went through highly classified areas. As I went down a long hallway, I looked at the pictures on the wall—very impressive pictures, all classified. Turning the corner, I went to my small team room, ready to continue my reconnaissance work after thirty-six months of war behind me. It was certainly different than my time in the steaming jungle or frigid mountains.

I looked at my watch as I dropped off my bag. It was zero four as I opened the compound door. There I punched in a series of digital codes. The latch unlocked as I walked into the armory of my team.

Weapons, weapons, everywhere, from top to bottom. I grabbed my 1911 pistol. Press. Check. Clear. I put it into my range bag, then dropped it into the back of the team pickup truck. I smiled as I drove through the dark compound to the secure area where they kept the ammunition. There, I grabbed my .45 ACP ammo and threw it into the back as well, before continuing on.

I passed a red flag that was always flying. It symbolized that the range was hot—that somebody was currently shooting there—and this was a twenty-four-hour-a-day range. I parked off to the side. Everything was computerized. I punched in a series of programs. The steel reacted, the steel dropped, the steel moved. I loaded up my magazines, put on my pistol belt, and stepped up to the firing line.

I hit program one. Load and make ready. Looking through the maze, program one started. As a target flipped up behind a car, I drew my pistol. First shot. It went down.

I scanned the sector. Second target popped up. I had maybe

two seconds before that target deactivated. So you had to make your shot before that. I made my shot. Target down. I did this drill over and over again, going through different programs.

After about an hour, I cleared my weapon and went back to the compound, got back into my cage, and put back my weapons. It was then about zero six. That was when the physical training started.

We had a state-of-the-art gym, instructors, physical trainers, strength coaches, dietitians, and even chiropractors. Everybody was right there. I was playing at that level now.

"Good morning, Tu," said a strength trainer. Even the warmups hurt with this guy. "You ready to get it on?"

*Do I do combatives this morning, or...?*

"Good morning, Tu," said a martial artist, at that time a well-trained second-degree black belt in Brazilian jujitsu. He had made a name for himself and was now hired on by this unit as our lead civilian combatives instructor.

I had been working with him before I was awarded and fired from my combatives-instructor position. But now I was in the reconnaissance section, and he was here to show me a combatives thing or two. Or three, or more.

"Good morning."

"You want to get it on this morning, Tu?"

*Oh God, he's going to ball me up. So do I go to strength training or do I go to jujitsu?*

Take a guess which I chose.

After he rolled me up into a pretzel for roughly an hour, I did my swimming workout in our Olympic-size pool. And then I sat in our state-of-the-art sauna. Only then did I go to the strength coaches and talk about my goals for the next operation.

Then it was time for a meal. Truly fine dining in this unit: the best food and chefs. And more than fifteen minutes to eat it.

Everyone and everything there was working to help you. And that is why it was the best unit of the United States Army.

Zero nine, the duty day starts. In reconnaissance section, everybody wore civilian clothes. You called each other by your first names. Back in Special Forces, you showed up in your duty uniform—your camouflage fatigues—and you called each other by your rank unless you're on the team. You called each other *sir* or *Sergeant Major.*

Here it was, "Good morning, Bob."

"Good morning, Tu. What are you doing today?"

"Well, I have some training with the photographers, learning remote OPs—observation points—to put in cameras at remote locations, unmanned, that are able to transmit a signal to a different location."

There, you learned, you trained, you repeated—all for the next war. At this stage I already had eight combat rotations behind me. If you got the call, you responded to the world.

I wasn't the door-kicker anymore. I was in a reconnaissance troop. I supported the door-kickers. For them, myself, my country, and the oppressed, I would find and fix, then lead the operators to finish some of the most lethal men in the world.

I was always studying how the enemy was fighting and attacking us. So the job was to stay ahead of them—studying the next technology, the geographical location, and the history. I studied how they were attacking, when they were attacking, and where they were attacking. The idea was to counter that during peacetime. We and the equipment were always loaded and ready to go. And when we came in, we came in with a new strategy and a new way to cure our enemies.

When America was attacked, the world responded. This was a global war. So if I said I needed a new type of technology on the battlefield, I had the smartest human beings in the world working on it. Some of the technologies you see today were developed during this time. That's why we are able to communicate better now, because we had unlimited funds back then to research, develop, and test this technology on the battlefield.

So we were hunting down our enemies with leading-edge technologies developed from the needs of guys like me doing special missions, targeting the enemy, and working with some of the smartest companies in the world who developed them. And I was employing that on the battlefield.

To me, this was true martial arts. This was truly studying your enemy. I never forgot when Miyamoto Musashi wrote "Know your enemy, know his sword" in *The Book of Five Rings*. I also remembered that Bruce Lee said, "The world is your teacher." The world became my teacher, and I wanted to make the lessons even better. I took Lee's and Musashi's teachings and employed them in Special Operations.

Much of what I did is still classified at the top-secret level, but I can tell you that, at this stage, I was wearing a fiber-optic earpiece, had a conductor loop around me, and drove around in a high-tech car that looked like it belonged in a James Bond movie.

I had learned to employ box position on targets—move, isolate, contain. I had learned all the tradecraft, all the streetcraft, and all the stuff that had been handed down since World War II.

Heady stuff, but I had to be ready because the next mission, and the next lesson, could happen at any moment. I learned that the hard way: sometimes you need low tech even more than high tech. Thankfully training was continuous, and I had a habit of getting involved with multiple exchange programs.

That's what led to me being in Credenhill, a village in Herefordshire, England, during the depths of winter.

"Ah, Tu, mate," a thickly accented voice said. "Did you open up that lock yet?"

"No, sir."

"Well, I tell you what, you got five more minutes to get it done because you're not looking good."

I had been cross-training with partner forces in an alternate means of entry. That didn't mean fiber-optic earpieces, it meant lockpicks.

It was a cold night, wet and windy, as I moved in, low-crawled up, jumped over a wall, and checked the door. It was locked. Immediately, I broke out my kit. Inserting the pick, turning the lock, I could hear one tumbler move. Pulling it back out, filing it down, looking at the lights, I tried again. Two tumblers moved. Wiping the rain off my watch, I checked the time as the 22 SAS Regiment's former operator, and now my instructor, sat in the shadows and watched.

Still locked. *Fuck.* Filing down the pick once more, I tried it a third time. *Crack.* Door opened. As I breathed, I felt that I was a go in this training. But during the after-brief, my instructor pulled me aside.

"You know, mate, you did really good, but you almost didn't meet the time. Second, did you check your surroundings like I told you?"

"Yes, I did."

"Did you really?" he replied with a grin.

That should have set off all my inner alarms, but I plowed right on. "Yes, I did," I maintained.

He did not reply. He simply kept eye contact with me as he neatly kicked over a pot of flowers by the door with the side of his foot.

There was a key underneath. *The* key.

"You got to check your surroundings, mate," he said with just the most subtle hint of a smirk. "It's about being situation-aware."

I was, and am, grateful to him, and all my instructors. As a Green Beret, I was intent on always being situation-aware, but now I was caught up in this advance-skill training, and it was taking me away from my basics. Never again would I make that mistake. It always starts with the basics.

Learning and training was always a joy. The real world wasn't always. I did a lot of rotations, and to tell you the truth, the surge—the 2007 increase of US combat troops in Iraq—changed everything.

# 21

I was thirty-one years old and two years into the special reconnaissance realm when George W. Bush had activated the surge.
Its goal was to try to end the war, but we had heavy, heavy resistance coming from Syria and foreign fighters.

At that time, my teammates and I were hitting targets twenty-
four hours a day. One summer night in Iraq, my team was moving
through a dark alley in a horrible part of Baghdad where many
soldiers had already died. The mission was to surveil a vehicle.

I was part of a four-man team moving forward, wearing the
dual-tube night-vision system. We were highly trained and knew
what we had to do. No communications. I knelt and could see
IR lasers sweeping across the streets as they scanned the area
under night vision.

As the team moved into a second position, the team leader
looked at me and gave a nod, so I moved up to the edge of the
street and the darkness. As I looked underneath my night vision, I could see there was a long, open area lit with streetlights
that I had to cross.

*Check your surroundings, Tu.* Roger.

Team leader nodded, and I knew I had to run across this huge
area, losing the cover of darkness to get to my work. *Oh well.*

Team leader gave me the thumbs-up. I immediately ran, infrared lasers sweeping and interlocking over me as I went. I could

still see the lasers as I slid into the pitch-black on the other side of the street. I wasn't exactly safe at home plate, but I was in one piece.

After studying everything around the vehicle, I looked across the street and gave the team leader the all-clear signal.

As the laser beams continued to sweep from across the street, I undid my body armor and helmet. I couldn't use them where I was going. Basically, I was kind of naked out there in a combat zone in one of the worst neighborhoods in the worst city in Iraq. I slid underneath the target, pulling my equipment with me. I was helpless. Well, not exactly: I had my pistol for close engagements and I also had a whole Troop of Operators scanning for threats underneath the cover of darkness.

My body was wedged under the vehicle we wanted to track. I won't go into detail except to say I slowly rocked what was called the beacon into a position underneath the metal beam at the back bumper. As I pulled out my receiver to test it underneath this vehicle, I heard voices coming from the courtyard.

The team leader went on the mic in my earpiece, quietly pushing two times, signaling *in threat range*. So I waited until the voices began to fade. Then I waited some more. When all was quiet, I activated the receiver. The GPS started transmitting.

I took a long, slow crawl back out into the lit-up street. I sought the shadows, maximizing darkness around the vehicle, collected my equipment, and put my night vision back on. I gave the team leader a thumbs-up. He gave me the all clear, then I ran back across this huge open area as the lasers swooped above me.

I slid into darkness across the street, and we moved back through the alleyway toward a predetermined pickup zone. We checked our equipment and weapons as the helicopters touched down. They had the best and most highly trained pilots. No more Laos cowboys for me.

Under the cover of night vision, we loaded in and shackled up. That meant we had a lanyard connected to the helicopter and our belts so if we fell we wouldn't go far. The bird lifted us into the night sky and over to our headquarters.

It was one of Saddam's palaces. Disembarking from the bird and going inside, I walked across marble floors. When I went to the latrine, the toilets had gold handles. This may have once been Saddam's palace, but now he was a prisoner and his sons had been killed.

Originally, our mission had been to find a high-value target. While that target had been killed the year before, that didn't mean we no longer had a use. There were other bad guys still around that needed to be found, fixed, and finished.

I checked my watch. It was three in the morning, which was our prime time. We liked to hunt bad guys at night so we were on a reverse schedule from most of the world. I figured I could shower the war off my body, get at least an hour workout in, grab breakfast, and then get some rest before my day started again.

So that's what I did before finally returning to my team room, which was crusted with sand from the frequent dust storms that blew through. I crawled onto my cot and thought I had just closed my eyes when my beeper went off. I was instantly awake and checked the readout.

I translated the series of classified numbers. I checked my watch again. It was ten in the morning.

*Oh my God*, I thought. *We're doing a daylight hit?*

I got my equipment then ran to the briefing room. The teams were sitting there, getting the atmospherics. It was a cool room, consisting of twelve TV monitors that had live feeds from everywhere. The people in that room had found a *possible target* in the area. That was the diplomatic way of putting it. What I can safely say is that it was a hostage situation.

Foreign fighters had kidnapped twelve civilians and were threatening to kill them at midnight if their demands weren't met. One of our birds—unmanned aerial platforms with high telescopic lenses—was live-telecasting the fighters moving the hostages into position outside the city.

Our mission was to conduct hostage rescue by helicopter assault force. The infiltration point was a small, open field located ten kilometers out. We were to tactically move and link up with the Army Rangers that had already contained and isolated the target, based off the mission timeline. We were to move to the target, kill the enemy, conduct hostage rescue, get the hostages safely back to EXFIL one kilometer out, then extract by helicopter.

We were ready to go until they told us to stand down and let the situation develop. Then the timeline was, if the situation developed enough, we would do an emergency assault. If they did not move the hostages, then we'd continue on with our previous timeline and strike with a more detailed plan prior to midnight.

But for now, we had to let the intelligence develop. In the meantime, we had a checklist of things to do. Prep explosive charges, weapons, equipment, communications checks, and conduct actions on the object rehearsals. Then, once that hard time hit, we'd move into infiltration phase.

I spent the day collaborating on the mission. That night I prepared to move in to contain and isolate one side of the village where the fighters were holding the hostages, so Alpha Team could conduct the rescue. At the same time, the Rangers were to lock down the general vicinity around the village. Within that village, our targets were three buildings.

We went back to the briefing room to get the final intelligence prior to moving out. As we started to load up our equipment, I could feel the Black Hawk's rotors spinning. As I approached the helicopter pad, the power of the chop from these rotors echoed through my bones.

Alpha Team were getting into their Black Hawks as we got into our assigned birds. I could sense my teammates looking at me in preparation for our thumbs-up ritual. We would grab and squeeze each other's thumbs because it was pitch-black in there.

The helicopter lifted off straight. As we were hovering, the Black Hawk came up and joined us, Alpha Team members staring at me as we floated across from each other in the sky. It was time for final comms check. With precision, the pilots moved the helicopters into a tactical movement formation. We swept over Baghdad, looking down to spot any possible threat as we approached the Palm Grove area eight kilometers outside the target location. The foreign forces preferred remote outskirts.

The helicopters dropped down low. We were to move in an attack formation as we neared the thick palm groves beside a little stretch of dirt road. As I scanned my individual sector for threats, I could hear the *thirty sec* command through my headset. Helicopter came in, touched down. We came out. Helicopter took off.

Now we were under the cover of darkness. It was completely quiet as we moved into the dense palm groves. We took a knee. All teams were quiet and using all their senses. This is a basic tactic of the Special Forces. We look. We listen. We smell. Even if we do not see or hear the civil war or the battlefield, we can still smell it.

We started moving down old dirt trails roads in tactical formation until we breached through the palm groves. We went eight kilometers through enemy territory under night vision. We breathed quietly but deeply, moving with antitank weapons and loads of C-4, enough to blow any building or bridge on the mission. We were coming in with firepower and the most highly trained operators.

We were in position, listening. As I moved up into an Overwatch position, I looked down into the village. Building one, building two, building three. To my east, Rangers were securing the area. But back at headquarters in Baghdad, they had their own Overwatch bird's-eye view.

Their word came to us. The terrorists were dug into the palm groves. This was an ambush. They were waiting for us to come and rescue the hostages so they could mow us down with heavy machine guns.

Now we knew. Thank God for bird's-eye view. We stood by, but we didn't stand still. The Alpha Team got ready to move in to extract the hostages. We got set to do what we do. The Rangers got set to support us all.

The minute signal was given. One minute before death happens. We waited as the seconds passed, down to five, four, three, two...

The palm groves erupted. A wall of our lead pushed out anything in the immediate area. Then the birds hovered overhead, shooting missiles into the palm groves. I watched it all under night vision.

First heavy gunfire, then heavy eruptions, and then cease-fire. I looked. Palms cut down and split in half. Vegetation cleaved and mulched.

The basic tactic of ambush after you engage the enemy is that you wait. You wait and listen. What you're listening for is life. I waited and listened. We all did until we heard, "All clear." The hostages were secured.

I checked my watch. It was freaking four o'clock in the morning. The sun was going to come up, and once that happened, we'd lose the cover of darkness. We'd lose our advantage. When we work at night with lasers and suppressed weapons, they don't see us coming. Now they would.

All right. *Get it together, Tu,* I told myself. *Move and contain.*

But then the grove erupted again with gunfire. Enemy gunfire. I could sense it but heard it too. *Boom, boom, boom, boom, boom!* I could feel the vegetation kicking up around us as the enemy blasted a volley of PKM machine-gun fire. We immediately went into our react-to-ambush drill. Dropping down and taking cover, we waited out the heavy volume of fire from the enemy.

As we got our bearings, I could hear the Air Force Combat Control Team leader on his radio.

"Immediate fire, Danger Close," he said. "Close air support."

"Roger."

The birds turned, moved in, hovered overhead, awaiting the signal to let loose.

"In position," I heard, then saw a laser shoot directly up into the air to give the birds the exact location of the friendlies.

"I got you," I heard a pilot say. Then they started shooting more missiles into the palm groves.

I could feel the ground shake. I could feel the earth split. I could feel fire. As the shock waves shook through my body, I was holding myself together, getting ready for what I knew had to come next.

The birds took off. At almost the same moment, we switched up our weapons and turned on our night vision—sweeping interlocking fire into that kill zone. When it was done, all I could see was the smoke from where the missiles had hit the palm groves.

"All right, we're going to sweep over here," I heard. "Tu, go ahead and take an L."

"Roger," I answered. It was a basic clearing technique. They would set an Overwatch position and fan out as I move in an "L" pattern with a teammate, and then we're going to sweep across, checking everything in between.

Let's call my teammate Matt.

As I looked over at Matt, he gave me the nod. Move. Plant. He saw me plant, he moved. He planted, I moved. What we were doing was called a leapfrog position. Then we were moving into the palm groves.

"No visual," I said flatly. That meant the Overwatch position had no visual to provide cover fire for us once we entered these palm groves. It was just me and Matt.

As we entered, I could feel the heat from the ground. I could smell the smoke. I planted myself as firmly as possible on the unstable terrain.

The palm groves were ripped to shreds. As I moved through the smoke and thick vegetation, I could feel torn, rended flesh that was both burning and wet. I looked over to see a ripped-apart arm. With every step, I could see limbs and guts scattered through the vegetation of this palm grove like sleet. Seeing it was rough. Smelling it was worse.

"Set," I said.

Matt moved, seeing and smelling what he was near.

"Set," I heard.

We kept going.

As I came out the other side, I gave the all clear. The other team came up.

"All clear," one said. "Hostages secure. Body count."

Body count is when we have to go back to our sweep sector and count the corpses with fingerprint biometrics. So back I went into the palm groves. I saw a man with his face blown-off. I grabbed what was once his hand, wiped the blood off the fingers so I could place his fingerprint against a scanner. This was a tough job, and, at times, it dehumanizes—to say the least.

I found a head. Scanned his eyes. Typed in data. Dragged dead bodies under the palm groves. I didn't smell the vegetation anymore. All I smelled was death. My nostrils were full of it. I ignored it. No, it wasn't easy, and the smell of burning human flesh does not go away, but no matter what I felt, my job that night was to count the dead bodies and that's what I did.

As I remember it now, it makes me sad. As I did it then, it made me proud. It fed my fire. We were killing our enemies at the highest level, fighting to protect our homeland. We were highly trained commandos. They didn't even have a chance. And that's why we were there.

"Tu."

It was team leader.

"Yeah," I answered. "Hey, man."

"Got the head count," he told me. "So we're moving out, but

you and EOD are going to stay." That was the Explosive Ordnance Disposal guy. Let's call him Will. "We found a weapons cache. Get down there and help out."

"Roger."

I joined Will, and we went into the basement in one of the buildings. There were rooms full of Soviet and other foreign weapons, homemade explosives, and more. Will brought up his device to calculate what it would take to dispose of it all.

The other teams were already moving out. Will and I were the only ones left on target. We prepped, using timed fuses.

"Tu," he said, "we have ten minutes, man."

"That's plenty of time," I figured.

"Not with this arsenal. We're going to have to run, bro."

"Roger."

Then we popped the fuse and ran.

We ran upstairs, we ran all the way through the village, we ran down the street beyond. We could see the other teams with the hostages already down the main road.

*Oh my God*, I thought. *It's six o'clock in the morning now. It's daylight.*

The humidity made it feel like more than a hundred degrees, which didn't make our running any easier. It felt like Baghdad itself was shoving a heat lamp into our faces at full blast.

"We got one minute, man," I heard Will say.

We reached the others, but Will and I kept running. They could take a hint. Immediately everybody started running with the hostages.

Three, two, one. *Boom. Boom, boom, boom, booooom.*

Will and I finally stopped and turned around to see a mushroom cloud—a mushroom cloud that nearly reached the clouds.

I stood there, going "woooow..." It turned from purple to red.

*Oh my God*, I remember thinking. *It's so beautiful...*

"Tu!" I heard, snapping me out of my reverie. "Are you fucking crazy? Let's go!"

As I watched, the palm groves started falling down. As the trees started toppling, I could see the shock wave from the explosion coming towards our position. Now we were running as fast as we could again, as the shock waves were knocking down trees behind us—the cracking, shredding sounds getting closer and louder until it felt like they were breathing down my neck.

I only managed to think *Oh my God* one more time as the shock wave entered my body. I could feel it going through me, squeezing, twisting, and even juggling my internal organs as I hit the dirt.

For a second I couldn't see or hear anything. I was covered in smoke and debris and all that stuff we just blew up. Even after a couple of seconds, I still couldn't see even three feet in front of me. When I finally stood up and joined everyone else moving down the road toward the extraction point, I was still covered in dust.

I forgot all about that when I saw the hostages. They were so grateful. Whenever any of the soldiers helped them down the road, they would grab the soldiers' hands and thank them over and over.

We saw the helicopters coming for us. They touched down, and we shackled back in. I looked over at a teammate. He gave me the thumbs-up, but I could tell he was burned-out.

Giving one last thumbs-up, the pilot took off, heading back to headquarters. After a forty-five-minute helicopter ride, we touched down and got out. We checked in, wiped the blood off our weapons, our uniforms, and our skin. We cleaned our guns and ourselves.

Our unit saved twelve men that day. Nothing glamorous. Nothing new. For us, it was normal. And not the worst thing we had ever experienced. Most of us washed our uniforms and headed for bed, but a bunch had to take sleeping pills because we were all fucking jacked up from doing this over and over for years.

As for me, I washed my uniform, then logged online to take a scheduled school midterm exam. Soon after, finally, I fulfilled my promise to my mother and graduated college.

War, death, college test. It was just another beautiful day in Iraq.

# 22

"Tu. Come on, man. Have breakfast with me."

"Oh, God. All right, dude, let me pack up my shit. I don't really have much time."

It was during the RIP process. Not rest in peace. Not yet. It stood for Relief In Place.

My teammate, who we'll call Peter, was a seasoned Green Beret but young to the unit. He was newly graduated, with only six months of operator training. He'd have two more months of advance training, just to be an operator in the unit.

Peter was a brother to me, and we first met one another as students going through the Green Beret pipeline. We quickly became close friends and moved up through ranks of Special Operations together. Although I appreciated and supported all my teammates, given our schedule and responsibilities, it was rare that we made true friends. Steve had been one, and now so was Peter.

Even so, I was trying to make every excuse not to have breakfast. I really did have a lot to do before my plane took off in a few hours for yet another mission. I had to inventory my weapons, check and double-check the reconnaissance equipment... but then I thought about how true friends were few and far between in this business.

"Aw, fuck it. Let's have breakfast, Pete."

After we sat down to eat, his first question was "So, how was it, man?"

"It's getting really bad," I told him. "You know, with the IEDs."

Those were improvised explosive devices. We'd lost some of our Iraqi Operatives from these so-called homemade bombs.

"Just watch the main roads," I advised him. "Hell, watch out for everything, because now they're starting to IED other places. You know, just watch yourself."

"Will do, man."

I sat with him as long as I could, then got antsy. I had a lot to do and a lot on my mind.

"Hey, bro, got to run," I told him as I stood. "I got to get back to inventorying stuff before I fly out."

He understood. Peter stood up, and we hugged each other.

"Much love, brother. Be safe."

If I had known that would be the last conversation I would ever have with him, I would have been a little more present. I also would have told him the whole truth—the fact that IEDs had not only killed our teammates but they had nearly killed me as well.

I had still been going after that high-value target who ran a terrorist-training camp and took responsibility for suicide bombings, hostage executions, and much more. At that time, he was the second-most-wanted man in the world.

Intelligence had said that he was going to be at a certain narrow street. Buildings on both sides. High walls. Everything was funneling into one alley.

I had looked down at my GPS, then looked up as the point man of this tactical vehicle studied the grid squares on his lap, then up at the streets, trying to coordinate the situation. There was trash everywhere, but only one funnel. I wasn't used to this terrain. Not during the day. But we had to go through.

As we had started moving, the vehicles started pulling away from each other, and we began wedging into what we called a tactical-formation movement. That was the technique we developed so that if one of us took an IED the rest of us wouldn't.

That day it was my turn to be the *one of us*.

As we started moving, I had seen a spotter—a kid. The kid was by the entryway. He started yelling.

"Push forward!" I had shouted.

If I hadn't pushed forward, I would've been caught directly on the IED's X-spot—its kill zone.

But even so, as I pushed forward, *boom!*

The blast hit me to the right rear. It spun the vehicle and almost snapped my neck.

But I hadn't admitted that to Peter. No, I had survived, I was a badass, so off I went on my mission and left him behind. I never got to be open with him again, and I only got to be present again when it was too late.

Our operators come out to bury their own. So soon I was standing underneath an oak tree in Missouri, looking at the flag over Peter's coffin.

As they carried his body across the field to its final resting place, another man folded the flag to hand it over to his mother as she cried. I heard the first round of the twenty-one gun salute, then said goodbye to my teammate and friend.

Over the sounds of the salute and his mother's sobs, I could hear yelling in the background. Hateful leeches who called themselves protestors were screeching disgusting insults and waving ugly signs like *Thank God for dead soldiers*.

They were a self-proclaimed Christian group of attention-seeking, mean-spirited extremists who said they wanted to make changes to the United States Army. They decided the best way to achieve that was to constantly spew bile on the loved ones of those who had given up their lives to protect them.

It was a long time coming, but that was the day the hate truly took over me. Their hate, combined with mine, infected me.

Looking back, I think somehow my martial arts fighting career had channeled all the hate to a place where it might do less personal harm. But now, without the mixed martial arts matches that had helped me dissipate my rage, the hate was eating me up inside.

That wasn't all. I had another secret that combined with the hate to poison me—mind, body, and soul. Because after that IED went off, I woke up in some sort of recovery room. The pain had been astonishing, even to me. If it hadn't been, I may not have reacted as thoughtlessly when somebody shoved a pill into my hand.

"What is this?" I had managed to say.

"It's for the pain, dude. Take it."

I had never taken a painkiller like that before. It did the trick. It did the trick so well that when it wore off and the pain returned, I didn't think twice about taking it again. And again. And again.

Even so, like so many of my teammates, I continued to do combat rotations. And, like them, I made the same mistake. As far as I was concerned, the pain pills were just another weapon in our arsenal. It helped us to keep going—and, at that time, we couldn't afford to think too much about the cost.

In fact, I was working so well that superiors, similar to the ones who had recruited me for the unit, thought I might be an even better asset with an even higher security clearance. So suddenly, I was going through even more highly sensitive training that would allow me, personally, to hunt down some of the world's most wanted men.

That training took eight months, and it was very technical. We had to find, fix, and put in the finishing capabilities, whatever they were, at the national level. After that, I was away, immersed in the missions, and not even able to talk with my wife. Without my martial relief and her marital love, I was cast adrift.

Even after the mission was technically over, all the hate and pain inside me just festered. And because I no longer had opponents to defeat in the ring, I found others to take my aggression out on.

"You don't know what the fuck you're talking about!" I yelled.

Ruthie stared at me from the passenger seat as I drove over the speed limit. "Why are you talking to me like that?"

I didn't know why I was talking to my beloved wife like that. Not then. All I knew was that I was angry. Always angry. I had reasons, but none that had anything to do with her. But that didn't matter to me then. Ruthie was safe. I couldn't safely unload on others like that, so I saved it all for my enemies and her. That's how blind my pain and the painkillers made me.

I shifted gears sharply, driving very aggressively. Ruthie held on, her lips tight, saying nothing.

"You don't understand anything," I snapped. "I don't understand why you are even talking!"

Ruthie didn't treat me the way I treated her or, for that matter, the way I treated myself. Instead, she asked me an honest question. A question she probably hoped would make me think.

"Why do you talk to me like I'm one of your soldiers?"

At that time, I was beyond thinking about anything other than the hate I needed to fuel the next mission. But she kept trying, and thank God for that and her, because the monster I was becoming returned over and over after every rotation.

I was always looking for the next mission. And I was never really present outside the mission.

She stood strong for herself. She tolerated it. She tolerated me. She saw the monster, but she didn't waver. She stood in front of the monster, never judging, but always being there for me.

Those were truly my war years. She saw me lighthearted before the war years. But now she saw me trying to deal with loss, hate, and the frustration of not being able to handle any of it.

But the combat rotations I could handle, so they kept coming. I can't tell you how many rotations: at least two dozen, through multiple war zones. And that's not even including all the operations outside the combat rotations. And often, what happened there was worse than what I've already revealed.

As I mentioned, the thing about operations outside the combat rotations is that you don't have war assets. You don't have drones. You don't have artillery. You don't have the quick-response force. You don't have any of that.

The only thing you have is yourself and, if you're lucky, maybe a small team. Your quick-reaction force was in some other country, even if they could get to you at all. That was the level at which I was now playing. No more training exercises. Everything was real now. Deadly real.

And every time I went on a mission, the monster grew stronger and more powerful. And every time I came home, the monster came with me. It sat in my soul.

Ruthie looked at me and could tell I hated the world. She could tell I hated myself. She could tell I was still a monster. But I didn't know if she knew that I was now also a drug-addicted monster.

After the war years came the dark years. The years I got lost inside my own personal hate maze. Ruthie was still my love, my wife, and my life preserver, so there was no way I wanted her to see how monstrous I was inside—not accepting that was really the only way she could actually help me. I was afraid that if she knew, she'd leave.

Instead, I just left her to think *What the fuck is wrong with you?*

I couldn't tell her. Because I was a badass, right? I was great at what I did, right? I was playing at the top level, right? But everything else that meant more to me than war—my love of life, my love of Ruthie, my love of justice and freedom was spinning out of control.

I only had hate in my heart because I was certain I needed that as a weapon. And I needed the drugs to keep the weapon working. I didn't know anything else. I was barely holding my life together. Something had to give.

Something did.

# 23

I had seen a message that they were opening up a crisis-response force for the continent of Africa. It was like what I had done in Okinawa, so I didn't have to think long about it.

*I'm in.*

But I had to do something big first.

"I want to leave the unit."

"What?" my Sergeant Major responded. Let's call him Jim.

I could understand his surprise. I mean, as far as he knew I was at the top of my game. I was cross-training different tier-one units around the globe. I was employing this training in real-world scenarios. I was highly sought after to find, fix, and finish high-level targets. I was *that* guy.

But I was also burned-out.

"I want to leave this assignment," I said.

It had been getting too much—the pressure at work, the tension at home, and the drugs everywhere. Running in small teams was becoming increasingly difficult for me as my monster only grew with every assignment.

Ruthie was just tolerating me at this point. I knew we were still in love, but she really saw the shift in me. I mean, she was not a twenty-year-old anymore. She had a college degree now, and she had started to become successful. More and more she was standing up for herself and standing up to me.

She told me flat out, "You're starting to change." And not for the better.

I was proud of her, but I was disgusted with myself. Maybe I thought that going back to freeing the oppressed rather than hunting down monsters would help.

Or maybe I subconsciously knew that the biggest monster was inside me.

Jim knew none of that. He couldn't quite get his head around my request.

"What do you mean?" he pressed. "You mean you want to leave the unit?"

Of course, I didn't tell him I was a drug addict either. After the IED, they prescribed me Percocet and now I was using it not only to numb the pain of the injury but also the pain of loss, guilt, war, hate, and everything else that was broiling in my brain.

"Well, you know," I told him, trying to be casual about it, "I am a Green Beret, and that's part of our career progression. I want to go back and do my team-sergeant time."

"Really?" he replied. "Why?"

That was a good question. One I don't think I knew the answer to yet. Looking back on it now, I think I actually wanted to go back and work with the A-Teams again—something I knew I did well, something I felt I could control better. I also did the reconnaissance stuff well too, but I always had the monster with me—and all too often he was driving and I was just a numb, even uncaring passenger inside my own body.

With him in control more and more, and me less and less, I had to subconsciously know that, eventually, things at the high level I was working at could go very bad.

Instead of admitting that, I simply repeated myself. "I want to leave the unit. How do I do it the right way, Jim?"

Jim thought about it for a second, then shrugged. "Well, you did your time, so, dude, it's on you, man. Whatever you want.

Thanks for your contribution, and you're always welcome back here."

The fact was that coming back to Special Missions wasn't guaranteed, but Jim backed his words with a *return to assignment* letter signed by the unit commander.

And that was that. No more great food, no more team of professional fighters and strength trainers and no more James Bond-ish cars. My orders came in to 10th Special Forces Group headquarters at Fort Carson, Colorado, and off I went, driving across the United States with my wife as the passenger in my Audi Q7, packed to the brim with luggage and guns, surrounded by beautiful landscapes.

I really didn't see any of them. Instead, my mind was consumed with hate and loss. I thought of Tung, Peter, and all the other teammates that I'd lost. I didn't think of Ruthie, even though she was sitting right next to me, holding my hand. As usual during that time, I wasn't present. Even though I was there physically, I was a million miles away from where she could reach me.

Because, in truth, the hate and loss were details. What I was really thinking about—what I was always thinking about now— was the next pill.

And it wasn't just Percocet anymore. Now I was also addicted to sleeping pills and antidepressants. Anything that the military gave me, I used to try to numb the pain in my body and brain. The pain of loss, the pain of war, the pain of hate, and the pain of life as I was now living it.

By the time we got to Fort Carson, I vaguely understood why they're called drug addictions. They get a grip and you become a hostage inside yourself. And the ransom comes one pill at a time, which only dug me deeper into the numbing pit I was increasingly living in.

My life had been so fast-moving that it had become a blur.

Now it was a fog. I could see and hear everything, but my senses were blunted.

We settled in Colorado, and I reported for duty.

"Command Sergeant Major is ready to see you."

"Yes, Sergeant," I answered hollowly.

As I entered the office of the 10th Special Forces Group Command, the Sergeant Major looked me up and down, taking in all my uniform's badges and qualifications—which were stacked all the way up to my shoulders.

"You've been out of the game for seven years," he unnecessarily told me. "Out of the game means you've been out of the regiment, on different missions for seven years." I knew that, of course, but it was only a setup for what came next. "I want to put you on probation. That's why I'm going to recommend you work in staff as a probation period. Let's see how you reintegrate back to regiment."

"Yes, Sergeant Major."

As I left the office, I knew Special Operations Command needed me to help stand up a new African crisis-response force. I had a reconnaissance skill that they really wanted. Special Operations Command tasked 10th Special Forces Group to set up the crisis-response force for the continent of Africa after the 9/11 attack on the US Special Mission Annex in Benghazi, Libya.

Then USSOCOM-Africa (SOC-AF) requested an action arm that had a finishing capability to enter into the continent of Africa and work as a Crisis Response Force. As far as I was concerned, that was my job. That was why I had left my previous assignment to come here.

My superiors appeared to agree with me. Probation period in staff never happened for me. I, along with a few other specially selected noncommissioned officers, helped stand up the new Crisis Response Force. What did that mean? New guns, gear, and a year of pipeline training to pass Special Operations Command.

The Sergeant Major was no fool. There had to be a reason

I had left my previous unit to come here other than "because I want to." On the outside, I was a highly competent, highly trained Green Beret who had roughly twelve years of continuous combat rotations around the world. I had the skills, I had the experience, and I had the tactics taught to me by the best in the world.

But on the inside I had painkillers, sleeping pills, and antidepressants that had helped create an aura of arrogance. The Sergeant Major may have picked up on that. It wasn't that hard to miss. The hate that I saw in the world was now embodied in me, and I wanted to share my self-loathing.

Besides, I had left the regiment for seven years. I had been working different missions, and most of my records were classified. So I had to rebuild them. That was a nightmare. Nobody understood. Nobody cared. Looking back on it, I don't blame them. But at the time, it only built on my hate.

Not surprisingly, reintegrating back into the Special Forces was extremely hard. Not only did I have to rebuild my history, I was in a bad place. I wanted to slaughter any pain—which now included any intrusive emotion. Something made me feel something? I'd pop another pill.

That was bad enough. What was worse was that I was now not only taking my pain out on the enemy and my wife, I was taking it out on anybody who didn't have a higher rank than me.

"Fucking push!" I bellowed at my junior communications guy as he struggled to keep up on a brutal six-mile, full-kit run. Full kit meant body armor, helmet, and weapons at full combat load.

"Yes, Sergeant."

That wasn't going to cut it with me. Not now.

"Get the fuck up and push!"

Once, I had said the same words with encouragement and empathy. Now I was saying them with disgust and derision.

My hate only continued to grow, so I gave it out to the team on hand-to-hand training and physical-training days. I didn't use the martial arts I had learned, I abused them. I directed it at anyone I considered weaker. And I considered everybody below my rank weaker. In between giving out hate, I continued to numb my internal pain, which now included my conscience.

But to everyone above me, I was badass. I was unrelenting. So after a year of selection, followed by a year of pipeline training, the new crisis-response force pushed into the continent of Africa. Within the first year I was in Cameroon, where I would conduct counterpoaching wars against Boko Haram—another al-Qaeda–affiliated terrorist organization behind not only ivory poaching but also beheadings and other atrocities on innocent people.

Our mission was to go in and train with the Cameroon commandos, then take this bilateral force and move up to the border of Chad, Nigeria, and Cameroon—where Chad rebels would frequently kill the wildlife to fund their terrorist-training camps. We were there to stop them.

After a month of continuous communications and reconnaissance training and working with the Cameroon commandos, we finally made our way up to the northern villages, where we swept and patrolled the areas. These villages were often attacked by Chad rebels who would snatch and sell the children into slavery.

At this stage, I had been in the military fourteen years and thought I had seen the worst in the world. But that was when I was watching with caring eyes. Now my eyes were deadened with hate. My inner monster fed on hate so it only got stronger.

It finally came to a head one morning.

"Tu," said a teammate, "we've got to get going."

"No shit," I replied.

Rather than get going, I just sat outside my tent, drinking some chai tea in front of a small campfire. I didn't want to go anywhere. I had had it. Pain was always there, but now anxieties were attacking me every night. It was too much.

So I just sat there until the sun finally peeked over the horizon, illuminating the incredible African landscape. It didn't matter to me. I really didn't see it.

It was quiet that morning, outside me. Inside me, the pain seemed unbearable. I was never a man of religion. It was hard to be, doing what I did.

But I was a man who wanted to seek truth in the world. And I never asked anything of anyone.

But I was so lost. I had to do *something*. So that morning, through and because of the pain, I asked the universe for help. As the sun came up, I managed to get past the monster just far enough to plead.

*Guide me...please...*

Then I just sat there for fifteen minutes, hoping for an answer. But the seed the Tibetan monk had planted in my mind back in India was still buried too deep in my internal hole to help or even to remember.

I heard no answer. It might have been given. It might have been given several times over the years, but I hadn't heard it then, and I didn't hear it now. I still wasn't ready.

But at least I was ready to be ready—for all the good it did a man holding himself hostage.

After fifteen minutes I had to go—physically and mentally.

Life went on. I loaded up weapons and equipment on gun trucks and spent another day patrolling through valleys, looking for the enemy.

Didn't find them. Instead, we found dead wildlife. That was all the terrorists left, destruction and death. I knew what that looked like. I knew how that felt.

I took another pill.

Eventually, I rotated out of Cameroon and went straight into Libya for six months, standing up their crisis-response capability—training militias and rebel forces who fought against Muammar Gaddafi.

I took another pill.

I rotated out of Libya and into South Africa just in time for Nelson Mandela's passing. They needed me to help protect President Barack Obama and our leadership who went there to pay their respects. I was part of a counterassault team working with the United States Secret Service, sleeping one floor down from the president.

In the past, that might have impressed me. Now I didn't care. And my pain and apathy were increasingly infecting every aspect of my life. My marriage was close to the breaking point. So was my reputation among my teammates. My drug addictions got ever worse, which meant, unavoidably, my performance continued to deteriorate.

I still didn't care. Maybe I wasn't even aware. All I knew was pain. So much pain. But I thought, after all this time, there was nothing I could do about it. I had to just keep plowing ahead until everything I cared about was destroyed.

The universe had other ideas.

# 24

I believed then, and I believe now, that nothing in the span of
the universe happens by accident. The energy you give is the
energy you receive, and ultimately, the universe will guide us
back to our true selves—even if this means killing off old ideals. Sometimes we may have to lose our false selves in order to
find our true selves.

All it took was one physical and mental checkup. I'd breezed
through these in the past. But the me of then was not the me
of now.

This time, they found traumatic brain injuries from the IED
I took in 2005. That was just the start of it. Hell, I had traumatic brain injuries from close-quarters combat, explosives-
breaching, heavy charges, high lead content from shoot houses
without proper ventilation, and the hundreds of free-fall jumps
with combat equipment. To top it off, the shrinks also diagnosed acute depression and anxiety.

Push had come to shove. I may have been able to handle even
more pain, but the mental and physical injuries had stacked up
so high, and my bad attitude had become so sour, that I really
had no place in the regiment anymore. Even I admitted that
they'd be crazy to keep me.

So I was thrown into a physical and mental medical gauntlet.
First stop, the Warrior Transition Unit. That was the Army's

place for veterans who were having a "tough time" physically and mentally.

I was thirty-nine years old, having spent eighteen years in Special Operations, and all that led to what looked like a Holiday Inn hotel lobby, except staffed by doctors, psychologists, and therapists. At least when I checked in they treated me with proper deference…as far as my monster was concerned.

"Hey, look," a First Sergeant told me. "Just make sure you make all your appointments, but otherwise you can do whatever you want."

I almost stared past the man. "I'll be there for formation at zero five," I told him flatly.

In the Special Forces you never really go to formation. You're hardly ever in uniform.

"You don't have to be," he assured me.

"I want to be," I told him bluntly.

The next morning, I put on my uniform. I looked in the mirror. The proud young Green Beret was gone. In his place was a hateful, drug-addicted, self-loathing veteran who wanted to fool himself, the staff, and his fellow patients.

I walked into the gymnasium where they were holding formation that morning. All the soldiers stared at me because I had all my badges and awards stuck all over my chest and arms. I was a highly decorated elite of the Army. I stood there, the center of attention, until another soldier hobbled up.

He was an amputee on crutches. Near him was another soldier with half his face blown-off. I could see the bones in his jaw through ragged skin. He had a handkerchief carefully positioned under his chin so saliva wouldn't soak his torso.

I quickly got over myself. I finally realized that all of us had been fighting this war, and now I got to see the other side.

Sadly, the monster wasn't so easily appeased. And, although post-traumatic stress disorder had been an official diagnosis since 1980, it was still sometimes seen as shameful, especially by those who suffered from it. After four months in the WTU, I understood why.

I had kept my appointments as instructed—with psychologists telling me I really wasn't going to recover because I had seen too much, and with doctors reiterating all my medical conditions while "treating" them by cramming more pills down my throat.

On the day of my release from the Warrior Transition Unit, I looked in the mirror again. I still wore my uniform, but the hateful, drug-addicted, embittered veteran had been replaced by a despondent, drug-addicted, demoralized veteran.

"Congratulations, Sergeant. All you have to do is sign your leave form."

The words cut through my stupor. I looked down to see my termination-leave form. It is the final leave granted to an armed forces member just before discharge, equal to the total unused leave accumulated during active service. I had a lot of leave, pay, and benefits—for all the difference it made to me.

Twenty-three years, for God and country. Twenty-three years, come and gone. Twenty-three years, and this is how I ended up.

I signed the form.

"That's it?" I asked dully.

"Yeah, that's it. You're out. Enjoy your retirement. You deserve it."

I got into my car and drove home. I parked in the garage, got out, ripped off my uniform down to my underwear and threw it in the corner. It stayed there for six months.

Enjoy my retirement? Was he kidding? Shame. That's what I felt. All-consuming shame.

You see, the teams run in packs, like wolves. And at one time I was the leader of the pack. But no longer. I had been at the top. Now I was at the bottom. My identity of more than two decades had been stripped away. I had no dignity. I'd lost my honor. I was a disgrace.

Wolves who are weak or no longer good hunters get kicked

out or killed. Back in feudal Japan, when a samurai lost his status, he was exiled to walk the earth alone. He was rōnin, which
means wanderer. Yes, I was no longer part of the pack, but I
was not yet a rōnin—because I was too depressed and ashamed
to wander much farther than my bed.

I slept for the next three months.

I was defeated, but my wife kept trying to get me to face my
past and move on. Slowly, out of my love for her, I would sham-
ble like a sleepwalker to the couch. But whether it was the sofa
or the mattress, I was basically lying down all day and all night.

"Honey, get up. How long are you going to stay like that?"

"Oh," I managed to grumble, "I'm just really tired."

"Okay," she'd reply with concern and caring. Then she'd
go to work and come home to find me where she had left me.

"Get up!" she'd plead or demand. Either way the only real
effect it had was to move me from the bed to the couch.

It was like my soul had been taken from me. I couldn't find
my purpose. My monster was starting to take even more control. And my only answer was more pills. Given my official
termination-leave diagnosis, getting more prescriptions was not
a problem.

Months passed. My uniform still lay crumpled in the corner
of the garage.

Where do you go after you free the oppressed? I went deeper
into depression and drug addiction. The medications were perfect for sitting in front of a television that wasn't even turned on.

Instead, I tuned in to my own regrets. They would play over
and over again in my mind—seeing the worst inhumanity on
constant repeat, until one day a thought, which was as loud as
a voice, appeared in my mind.

*Get up.*

I froze. The words first came in some sort of silent meditation. But then it got gradually stronger.

*Get up.*

Was it the monster? It couldn't be.

*Get! Up!*

So I did. No one ever said I didn't follow orders.

I stood there, tired and weak, until something started me shambling. I walked aimlessly around my dark house. My hands were trembling, then shaking. I figured it was for the next opiate hit.

I turned, seemingly toward the bathroom where some of the pills were, then realized where I had wound up: I was in what I called my war room. It was filled with mementos of the twenty-seven countries where I had fought to free the oppressed. Tribal beads, writings, spears, guns, knives, and many more souvenirs from around the world were all neatly displayed as if it was a museum.

*How'd I get here?*

As I looked around, I saw different relics—memories of running with the natives, rescuing hostages, defusing land mines, and many more acts of selflessness. Then my eyes focused on the books I had collected since childhood. I hadn't noticed them when I first came in, but I did now. The fog was suddenly gone.

Something was drawing me toward them, like a shaft of light in a dusty old bookstore twenty-six years before.

I saw my hand opening the book cabinet. I saw it reach in. I slowly pulled out the same volume I had pulled out as a thirteen-year-old.

*The Book of Five Rings.* Written in a Japanese cave in 1645 by the world's most famous rōnin, Miyamoto Musashi.

Coincidence? Possibly, but I'm certain that the next thing that happened wasn't. It was as if the universe had let me go as deep as I deserved, but not an inch further. I immediately remembered what Musashi had written days prior to *The Book of Five Rings*, on a scroll that has become known as *The Dokkodo: The Way of Walking Alone.*

"There is nothing outside of yourself that can ever enable you to get better, stronger, richer, quicker, or smarter. Everything is within. Everything exists. Seek nothing outside of yourself."

The words spread in my mind like a blossoming flower. All my life, I had looked for meaning everywhere else. I had fought for it in twenty-seven countries. No matter where I was or what I did, I had always looked for the meaning of life.

And then, finally, the words of that Tibetan monk also bloomed.

"You don't know the meaning of life unless first you know who you are."

I had spent all my life looking outside myself to free the oppressed. I now knew I had one more place, and one more oppressed person, to free.

# 25

*Window of opportunity.*

A small chance to make something happen.

I learned this in the Special Forces, lying out in the jungles of Zamboanga, the Philippines.

It was completely dark, and we knew that there would be just a small window of opportunity before dawn. That moment when our eyes have adapted to the dark, the enemy is still asleep, and there is just enough illumination to identify buildings and enemies. It was in this moment between dark and light that we attacked.

I'll never forget that moment in my home of total realization. It was just a small window of opportunity. It comes fast, and it goes even faster. I knew I had to take advantage of it in that moment. I felt it coming, but already it was almost overwhelmed and nearly swallowed up by shame.

*Who am I?*

A warrior? A failure? An addict? I needed Miyamoto Musashi's words. Such simple words.

"Determine that today you will overcome yourself of the day before."

I tried, but I couldn't see my way through the forest of my deadened mind. I had lost my way.

*Where am I?*

"Anyone can give up," Musashi wrote. "It's the easiest thing in the world to do. But to hold it together when everyone else would understand if you fell apart, that's true strength."

Yes, I had lost my way, but now I knew where I stood. I had a choice. I could go forward or fall back.

"You must understand that there is more than one path to the top of the mountain," Musashi had written.

Suddenly, with certainty, down to the present moment, this small, once-cloudy window of opportunity became crystal clear.

I remembered all the windows I had breached in my training, then breached this one. I ran upstairs faster than I had moved for months. I threw open my medicine cabinet. All the drugs the military and civilian doctors were willing to prescribe me were falling out. Scrambling for a plastic bag, I threw all the medications in, then raced around, finding the other places where I had put pill bottles. I dug through my clothes, finding my secret stashes, then threw them into the bag along with all the others.

The window was starting to close. I felt it. The window was shutting and new addictions were coming. If I waited even another few seconds, this opportunity would lock, and my resolve would collapse.

I ran to the toilet. I looked down into the bowl.

Clarity.

"It may seem difficult at first," Musashi said. "But all things are difficult at first."

It was just like how my eyes had adapted to night vision. Suddenly—wow!—I could see. My orders were so clear now.

Dump it. *Dump it!*

I followed orders.

With hands that once had been weak I now unscrewed each bottle top and poured every one of those meds into the toilet. My hands began to shake, but they kept working. My vision began to get fuzzy, but the target was large enough. I stood over the toilet bowl, dumping the meds. I dumped every single pill into the porcelain maw.

I didn't even pause when my fingers went for the toilet handle. My eyes, and my soul, watched all the meds flushing away. One second, they were there. The next, they were gone.

I exulted in the moment of freedom, triumph, and success. Then I felt my inner monster looking down on me with a knowing smirk. It would not give up so easily. I could flush my future fixes, but getting rid of the grip they still had on me would not be so simple.

I waited for what came next. I didn't have long to wait. Within hours the withdrawals set in. And stayed.

The first few days were all shitting and spasming. I lost control of my physical body, and nearly my mind. As I tried to break the grip of these withdrawals, I was shivering, then shaking. There were hot spells. There were cold sweats. Vomiting became as expected as breathing.

Ruthie was there throughout. When my addiction started, I had hid it from her. I had learned to be powerful and deceptive. I had to stand in front of rebels. I had to talk to generals. I had to be a symbol of power. In order to do that, I had to be deceptive. I had to put on a mask.

And all too soon, I was keeping that mask on for my wife. I deceived Ruthie about my drug addictions. Did she know I took painkillers? Yeah, but she didn't know I abused them. When I started withdrawals, she said she knew that something was wrong with me because I could not keep the mask on anymore.

Her snapshot of things was that she'd seen this badass warrior problem-solver who'd been deployed all over the place. Then, seemingly, in a split second, his whole life was crumbling right before her eyes. *What the fuck was that about?* She didn't have a support system anymore because we'd retired out of the military. But she was too strong, smart, and prideful as an Asian American, entrepreneur, and businesswoman to give in to this shit.

So she became the firm voice that told me, "You're stronger than this." It became almost yin and yang, where I had been a strong energy that shifted to a weak one. She became the strength. She became my light. And I listened to her even though I didn't believe in it at first. But I believed in her. And she guided me out.

She became my reason to keep going. I had come to hate myself, but I never stopped loving her. She was my beacon. And through her steadfast courage, I began to see glimmers of light, like glow sticks that always led me back home.

I realized that these momentary glimmers were the renewing of my previously captive mind. So in between withdrawals, when I got the chance and the clarity, I decided to start seriously studying meditation. What had that Tibetan monk been trying to teach me all those years ago? What had the tribes in all those countries I'd been to been showing me?

All their warriors would come back from battle, and the tribes would heal them. I never physically witnessed it, but I would hear the cries from these warriors as they supposedly transcended their evils and recovered from all the things they saw in war.

As my body shook, before and after the vomiting, I would open up old cabinets. I would search through old bins where I had piled all my journals. Yes, in addition to college textbooks, I had many journals, filled with words I had written before, after, and sometimes even during battles around the world.

Thoughts on war "decorated" with tears of blood from my hands, which were now smeared and dried on the page. They were also illustrated with sketches of buildings and temples—even ideas for new equipment, especially when whatever gear I was using fell apart.

As I scanned these painful, powerful memories, once again I heard my mother's words.

*If you have education, you'll never be oppressed.*

Then, as quickly as the light appeared, it was snuffed out by more vomiting and uncontrollable shaking. But even during new bouts of withdrawal, the light gave me something to fight toward. More and more I was able to go back to reading my words and reflecting on them as if they had been written by my masters, my mentors, my sensei Musashi, and my sifu Bruce.

Those moments of reflection turned into hours, days, weeks, and even months. I sat and read my blood-smeared words, the red stains symbolizing all that hate, all that loss, and all that love of God and country.

As I put down one journal, I picked up another. On to another country in my memories. My life was written in these words. My ideas were captured. They were like time capsules. Then, invariably, the detox crash came back.

Vomiting. Reflecting. Shaking. Studying. That was my life then.

I would read about meditation, mindfulness, and gratitude. I was gathering intelligence on how the body–mind connection worked. I lost count of the hours I spent watching lectures online about how the mind and body were connected, and how depression and trauma set into the brain. I learned how the mind worked—about how the subconscious remembered even when the conscious didn't.

It was just like when I was back in Special Forces. Even the subject was the same: how to survive. Well, maybe not just like that. Because now it was also about how to flourish. It was like climbing out of being buried alive inside myself.

How did I know when I was out of the worst of it? Easy. Amazon came knocking.

"I got to sign for this, huh?"

"Yeah," the deliveryman said. "You got to sign for this, sir."

Oh, I came to love those deliveries. This day, I happily accepted the package, dropped it in my living room, and quickly opened it up. I knew what it was. I pulled out the meditation cushion I had ordered. After all the years of trying, I was really going to start meditating. And not vomit or shake while doing it.

Ruthie and I had put as much of my recovery time as we could to good use. Our new home was roughly about a mile and a half up in the Rocky Mountains, and it reflected our love of beauty, art, and culture. I picked out the best place for my meditation: on my deck overlooking my Japanese Zen garden. Hey, if I could make one for my mother all those years ago, I could make one for me. It was even better since it was backed by a beautiful grove of aspen trees.

*I'm ready*, I thought. How hard could it be just to focus on breath? I had googled for dozens of hours about how to do just that. I listened to lectures on mindfulness and meditation and how that new mindset could help change who you are or who you became. All my studies and all my intellect led me to this course of action.

I studied timing. When was the best time to meditate? Well, probably the morning because your analytical mind is at its lowest frequency. It goes into a beta mode, almost like a sleepwalking state. At least that's what I had read and heard. And all you do is focus on the breath. Really, how hard could that be?

I would find out, starting the next morning at oh-four-hundred.

Turned off my alarm. Made my coffee, ran downstairs. Little Rōnin was running with me. I petted the dog. I let him and Cricket, our other dog, out. Used the bathroom quickly. Let the dogs back in. Grabbed my coffee, saw my dogs running back to bed, saw Ruthie still sleeping.

It was 4:15 a.m. Time for meditation. Right on my deck. It was so dark out there.

Okay. Sat down. Breathed.

Inhale. Exhale. Inhale. Exhale. Man, it's really windy out here.

The temperature—pretty cold.

I remember that time when I was overseas. It was cold and windy just like this. I remembered the pain.

Okay. Stop getting distracted. Concentrate. Get to it. Inhale. Exhale. Another thought. Another thought. Another thought.

It was an hour of meditation-disrupting thoughts. I came into the house worse off than when I went out. *That's terrible.* I quickly learned that thoughts are tied to the body, and each thought is tied to a memory, and each memory is tied to an emotion that can be felt throughout the body.

I had read about this, but I had not experienced it—until now. But that's what meditation does. It makes you aware. But what happens to meditation if these thoughts play out over and over?

How hard could it be? Fucking hard, even without going cold turkey at the same time.

The next morning, four fifteen, I tried again, but this time the voices in my head were even louder. They were so loud I started journaling them. Why am I failing? Why can't I focus on only my breath? Come on! Honest to God, how hard can it be?

I tried and tried. I never stopped trying. But I kept failing.

*I don't fail.*

My mind just wouldn't shut up. Days turned into weeks. Four fifteen every morning. Defeat over and over.

My answer was studying and journaling. More hours of intelligence-gathering online, listening to lectures, running at five in the morning. I'm on a treadmill with my headset, listening to podcasts, listening to spiritual healers, listening, listening, listening.

All this intelligence but no answer to my question: Why can't I turn off my mind?

Months turn into years. Every day. But believe it or not, I was okay with that.

You see, a warrior understands that it takes ten thousand tries just to start to develop. And it takes a hundred thousand times to polish.

"One thousand days of lessons for discipline," Musashi wrote. "Ten thousand days of lessons for mastery." As usual, he was right.

So I had to do it. Even if it defeated me every day, I still did it. And I would study it so my enemy became clearer.

It was me. My enemy was me. It was my thoughts. My thoughts, which were tied to my every emotion. And every emotion was tied to every memory. And every memory was, yes, tied to feelings that could be felt throughout my body.

That's what trauma is. And I had plenty of it. My cup runneth over with trauma, both physical and mental.

How could I defeat something so powerful? How could I control something I didn't remember, buried in my subconscious, running almost all the time? How could I have control over the person I had become?

Journaling. Studying. Listening. Learning. Daily attempts at meditation. It all added up to one hope. I may not have had control over what I was. But I might, just might, have some control over who I would become.

In between daily meditation defeats, physical training, and journal reading, it came to me. I decided, *Hey, why not start a business?* I mean, I'd always wanted to be an entrepreneur. More and more, those thoughts that interrupted my meditation were becoming helpful. And there was one I never forgot.

*Be something more.*

Along with all my war journals and thoughts and memories and drawings of forbidden temples and castles and range rules, I had all these memories that I had written below the red lens of a tactical flashlight in a rainy jungle. I had written about my day, about war, about loss. But I had also written about shit that didn't work.

"What do you mean it don't work?"

"Look, dude, I'm telling you, I just got this gear issued, and after two combat deployments, it's falling apart on me."

"Well, you're, like, free-falling and you're, like, swimming in it. You're, like, freaking doing close-quarter battles, and you're climbing and doing reconnaissance with it. You're throwing this body armor back and forth. Yeah, it's going to rip on you. And tear. And fall apart."

"So what can I do?"

"Well, hell, like, get on a Rigger."

Cool. I always loved the Rigger. Every time we would deploy to any location, if we were able to, we loved bringing a Rigger along because these people specialized in repairing our parachutes. Hell, they specialized in repairing everything.

And what came with a parachute Rigger were these high-industrial sewing machines that I always wanted to learn and use. So I set out to make a new best friend: a Rigger.

"So how do you learn? How do you do this?"

"Well," the Rigger told me, "it's called bar tack stitching."

"Huh? What does that mean?"

"Well, you have to do this type of stitching to hold this amount of weight in this pouch."

"Oh. So that's why this belt is designed like this. That's why that body armor was designed like that."

"It's designed like this because it has multiple layers."

Made total sense. With that new knowledge, I was able to repair my gear. I was able to cut up, then modify the gear. I was able to do all sorts of stuff.

During wartime in Iraq, we were doing high team clearance. That means that, under night vision, we would take tactical ladders and insulate them. Just like ninja, we would insulate all the joints and the attachment points. So when we quietly laid these ladders against a wall in total darkness, they didn't make a sound.

We would climb up, and once we got to the rooftop, we could see the Iraqi locals sleeping. We would step over their bodies. They wouldn't wake up. I understood that under stealth, moving at close quarters at that speed required that your equipment didn't rattle around or fall apart on you.

So I started designing gear and equipment, and a lot of this understanding and these ideas were inspired by the words and drawings in my journals. I decided to start a company to take what I knew and teach it to the world.

I took everything I had learned in the military—and, maybe more importantly, everything I had learned about learning and putting that to effective use—and focused it on the business world. I learned a lot about business for many years without really realizing I was taking it in.

And my wife was a not-so-secret weapon. She understood business, contracts, and more. She had a master's degree in accounting, so she knew numbers, ledgers, and bookkeeping. She had been working in the public sector for many years, so while I knew soldiers and officers, she knew customers. I was the face. I was what people gravitated toward. And she was able to take my face and my ideas and turn them into a viable business.

I took my life savings and bet it all on my belief.

I knew I wanted to go into the tactical industry so of course I approached it like a military mission. I concentrated on the manufacturing world first. I took the words that were written down many years ago in some war-torn country, fighting against some Indigenous force, and put them into an engineer's hands to make them into a physical item.

But my research had already taught me that if you had hundreds or thousands of these items that you had invested in, you needed to get your return quickly; otherwise, you were going into debt. That led me to my next strategies. Marketing. Brand-building. Developing the business and the business mindset. I became the marketing guy.

It seemed totally opposite to everything I was ever trained in. How does a commando go from running with rebels and native forces and hostage-rescue ops to business? I'll tell you. Reconnaissance.

In reconnaissance, you have to understand how the camera works. You have to understand lighting. You have to understand ISO shutter speed, and aperture. You have to be creative in the content. You have to understand videography. You have to understand geography. You have to be able to capture images of the enemy by any means possible. And you have to be able to download this data into a postediting video-processing application. Then you have to compress it and transmit it secretly over a horizon to a satellite back to headquarters.

Sound hard? No, that was easy. But how do you brand-build? Well, I could go from door to door and tell everybody what I thought, or I could create a website. The military had trained me for that too, by showing me that nothing is impossible if you are intent on a goal, and there's plenty of information about how to achieve it.

I studied how to build a website, then got online to do it—how to design and implement one, add a shopping cart, all of it. I took my training from years of doing low-vis reconnaissance and hunting down bad guys and turned it to manipulating ISO apertures and speed on an SLR camera to take product shots of my gear.

I knew how to work advanced programs like Adobe Photoshop and Premiere, so I was able to crop, edit, darken, and highlight certain areas. I was able to make an appealing product page and I was able to compress the files and put that onto the screen.

Voilà! An operational website.

Yes, I make it sound easy, but it wasn't easy. It was hard. It all took years because I had to teach myself. I stayed up late studying how the market worked and who were the key players in social media. And I studied the analytics of YouTube and how that was tied to products, and how that product pushed to a brand, and how that brand grew.

Thankfully all that information was on the internet—the same place I wanted to put the website. And my goal was to not only share my experiences but also my journey toward peace of mind. For many years I'd fought, using different weaponry. Now I was trying to add spirituality to my arsenal. I would sit there, seeking peace, while building a business.

One day, while I was trying to concentrate on my breathing and not to think, I thought, *Hey, why not use the teachings of Bushido, my study of balance, and the search for my spiritual self to create new business ideas and ideals?*

So I started arming myself with those things. I strove for a balance between body and mind, which meant I had to get both up to their optimum. So after my four-fifteen meditation attempts, I returned to running, but added listening to podcasts with doctors, scientists, and warriors. Running, listening, running, learning. Then I returned to a powerlifting regimen, getting my body back into warrior shape.

You see, the art of Bushido, the way of the warrior, was developed by samurai as a code of living from birth to death. It was intended to not just be something physical but spiritual as well. It was to transcend into a spiritual world alignment along a warrior's path.

*Bu*—to stop the spear. *Shi*—to walk the way. *Do*—to take someone's life lesson and to give back for the sake of humanity. *Bushido.*

Finally, I decided who I truly wanted to be.

# 26

"Honey, I think I want to be a teacher."

"What?"

"I want to be a teacher."

"What do you mean? What are you going to teach?"

"I pretty much don't know how to do anything but combat. So why not teach combat, or teach in the way of Budo?"

"What does that even mean?"

"Hon, I've told you a hundred times what Bushido means. I've told you a thousand times what Budo means...!"

"Ah," she said with a knowing smile—a smile that knew me. "Whatever. Then be a teacher. I think you'll be a good one!"

Armed with her words of encouragement, I did, using the internet and my contacts to set up classes. And she was right... but not at first.

"Ready on the right. Ready on the left. Steady your hand!"

The civilians looked at me with uncertainty, even confusion. That's how I thought of them at first. Not as *students* but as *civilians*. I started teaching civilians the only way I knew how: as if they were rebels. As if they were militants.

"What's wrong with you?" I demanded. "Do you not understand my words? Ready your weapon!"

That, too, elicited an uncertain response.

"Shooter?" I asked quietly as I smiled like a wolf coming upon a sheep.

"Yes, Tu?"

"What is wrong?"

"I'm just fucking nervous!" he exclaimed. "You're standing next to me!"

I mentally shrugged. Even if someone didn't know my background, I accepted that I could be an imposing presence.

"Tell me, do you not understand the words?" I repeated. "Ready your weapon." When the expression on the civilian's face told me even that confused him, I translated. "Unsafety that gun."

He finally did as I asked.

"Okay, everybody, on line. Range is hot. Press the weapon." As the civilians pressed the weapons, I continued my instructions. "Take it to the wall, hold at wall on trigger."

I watched them carefully.

"Fire," I said.

Not one person hit a target. *What is going on here?* I had been walking back and forth all day, teaching the fundamentals.

"Do you not understand the fundamentals of marksmanship?" I asked. By the looks on their faces, I guessed they still didn't. "What are the seven fundamentals?"

I was looking at a woman. She looked back at me, her eyes wide, her hands shaking.

I walked up to her. I stared her up and down. I spoke carefully.

"Do you not understand my fundamentals?"

"No, sir," she said in a small voice. "No, I don't understand. Can you say it again?"

"Sight alignment to the target," I snapped. "The target is crystal clear. Transfer that crystal clearness to the rear. Push that through to the front sight till it's crystal clear. Front sight, crystal clear. Crack a round. Do you understand? Take it to the wall."

"Uhhh," she said uncertainly. "Okay..."

I shake my head when I think back on it now. At the beginning of this new challenge, I kind of trained them the way I knew how. Which was extreme, but coordinated and calculated in my training methodology. In the Special Forces, I had to quickly organize—whether it was a team, a regiment, or even an army, and be able to take them at the intelligence level to a combat zone.

But in the public sector, I treated it the way I had treated the rebels. I figured that if I went into their areas and trained communities, they could better protect themselves. But there's a big difference between rebels wanting to learn how to fight for their freedom, and Americans who had been free all along wanting to learn how to protect themselves. As a student, learning was my thing, right? But now as a teacher, I had to learn how to teach.

It took me a while. It took many classes. Luckily, I had my reputation as a Green Beret to bring them to my lessons. Now I had to learn how best to communicate with them. And just as importantly, I had to be smart enough so they would tell others to learn from me.

"Run."

"Excuse me?"

I was looking at a forty-five-year-old man.

"Run," I repeated. "Run with me to the first obstacle."

We ran. He could barely keep up with me, even though I was moving at almost a walking pace.

"Now at the pull-up bar, sir," he told me.

He barely mounted the pull-up bar.

"Five pull-ups," I instructed. That was the task. Five pull-ups. He couldn't do it. "Two pull-ups," I amended.

"Okay. Two pull-ups. Unmounted the bar, sir."

"Run to the next obstacle."

Again, he barely kept up with my stride.

"Pull out your pistol. Engage the five steel targets in front. Do you understand?"

He could barely catch his breath.

I looked around at my civilians and tried to understand. Americans. These were the people I'd fought for—had been willing to die for. They were all looking back at me in different stages of confusion and suffering, with tears of pain and gratitude in their eyes simply because they could come and learn from me.

It's said that when the student is ready, the teacher will appear. Well, from my experience, it's when the teacher is ready, more students will appear.

I had a lot of learning, and teaching, to do.

At first, we took small steps, locating all the classes near home. I'll never forget the day I realized this new endeavor could work. I was standing in a Colorado blizzard. Colorado weather is always shifting and changing. It goes from one season, skips another season, then ends with summer going right to winter. One day it's nice, the next day it's a blizzard. Well, this day was a blizzard, and it hit hard and fast.

I looked to my right. With the snow slicing almost sideways, Ruthie was barely remaining upright as she stapled the targets to posts that were shaking in the wind. I looked to my left. Forty students were standing there. All had come for a combat rifle class to be taught by no one else but me.

Even as early as that morning, I had been tempted to cancel the class due to safety reasons, but as I was logging online to see the student situation, I saw that all of them were coming, snow or no snow. So I was standing there, looking at all of them through a blizzard. Every single one of them had made it here.

Then I looked past the students to my wife, covered in snow.

"Honey," she said, "all the targets are up."

And when she said they were up, I knew they would stay up. That's what she did. That's what she'd always done—even when I was treating her like one of my soldiers. I would never do that again.

From that class on, she was with me. As we traveled, I taught her how to work a high-end camera, understanding polar and UV lenses, angles, and composition so she could film me. Then I could process these videos and post them online. I understood the power of social media, so I would teach her as I would teach the classes and teach myself.

Sure enough, one class led to another. One student would tell a friend, and so on. New York. Tennessee. Florida. Texas. Anywhere anyone wanted me to teach, we would go.

"Ready on the right?" Ruthie yelled. "Ready on the left?"

She was telling them to get on the firing line because some of the instructors I had recruited couldn't make it out to this course. When she had to, she filled in where she could. And for this day, she was getting the students on the line as I stepped up, secure in the knowledge that I now knew how I wanted to teach.

"It's such a beautiful morning, isn't it?" I told them, setting the tone of the training style I had developed. "How heaven and earth align. The universe must want me to teach you something."

So I did—as they ran, as they moved their weapons, as they dropped down into prone position, as they rolled over left and right, as they shot strong hand/weak hand, as they learned efficiency, as they moved at a high accelerated heart rate, flipping tires, moving, popping smoke.

As they crawled through the vapor, they shot, understanding ballistics, angles, and dominance in a gunfight. I helped them see what they were made of—at an accelerated heart rate. Some struggled, but most kept up.

"These are the teachings of Budo," I would tell them. "It is not just the way of the weapon. It is the way of self in these conditions of hardship."

I had learned that the tough way. During my ongoing recovery I had added more voices to my mental mentors. Confucius joined Lao Tzu, Musashi, and Bruce. Confucius once said, "To put the world in order, we must first put our hearts right."

I had learned how to teach through trial and error, but now I was cruising with satisfaction. And the better I felt about what I was doing, the better the students seemed to feel—and the more students appeared.

Even so, every day I would try to meditate at 4:15 a.m.—sitting with a loud, loud mind trying to calm it down, while attempting to focus on my breath. But the inner voice was so deafening. I felt defeated, but my discipline kept me going.

*Try to inhale and exhale. What am I doing wrong? Am I not being grateful enough today? I said I forgive. Am I not forgiving enough today? I don't understand.*

It had been three years since I started seriously trying to meditate in the wake of my drug withdrawal. I practiced forgiveness. Not only as a Special Forces soldier but also as a refugee who'd escaped genocide and a child surrounded by racism, I sought the strength to forgive. And I knew that it was through my struggles as a child that gave me the energy that I needed because I wanted to be a better human being. It wasn't just about being an entrepreneur and running a successful company anymore. It was about internal growth.

And speaking of growth, my classes were growing. Through YouTube and Instagram videos, the word was getting out. The students now knew what to expect from me because they saw me in action on the internet.

"Within each space," I reminded them, "within each lifetime, we must make the best out of everything and everybody. And every act we do ripples through generations. One moment can change the day, and one day can change a life, and one life can change...well, the world. Have a beautiful day, everybody."

Then I stood, gratified, as the students bowed out one by one—literally bowed out. Then I let them take pictures, always flashing the peace sign as in so many selfies. I noticed my wife waving at me.

"Honey, honey, honey," she called, "come over here. Come over here."

I went over there. Before I could ask what was up she said, "You need to talk to this gentleman."

"Yes, sir," I said, pegging him for a police officer. "How can I help you?"

"My name is Jeff," he told me. "I'm with the Duncanville SWAT team. I wanted to let you know that this is what we're looking for."

"Jeff, is that correct?" I answered calmly.

"Yes, sir."

"What are you looking for?"

"We're looking for this, sir. We're looking for the next evolution in close-quarters battle. Your tactics and your mindset is what we're looking for. Free flow CQB, your methodology, how you move through the target like water, how you flood the area, how you interlock fire, how you move your weapon at close quarters? Sir, this is what we're looking for."

"Oh," I said as I stared past him. "Okay…"

You see, weapons, war, tactics—that was my brand. I'd dedicated my career to it. But what I didn't have at that moment was peace. So inside, I was suffering. At that point, I wasn't interested in getting involved with training, tactics, strategy, and killing. I didn't want to get involved with that anymore.

"Well, I'll tell you, Jeff," I replied. "You know, thank you for coming out, but I'm just really not, you know, interested in that right now. Just done it too much, you know? Kind of working on myself these days."

"Oh," he replied, clearly disappointed. "Well, you know, if you ever change your mind, sir, here's my card."

"Well, I appreciate that. Thank you." I put it in my pocket as everybody drove off. The sun was going down.

"Ready to go, honey?" Ruthie asked as she loaded up the targets.

We got in the car and headed home. Ruthie let it rest and simmer for a while, then simply said at the perfect moment, "Honey, I think you should go to Duncanville."

"What?"

"You know, Jeff and I have been talking, and they really could use the help."

I could ignore Jeff, but I would never ignore Ruthie. She always guided me well. She always pushed me in the right direction.

So that's what I did. I started teaching the SWAT team in Duncanville, and once one customer was satisfied, more lined up. Jeff became my friend and, eventually, my assistant instructor. We started traveling to major cities and training SWAT teams, counternarcotics teams, US Marshals, Texas Rangers, and police departments all over the country. As we traveled, our world opened up even more, and I was invited to officers' tactical-training conferences. The soul drives the weapon. So as I teach, these officers grow.

I also posted more of my blade tactics online: how to properly insert a blade, how to twist and turn a blade into an organ, which organ to attack, where to collapse the lungs, how to move the hands and parry in order to cut mobility from the limbs, and how to rip metal through a torso.

Now many more students showed up as Ruthie and I continued to travel across the United States. As a teacher of how to unarm an opponent, then kill an enemy quietly with a blade, a gun, a rifle, or my hands, things became so fluid and moved so naturally I understood what Bruce meant by "Be water, my friend."

By that point in our lives, Ruthie and I had spearheaded a successful company. Most of the journals that I put into an engineer's hands resulted in a physical item that we were able to market because I was able to build a brand by sharing myself in my training videos. We were so successful that we were able to kick off our own internal manufacturing and hire our own engineers.

As we traveled and built upon our brand, our products, and my teaching, we started picking up contracts from militaries around the world. There was only one major arena that I hadn't been able to crack yet. But that was about to change.

"Honey," Ruthie called one day, "can you come in here?"

That day, like so many others, I was drinking coffee after my failed morning-meditation practice.

"Yes, honey. What is it?"

"A talent agent from the History Channel wants to interview you."

My inner monster immediately sought to isolate me. "I don't want to do that."

"I think you should do that."

She had been right so often, the monster knew it had to change tactics. "What does that even mean?"

"I don't know. They're talking about a TV show."

"I don't want to do that."

"I think you should do that."

"Oh. When?"

"Next week."

I had a week. I had a week to try to get out of this. Despite what I look like, inside I was always that little Asian boy that got picked on or spit on. The persecuted little boy who got isolated. Even on the A-Teams, no matter how big, strong, or bad-ass I got, there would always be some sense of *You're different. You're not one of us.*

So every chance I got in the following week, I said, "Honey, I don't think—"

Ruthie replied, "I think you should."

As I washed the dishes, I said, "I don't think—"

"I think you should."

As I took out the trash, "I don't think—"

"I think you should."

Ruthie was always right. The next week: Zoom call. Talent agency. History Channel.

"Who are you?"

"Tu Lam."

Their response, as I discovered, was classic Hollywood-speak. "Who is Tu Lam, and what does Tu Lam do?"

I told them. Their eyebrows started to rise and they leaned in as I went through my military background, training, and unconventional warfare tactics.

They got down to business. "What is your understanding of blades?" one asked.

"What?" I replied. "How to kill a human being with a blade, or how to survive off the land with a blade, or the history of a blade, or maybe the geometry of a blade and how that's tied to a culture or religion or practice, or maybe the blade and how that's tied to a belief?"

A guy I would learn was a producer stopped me.

"What did you just say?"

"I don't know what I just said," I answered honestly. "I was rambling. What did I just say?"

"You know that much about the blade, the history, the mythology, the culture?"

"Yes," I said. "I'm a Green Beret. I've traveled to twenty-seven countries. I studied the blades in each. I had to live off the land with the blade."

One of them tried to get clever. "What do you know about a Kukri blade?"

"I teach how to kill livestock with a Kukri blade. I had to survive. I had to cut vegetation in jungles and build a hammock in rainforests using a Kukri blade."

"Rainforests? Jungles? What were you doing in rainforests and jungles?"

"I was learning how to track a human being. You know, Special Forces stuff."

Well, needless to say, that audition went well without me really trying. Next thing I knew I was on a Zoom audition with

Bill Goldberg. He was already named the star of the *Knife or Death* spin-off they were planning from their already successful *Forged in Fire* series.

Bill Goldberg? Everybody I knew had heard of world champion wrestling superstar Bill Goldberg. I grew up watching Bill Goldberg. He revolutionized his industry. He was a great athlete and a great entertainer. His traps were amazing. Everybody knew him by his trapezoids, his badass tattoo, and his catchphrase, "Who's next?" Me, with Bill Goldberg? Imagine.

"Hi," I said on the Zoom call in a fanboy voice.

"My name's Bill," he said.

"Well, of course I know who you are. My name is Tu. Hi."

We hit it off, and I went on to the next step in the process, the chemistry test. They had a YouTube video of guys running around with knives, and we had to commentate. That was to see how we communicated and whether our knowledge blended or conflicted.

It blended. The TV show was a go. Or, as they said in show biz, *green-lit*.

Let me tell you about my first day on the set. They flew me to Atlanta, Georgia, put me up in a really nice hotel, and picked me up in a limo.

"Mr. Lam?"

"Yes."

"I'm your ride."

Of course, I went to grab my stuff.

"Oh, no, no, no, sir," said the driver. "Please let me pick up your luggage for you."

"I have it."

"No, no," he protested.

"I'm not used to people carrying this," I said in my Special Forces voice.

That stopped him. "So let me get your door," he nearly stammered.

Driving across Atlanta, I admired the city. So historic. You know, I used to study every city that I went through during training. And if I found it fascinating enough, I would actually go out with Ruthie to these locations and explore them.

As we drove into a fenced compound, a security guard came up. "Talent," the driver told him.

That word, relating to me, gave me a rush of pride...and shame.

"Good morning, Mr. Lam," he said to me.

"Oh, good morning."

From there I was driven to a line of movie-star trailers. One of them had my name on it.

Well, I acted like any commando would, looking all around at the trailers, the construction, the street, the angles, the security guard, the equipment, the people. I was not in Kansas anymore.

"Sir," said the driver, "I just moved your luggage into your trailer. Anything else I can get you?"

"Can I get water?"

"Oh, your fridge is totally loaded with water," he replied, "as well as the snacks you like."

"How do you know what I like?"

"Remember that survey we did? The one that asked what you liked to eat?"

"I thought that was for my diet."

"No. It's stored in the trailer. It's all set for you."

It was very nice. I just sat there in my star trailer, which had a bathroom, shower, couch, bed, television, fridge, air-conditioning, and a Mr. Lam—Mr. Talent—letter of welcome.

Bill Goldberg came in and introduced himself. Around fifteen minutes later, the wardrobe crew came in.

"What are you going to wear?" the wardrobe guy asked.

I raised my eyebrows and opened my arms to show off my baggy street clothes. Had to be able to move quickly in my line of work, you know.

That would not do for the wardrobe guy.

"You need to show off your body a little more," he said. "Somewhere in those baggy clothes, there's a star waiting to be born."

"Sir?"

"Yeah," he said without blinking. "The producer wants you to wear tighter shirts and, uh, show off a little bit more of your guns and tattoos. Hey, this is Hollywood, you know."

Actually, Atlanta, but still. You see, the thing is, at that point in my life, although I'd had a full career as a Special Forces Green Beret, done a lot of stuff that a normal human being hadn't done, and got to experience the world, I still struggled with insecurities.

All too soon, as I stood there in my new tight gun-and-tattoo-showing shirt, with fifteen cameras in front of me and barrels burning all around, shame still stuck its tongue out at me. The inner monster still smirked.

Even so, it backed off a little when Bill Goldberg gave me a fist bump. "You ready, bro?"

But my anxiety wouldn't budge. I could feel it coming in like the tide.

*Oh no, am I going to freak out in front of all these cameras? This is kind of live. Get your shit together, Tu. Breathe. Breathe. Be present.*

Turned out all those hours, days, months, and years sitting on my meditation cushion were not a complete waste. Like the rest of my life, when it came time to follow orders, I followed orders.

Next thing I knew I was cohosting a show, standing next to Bill Goldberg as he worked up the crew and cast, before handing it off to me to talk about geometry, construction, history, and philosophy.

Seemingly, even the monster had to admit it was really cool.

# 27

Seemingly overnight my hundreds of students were joined by thousands of fans. I knew this firsthand because, in between filming, Ruthie and I continued traveling in order to train communities, and the crowds would grow. Students would even bring me gifts.

"What is this, sir?" Now I always called my students *sir* or *ma'am*. They weren't just civilians to me anymore.

"It's a combat boot I painted," said the young man.

It was amazing. He had painted my rōnin symbol, and even my face, on a combat boot. It seemed weird to me at first, but I had to admit, it was beautiful.

Even college kids were now coming up to me with drawings, among other things. One built a big titanium-ribbed Asian-style folding fan, complete with calligraphy. I still have that displayed in my office. More and more students would hand me artistic examples of their appreciation, then all would bow out after every class—as if they were in a dojo.

As my fan base grew, I continued to edit, postprocess, and post videos of it all on YouTube and our Rōnin Tactics website. And I would have been happy, grateful, and content to leave it at that until Ruthie got a great idea.

"Honey, I think we should go to Japan."

It was as if she had read my subconscious mind. There were

two things I had always wanted to do, and they both could only be done there. I had never been there as anything other than a Green Beret, but now I was a successful teacher, brand ambassador, and even a TV costar. This visit would be a whole new ball game.

"I'm going to contact Kiku," I told her, referring to the first thing I had wanted to do.

"Who?"

"Kiku. We met him at the SHOT Show in Vegas," I reminded her.

The SHOT Show was the annual Shooting, Hunting, and Outdoor Trade Show, and was one of the biggest events of its kind in the world.

"Yes," she recalled. "He wants to make a sword for you, you know."

Oh yeah, I knew that all too well. In one of the stories about Miyamoto Musashi, he said "My sword is one with earth and heaven." That inspired me. I would love to coordinate with Kiku on making it a reality.

Kiku was Kikuo Matsuda, one of the most famous and respected blademakers in the world, and he was willing to forge one Heaven and one Earth Wakizashi sword for me, by hand, because samurai carry two swords—one in service to their Daimyo and the other in service to their Lord.

"Okay," Ruthie replied. "But I want to go to Tokyo and go shopping, and I want to go to Kyoto and eat some sushi there, and I want to visit the temples. So don't do all that rōnin stuff the whole time, you know? I want to enjoy our vacation too."

"Yes, honey," I said, already thinking ahead to make sure there would be plenty of time for her and me.

So the plans went ahead with gusto. But since I was now a presence in the tactical industry and a new face on television, a journalist was assigned to chronicle the trip. We invited some friends who joined us from San Francisco, and all too soon, followers from around the world were watching us travel through Japan.

And not just them. Major weapons collectors and sellers in Japan knew I was coming, invited me to visit them, and closed their collections for private showings. I would stand in their amazing establishments, some three stories high, filled with swords dating back hundreds, even thousands, of years.

I saw things that had been hidden since World War II, since all these swords had to go underground or be destroyed because of clauses in the peace treaty between the United States and Japan. As I sat amid this ancient armor, with swords from famed battles all around me, the journalist took photos of my every move while collectors regaled me with the fascinating history.

Then, when we traveled, dojos would shut down and privately perform for us. We finally made our way to Kiku-san in his home village, Seki City, known as the City of Blades, more than two hundred miles from Tokyo. There, Heaven and Earth would be forged.

"How long will it take?" I asked.

"A year."

"Excuse me?"

Yes, a year. In addition to Kiku's painstaking, precise, ancient handmade art of *Hamaguri-Ba* sword-making, the finished work of steel art had to go through all the official certifications and receive approval from the Katana Association, before the blade, which was tied to Japanese history and culture, could go to America.

A year. Well, that was not too long to wait for Heaven and Earth.

After that, we felt free to travel everywhere in Japan, running from one bullet train to another with our friends. And everywhere, there were fans who knew me both from the tactical industry and the History Channel.

So it was natural I set up some training events. People flocked to them. They always sold out. And afterward, the students all wanted selfies with me—everyone, including me, flashing the now stereotypical double-handed peace sign. In fact, I almost missed a train due to signing one last autograph. Bullet trains don't wait for anyone, you know.

As always, after all my years of training, I treated this vacation like an operation. I researched everything. I needed extra adapters, memory sticks, batteries, portable battery chargers, and more. Soon I looked like a Special Operations soldier going through a reconnaissance mission.

I was in the right place for it. Japan is one of the greatest camera and tech centers on earth. I needed a primary-capture unit and got the best Canon camera I could find. I needed a secondary-capture unit, which to me meant a GoPro. I had pictures and videos I wanted to post, and for those I had a *P* primary camera, an *A* for alternate camera, a *C* contingency GoPro camera, and an *E* emergency phone camera. Every trained commando has a PACE plan.

You can take a Green Beret out of his training, but you can't take the training out of a Green Beret.

The Japan visit was a thrilling whirlwind, until it came time for the single most important thing I wanted to do there. I found myself sitting alone at three a.m. in a private Kyoto courtyard overlooking a quiet, precisely designed and maintained garden.

I smiled to myself as I thought back to the years when we used to stay in cheap hotels. Now we had become successful enough to experience the kind of life where I could look down into a private garden outside a beautiful bedroom as koi fish swam around in a pond—and my wife could have the best sushi imaginable.

My hands were shaking that morning as the fog settled in. As long as I kept running, moving, researching, planning, teaching, and taking pictures I was okay. But it was in these quiet, still moments that the darkness threatened to move in again. It had become more than a threat. It was all too regularly a promise from my anxiety.

*You are not worthy.*

Those were just four of many words that disturbed my meditation. But here, now, I could face them because this morning I was going to go meet Miyamoto Musashi. It was this morning that the ways of the old combined with the ways of the new. This unworthy present-day rōnin needed to speak to this worthy past rōnin. I had questions. I needed answers from the man I most admired.

I counted the minutes until our driver collected me, Ruthie, and our friends in front of the hotel and drove us to a private aircraft. Then we flew nearly five hundred miles through the rain and fog to Kumamoto—which was just a short distance from the western edge of Japan.

Our destination was Reigando. *Rei*, spirit. *Gan*, rock. *Do*, way. In translation, most called it the Spirit Rock, or the Spirit Cave. Some split the difference and called it the Spirit Rock Cave. By any name, that was the place where Miyamoto Musashi wrote *The Book of Five Rings* in 1645, then died ten days later. The same *Book of Five Rings* that came into my life when I was thirteen years old.

I wanted—I needed—answers. I longed to feel his healing energy. Because, right now, my internal pain was a constant. The more successful I became, the more insecure I got. It was my fourth year of meditation and daily practice of discipline and mindfulness. Four years of doubt, shame, anxiety, even hate. Four years of angry voices. And if they weren't getting louder, they were getting more insistent.

The military shrinks had said I would never recover from what I had survived. I wanted—I needed—to prove them wrong.

I could hear and feel the jet wheels touch down in Kumamoto. The craft braked as my body shifted and Ruthie grabbed my hand. I smiled. She was always nervous about any flight. Takeoffs and landings were the worst for her.

"Ooh, that scared me," she said.

I knew how she felt, but for me it wasn't about planes. I had jumped out of so many, they weren't my concern. My concern was that, again, there would be no answers, or maybe even worse, there would be, but I wouldn't hear them.

All too soon we were meeting our personal driver. He could have been any middle-aged villager, except he stood by the wheel of a nice black car.

"Good morning," I greeted the man.

He said something in Japanese as he bowed. That's when we discovered he knew no English. Even so, we loaded up our luggage and cameras in a misty rain.

"I got you coffee, honey," Ruthie said as she appeared beside me.

"Where did you find that?"

"There was a Japanese vending machine. Be careful. They said this brand is toxic."

*Perfect*, I thought. Suited my mood.

"I love toxic," I told her. "Thank you, honey."

"You're welcome," she replied.

I sat in the front passenger seat. I always liked to be up front. The driver glanced at me. I doubted that he noticed my anxiety had started to grow, so I sat in pain, studying him.

We were climbing up toward Mount Iwato in the misty rain, so he had to drive carefully. He said something else while keeping his eyes on the road. I was about to tell him I didn't know Japanese when Ruthie reminded me that she had brought a translator device.

We also had a portable digital cellular module with us that gave us broadband internet no matter where we were in Japan. Even if we were in a tunnel, it was guaranteed to transmit broadband internet. She used it now to understand what the driver was saying. Going back and forth with it went a long way in making the trip tolerable for me since our conversation started sounding a little like a comedy routine.

"I am excited," the driver had told me.

"Why?" I asked.

"I never been."

"You never been where?"

"To the cave, sir."

My inner voices and I started to judge him. "Do you not live here?"

"Yes, sir," he replied. "I'm from here. I was born here."

"And you have never been to the cave?" To my disapproving mind, it was like a New Yorker who had never seen the Statue of Liberty.

"No. This is my first day. The first time I ever been. I'm so excited."

At this point in my daily meditation attempts, I had become even more aware of energy—my own and those around me. I felt his excitement. I also felt my judgment. My inner voices made certain of that.

*How could you not go visit Miyamoto Musashi? How could you not learn the ways of the warrior?*

I tried to distract myself by becoming more of a Green Beret. We were heading toward Unganzenji Temple—a Zen Buddhist retreat created in the 1300s on the western slope of Mount Kinpo. As we drove through the mountainous landscape, I looked at my metrics meter for the elevation. I looked at my GPS. I looked at the navigation system. I looked at the bends and twists in the road. I looked at the shift in biometric temperature. I looked everywhere but inside myself.

"Yes," I heard Ruthie translate, "that is why I am excited to come here."

The driver had been talking to me. He had been telling me about his childhood.

"That is very nice," I said automatically. "Thank you." But in my mind, I was looking for vulnerable points in the road as he drove us through the fog maze.

Even through the mist, I could see why Musashi retreated here. It was high in the mountains. It was away from all things. It was away from the world we created for ourselves. It was away from voices and opinions. Except from the ones that came from inside ourselves.

I quickly turned my attention to the driveway that we pulled up to. It was covered in fog. We had reached the entrance to the temple, surrounded by orchards, forests, and fields. I imagined that back in the days it was created, it must have been almost pure wilderness, but now a large parking lot gave proof of its present position as a popular tourist attraction.

The driver parked right in front of a big squat white statue. I stared at a seated Miyamoto Musashi that filled the windshield. I immediately moved to get out of the car.

"Honey, you're going to get wet," Ruthie cried. "Let me get the umbrella!"

She got out of the back seat as the driver came around the front. They were like a silent-film comedy team as she tried to get our umbrellas out of the trunk, while the driver opened his own umbrella to protect her from what she was trying to protect me from.

I didn't care about the mist. I stood there and stared at the statue of Musashi. Fifteen feet high, he was cross-legged—one hand lying on the other on his lap, palms up—seemingly in meditation. His sword was, as always, tucked in his sash. I saw a rope dangling in front of him and raindrops course down the rope like a clear liquid snake. I remembered what had been written in a travel brochure.

*Shinto teachings state that if one says one's requests and shakes the rope, then claps one's hands, one's request will be sent into the spirit world.*

I reached for the rope.

"Honey, you'll get wet!" Ruthie was moving toward me with an umbrella. She grabbed my hand and pulled me away from the rope. "Come back here. Oh my God. What are you doing?"

I shook my head. The Shinto spell was broken. Now all I saw in front of me was a squat crude statue next to some vending machines at the edge of a parking lot.

No matter. I pulled up my new Canon camera, with its digital capacity and higher complementary metal-oxide semiconductor processing capability, and quickly inserted a special lens that had a weatherproof sealant. I had studied this camera. I had used an older version of it all over the world, and it had never failed me. This was the most updated one I could have brought. This was the camera I was going to use to capture my meeting with Musashi—starting with this parking-lot statue. It would make the piece look better than it did in real life.

I lifted it to my eye. I pointed it at the statue. I pressed the shutter button.

Nothing happened. No comforting click, no familiar sound of a memory being captured. Nothing. I looked down at the LCD screen.

*Error Message* it read.

*What? There cannot be an error message.*

I looked down at the screen. *"0-1-5,"* I read.

*What does that mean?*

One of my friends quickly pulled out his phone.

"Oh, dude," my friend said. "You got to take that back."

"What?" I grabbed his phone. I quickly read the message. That code meant *manufacturer error.* This couldn't be happening. I had researched this!

The camera was plucked from my hand. I snapped my head around and looked down at Ruthie. She looked up at me with a kind, understanding smile, holding the traitorous camera.

"Honey," she said softly, "I'll take photos for you. No worries. Just enjoy the moment."

I stood there. It couldn't be. I had researched and double-checked this. Besides, I had my secondary plan—the GoPro. I pulled it out. Fired it up. It worked, right?

Ruthie grabbed that from me too. Anyone else trying that

might have lost some fingers. But Ruthie knew me too well, and I loved her too much.

"Enjoy the moment, honey," she repeated.

For a split second I was on the edge of a cliff. Then, for want of a better description, the spirit of Musashi filled me. I mentally stepped back from the precipice.

"You're right," I said.

It was written that, at a certain stage in Miyamoto Musashi's life, he retreated. After a lifetime of war, he came here. And he focused within. After he found his peace on these grounds, he wrote *The Book of Five Rings*. It had guided me, helped me. But at this stage I felt so much pain I didn't know how best to honor him.

But I knew it was not by taking a lot of pictures to distract myself from why I came or by getting into an argument with my wife in the parking lot.

For many years I had tried to meditate, just like Musashi had. On these Buddhist grounds he had focused, and in doing so, had developed himself as a human being. I also tried to focus within. And yet there was something in me that wouldn't allow me to let go.

I turned from the parking-lot statue and walked onto a path toward the temple. It quickly became steep. All around, among the moss and rocks, were hundreds of stone *rakan* statues of Buddhist disciples.

They were everywhere, their energy leading me on through bamboo groves and sacred grounds. I made my way slowly through the slippery, narrow, steeply rising path of stones, interspersed with remnants of a coral reef that had once been underwater. I looked up to see the entrance to the temple at the top of the stone staircase, flanked by *nio*—frowning guardian—statues. They were demon warriors guarding the gates.

As I made it to the top, there was an old monk awaiting me. He could barely sit up as my friends from San Francisco checked in with him. Ruthie ran to an adjoining souvenir stand that sold special editions of the book. This seven-hundred-year-old temple had become a tourist trap for students of Musashi like myself. I thanked the mist and rain since they had seemingly kept the majority of tourists away that day.

My specially researched and chosen camera didn't work, but that didn't stop Ruthie from taking selfie pictures with her iPhone. As she did, I poked my head in the back of the area and saw where the old monk lived. He literally slept a few feet from where he now slumped. His sleeping mat was already rolled up— just like they would have done hundreds of years ago.

Temple rituals rarely change. I could smell the incense in the air that morning. Based on the smells, sights, and the manicured condition of the gardens, monks were still here—unless the *rakan* and *nio* were maintaining the space.

"Honey."

I looked down. Ruthie handed me a ticket to the cave. Then the monk stamped a copy of *The Book of Five Rings* with a special seal that was only available here.

I had purchased copies of the book from around the world. I had bargained and gambled with side-market merchants to find the book in Libya. I ran with linguists and taxi drivers to go in record, book, and antique shops to try to find copies. And now I had a monk-stamped edition at the site where the author had written it.

Its words came back to me, but here, now, seven words stood out. *Do nothing that is of no use.* The only way that could be true was if nothing had happened to me, and nothing I had done was of any use—unless I made it so.

From there we walked down a hallway that led to a garden, where there was an exhibit of Miyamoto Musashi's artworks. His swords, Heaven and Earth, were neatly displayed. His writings were all there. I felt his energy. As we walked past all this evidence of his accomplishments, I thought of Musashi's journey again. After being undefeated in more than sixty duels, he had retreated here. He meditated here. He became an artist, poet, and writer here. His words influenced me, along with millions of others. He had reportedly found inner peace here.

But it was also said that, after the third year of living within these sacred grounds—cultivating gardens, worshipping, meditating, and finding his inner self—he took a torch and walked through the dark, up steep, slippery ground. He had found a passage where he discovered a small opening on the side of the mountain.

I followed in his footsteps, walking through the garden and approaching that same opening.

"Honey."

I looked down at the caring face of my wife.

"Why don't you go there by yourself first?"

I looked from her to our friends. They all looked encouragingly at me.

"It's okay," they said. "We'll wait."

I looked over them to the driver. He was holding my umbrella. He smiled and nodded with excitement for me.

I stepped off into the mist and started to climb up the final steps. Even with handrails installed for tourists, the climb was tough. It must have been even harder for Musashi himself, with a torch in one hand and no banister to hold onto with the other. But like him, I approached the entrance and finally entered the cave.

It was small and green. When the light finally hit it that morning, it turned into a jade jewel. The floor of the cave was now covered in wood so tourists could easily walk around. In the back there was a place for small shrines to worship the eternal or the dead. Vines were overgrown on the stone ceiling and walls. On these vines were tied pieces of paper with Japanese writing on them, and they wound and stretched all over the cave. All around them algae and vegetation continued to grow, encircling the biggest, most central thing there.

It was a rock—a large boulder on the cave floor, about four feet high and five feet deep, almost ten feet wide. There were indentations of various sizes all over the top and sides.

I could easily imagine Musashi sitting on top of this stone throne, meditating out onto the wilderness beyond.

I took off my boots as I approached the Spirit Rock where he had written his book by candlelight. Without shame or doubt I climbed the rock and sat where I imagined he had sat. It felt as natural to me as my favorite chair. I looked through the mist and past the rain to see the lush green and brown sacred grounds.

And then, for the first time, as if it had been waiting for this exact moment, I transcended into breath.

It was as easy as that. I had never been able to lock onto any single thought before. My mind had always been too busy. I thought it would be this time as well, but no. I simply transcended into something between breaths. I recognized, and accepted, it immediately.

It was the void.

Inhale. Exhale. And there I saw it. Right inside me. The monster.

As I held it in this place of emptiness, in this place between breaths, it spoke to me.

*How can you forget the world? You say you forgive, but how can you forget the world? Remember, they left us for dead. They killed our people. Thirty days you drifted at sea with your family. How can you forgive the world when they spat on you?*

The Spirit Cave was where I heard the clear voice of the tormentor within me. And it kept whispering, reminding me of the pain and the suffering.

*Do you remember? Do you not remember the twenty-seven countries you and I went to? How can you forgive the world for the children that were murdered in front of you? How can you forget the pain that you felt inside? It is what keeps us alive.*

But it was also on this morning that I was able to focus into my book of void. I breathed in and transcended regret or even thought.

And as I did, the angry voice became muted, and its energy became less powerful. I transcended into the Spirit Rock. As I continued to sit there in breath, the hateful energy diffused and ultimately dissipated within me.

And through that process, I quieted the noise from others. It made me realize that I didn't need acceptance from them, I needed acceptance from myself. I needed to heal that boy inside me who was traumatized by oppression and war. I had to become a hero for that traumatized boy.

I finally got it. I was not filling up my void with drugs and addictions anymore because it can't be filled. And that shadow that I sat with had now become my best friend. It had always been my best friend.

It was on that morning that I closed my war years—and truly forgave the world for its cruelties.

# 28

I could forgive, but I never could—and never would—forget. Although my hate monster had been changed, it was and would always be with me. Now I just had to find a way to help that strengthen more than weaken me. In the meantime, I had a business to continue building and a life to lead. And the best way to do that, just like always, was to keep learning.

I was back home, looking through the books I had collected while I was in Japan. I knew *The Book of Five Rings* by heart, but another I had always found really interesting was *Hagakure* by Yamamoto Tsunetomo. He had been a retainer to the ruler of Sega Prefecture in 1716, and the book, which was often called *The Book of the Samurai* or *The Way of the Samurai*, was a collection of stories about the Bushido code. The title, *Hagakure*, is literally translated as *hidden leaves* or, more poetically, *in the shadow of leaves*.

What I found really fascinating was that it was written roughly a hundred years after the Sengoku era—the warring-state period of Japan which started around the middle of the fifteenth century—telling of a code of behavior that these warriors had never even lived. This book was for peacetime samurai, trying to describe what it meant to live the Bushido way. That certainly rang a bell for me.

Back at the height of the samurai era, they swore their allegiance to, and served, the Daimyo—feudal lords who ruled most of Japan from the tenth century to the mid-nineteenth century. Their creed? To lay down one's life for one's lord. Anything else went against the Bushido code.

But what happened if you didn't believe? What happened if the daimyo hurt the people he swore to protect? What happened if he tortured or murdered innocents? Samurai were warriors but also human beings. And as an honorable human being, how could you live with that?

Most of the greatest samurai movies ever made were about what happens when the power of the daimyo corrupts absolutely. In Japanese history, and their movies, there had been stories of samurai who broke the oath of loyalty, which is a virtue of the Bushido code. Compassion is another virtue of this ancient code of samurai. So, when they chose to walk the path of compassion over duty, they became lone wanderers—rōnin—shameful to the sycophants and the judgmental.

I identified with them. As a human being, I chose to walk a path toward heaven. I chose to serve others as a teacher of the way. But how? How could I effectively teach others what it meant to be a warrior? How could I improve what I had already been doing to make it even more helpful and constructive?

I reflected on this for many days. How could I teach lethality and compassion at the same time? How could I teach violence and benevolence? How could I be that teacher? How could I not allow the wrong skills to fall into the wrong hands? How could I not protect others? How could I best serve others?

Days turned into weeks as I meditated on it, my monster friend watching over our progress from the dark edges of my mind. I needed to turn thought into action. I began to journal—writing down what it meant to be a noble warrior, and to live as a warrior in the code through wartime. I had traveled to twenty-seven countries. What had I learned?

Compassion. Compassion is one of the virtues of Bushido,

and compassion is what led me to all those countries. Compassion and honor had led me to fight for the oppressed, to live in honor and make a difference in this world. And to be willing to die for it.

I started to break down my art of Budo, my combat skills.

I analyzed the guerrilla tactics and unconventional warfare. I needed to explore a deep understanding of intelligence and how that both effected and affected the battlefield. The terrain, the men, the timing, everything.

Every samurai, every rōnin, has their own journey. My journey was to seek perfection. Human perfection. It was discipline, and it was war. I realized that in Special Operations history, I was in the generation that saw the most war, the most combat. Was it any wonder I was really messed up when I got out? I saw the worst of humanity. But the ideals that were now resurfacing had always been there for me since the beginning. Bushido's teachings had always been there. I had just forgotten them.

But I remembered them now. Musashi, the monks, and Bruce always told me *If you want the world to be a better place, it starts with you.*

I went through all the martial arts I had learned. Sticks and blades and impact weapons in the Philippines. Silat and empty-hands combat in the jungles of Indonesia. My understanding of angles and Bruce Lee's Jeet Kune Do intercepting fist. My mindset in the underground Toughman matches. How my close-quarters defense became my offense.

I remember taping out two locked triangles and working out every attack angle, then applying that to properly close and control an opponent's space, like a fencer. The aggressor looked for lines of attack on their opponent. But as an observer as well as an aggressor, I moved on the angles of the doors, windows, and breach points to control the space while maximizing cover and concealment—all through games of angles.

Within any style of martial arts, it starts with form and proper structure. Without structure there could never be speed or power. I studied, planned, and practiced until I felt it was time to put it to the test. Everything is the human body, the human mind, and the world around them. You have the chance every moment to study and make the best use of them.

I stood before students on a breezy fall morning in New Jersey and demonstrated the form of empty hands I had been developing—what a friend called *Tu-fu*.

"One must have structure," I said. "Structure in stance and balance. Structure in the hands in relation to the weapon. Structure in form as it relates to grip and pressure on the gun as it snaps the weapon back to the threat."

I looked at the nearest student. She was a police officer. I could feel her energy; it was tight, high-strung.

"Do you understand, Lieutenant?"

I glanced at all the other police officers. Some had driven for days just to attend this class. Some were willing to stay awake after pulling two eighteen-hour shifts just to grasp the depths of a rōnin's teaching.

As I stood there on that beautiful morning, it suddenly hit me: I had become the warrior in the garden.

One day when I was a child in Fayetteville, North Carolina, I had retreated from my difficult life into a library. That was where I had come upon the story of the warrior in the garden. In it, a master and his student were walking through a beautiful Zen garden.

The master said to his student, "How beautiful the morning, the sky, the flowers?"

The student asked his master, "How can you say everything's so beautiful when all you do is teach us the ways of combat?"

The master smiled, kneeled down, and plucked up a flower—effectively ending its life—then replied, "It's better to be a warrior in a garden than a gardener in a war."

Since then, I had seen the proverb pop up here and there,

most memorably attributed to Bruce Lee, but for me, within this space, I had found *the* way. I had found my way. I found a new, or renewed, purpose. It was to travel to communities and train police officers who had sworn to protect the people. It was to travel to train law-abiding citizens so they could better protect their families.

I had done that before, for years in fact, but now, thanks to Musashi's cave, I was doing it in an improved way. I was consciously doing it so that kindness prevailed. And incredibly for a hate-filled warrior, I found that when kindness powered me rather than cruelty, the teaching was even more effective.

My martial arts ranged from long-range precision shooting to close-quarters gun fighting, maximizing angle speeds and darkness. I drew my knowledge in combat shooting and applied that with structure in martial arts of effortless movement.

Bruce may have spoken of the warrior in the garden, and he also said "Be water, my friend." But Musashi got there first.

"Taking water as the basic point of reference," he wrote in *The Book of Five Rings*, "one makes the mind fluid. Water conforms to the shape of the vessel, square or round; it can be a drop, and it can be an ocean."

Only more than three hundred years later did Bruce teach "Empty your mind. Be formless. Shapeless. Like water. You put water into a cup, it becomes the cup. You put water into a bottle, it becomes the bottle. You put it in a teapot, it becomes the teapot. Water can flow, or it can crash. Be water, my friend."

My wife and I continued to travel, teaching military units, law enforcement, SWAT teams, and special task forces. Now I not only taught weapons and tactics, I also drove home the importance of operations and intelligence during mission planning. When I first started teaching, it was more Budo-based, more offense-based. It was what I did in the Special Forces.

But when I retreated to Musashi's cave and was hurting so much, I realized I had to shed who I was. That cave was a turning point, so my teaching changed. Now it was driven by compassion and what I felt was the universal law of everything. The ripple effect. Because now I knew that if I taught civilians a certain mindset, which was Bushido powered by compassion, that could ripple through generations. That's what I took out of Musashi's cave.

For me, Bushido was to take your whole life lesson and give back for the sake of humanity. To take all your pain, all your suffering, everything you experienced, then turn it around and still choose this higher power. Even if life gives you shit, you're able to turn it into fertilizer and give it back to the world in the virtue of compassion. Bushido allowed me to find my peace as well.

But that was not all I found. I revisited what Bruce Lee did in his movies, the films where he actually espoused his teaching and reflected his philosophy. I studied and incorporated his "way of the intercepting fist"—stopping an attack at its source rather than waiting for the attack—and especially his core lesson of "learn everything you can, then make it your own."

I was making it my own and teaching others to make it their own. Don't just copy me: take what I teach and incorporate it into yourself. Not everyone could look like me or had been trained like me for as long as I'd been trained, but my students could, and should, formulate their own styles, based on who they were, what they felt, and what they could do best. And we taught that to major police departments and special task force units, running and gunning from coast to coast.

"Shots fired, Lieutenant. What the fuck are you going to do?"

We were standing at a command post.

"Isn't that the trigger, Lieutenant?" I pressed.

The *trigger* is when an event has happened that would cause the SWAT team to make a direct entry.

Through the rain, I could hear the snipers' Overwatch team.

"I have you covered."

That allowed gun coverage to primary breach.

"Emergency assault!"

The emergency assault is to quickly place explosives to make entry into the structure. In this training scenario, there were paper targets throughout this three-hundred-and-sixty-degree shoot house. It was a one-story shoot house with a catwalk, where instructors could observe the students as they moved through the space so we could evaluate their tactics and strategy.

Because of my night vision, I could see the A primary breach team moving up with speed to the front door. B-Team split to support A-Team and were now quickly placing an external explosive device on the door.

The explosives went off. A-Team flowed in breach point. Snipers outside in the rain scanned for exterior threats. Through my night vision I could see the interlocking IR lasers. B-Team moved to primary breach point to support A-Team as they fought to secure a footing in the building.

"Get behind cover!" I barked.

Through the darkness a student looked around, didn't see me; I was invisible. I moved with stealth in the dark. I knew where the players were. I knew where the teams needed to go at this point. The teams cross-covered to support each other's movements. Stacking on the door, the teams made entry to move to their points of domination while engaging multiple targets presented to them in this maze of a shoot house.

Number-one man checked a door, shook his head. Number two came up and readied his shotgun. As I looked around, I could see another team member poking his head around the corner. He stiffened when he heard a soft voice coming out of the darkness. My voice.

"If you're going to provide security, provide security. Stop looking around. Understand?"

"Yes, Tu," the police officer said.

I disappeared back into the dark.

Shotgun went off, door kicked. Flash-bang went in, followed quickly by officers.

Points of domination. Interlocking fire.

"Clear!"

"Clear."

Lights came on.

"Good job," I said. "The thing is, some of you guys over-exposed at the breach point. Make sure you clean that up. Too many lights. Need more light discipline. Number-one man, what were we thinking at the door?"

"I wasn't thinking, Tu," he answered.

"Damn right you weren't. Damn right."

Two weeks later, we were running in Baton Rouge, Louisiana, teaching counternarcotics teams how to quickly take down vehicles.

A few weeks after that, we were running in the rain through smoke and live-fire exercises with members of New York and New Jersey PD.

This went on for years, and we were feeling satisfied. It wasn't until I was teaching close-quarters weapons in Nashville, Tennessee, that it changed again.

I got the Nashville students to understand angles until a student snapped around a corner and illuminated a room with light.

"Too late."

The student looked at me. "Sir?" she said.

"Too late now," I repeated. "See, ma'am, once your light turns on, your weapon needs to be a presentation, finger-prepped, understand?"

"I do, sir."

"Try it again."

Lights went off, she entered the darkness. As she moved up, she angled the door, presented the gun. As I could see the glow of reflection at the front site, the lights came on. She fired the weapon, the lights went off, and she moved to dominate the room—maximizing cover, maximizing concealment.

"Good job, ma'am," I said. "Next shooter up. Load and make ready."

We were five hours into the session when I presented them

with a new lesson that, like so many others, I had learned the hard way.

"When you step up to any situation," I told them, "you must approach it with no mind. That means that the mind must never be cluttered. The only way to achieve your goal is to let go. Every day you must look past the way of the weapon—you must unclutter your mind."

I let that sink in before continuing.

"When you drive your car," I asked them, "do you sometimes daydream? The body reacts to the route and the speed without thought. You approach your workplace or home without thought. Has that ever happened to you? That's the state of *mushin*—the Japanese word for *no mind*. When all thoughts and emotions are eliminated, then your training can truly kick in. So if a weapon is a state of normal, it becomes a state of no mind..."

It was at that moment, as I looked around at these officers, that I could feel the shadow suddenly grow inside me. The monster wanted to come out. I realized no matter the peace I'd made in the Musashi cave, the monster still had a grip. Sometimes light, sometimes firm, but it never let go. And as I spoke of the state of no mind, as the students readied their weapons on line, I quickly and subtly signaled for Jeff to take control, then went away to a quiet, secluded area off to the side.

I sat. I inhaled. I exhaled. I looked around. It was a beautiful spring morning. Inhale. Exhale. I could feel the energy around me. I waited until I felt the pause in the moment—the void in the space of emptiness.

There it was again. The monster. The pain. The oppression, the suffering, the trauma, the cruelties, the hate.

As I inhaled love, life, and beauty, as I extolled compassion, I felt it again. Suffering.

I had more work to do.

# 29

We continued to travel, teach, record, postprocess, and place my teachings of Bushido and the way on social media. Despite my inner issues, that message somehow just grew in popularity. Apparently, a lot of people were interested in Bushido—at least Bushido the way I taught it.

At the time I had no idea just how much popularity it had until one day, Ruthie called out to me again.

"Honey."

"Yeah?"

"You need to come read this text."

"Can't you just read it for me?"

"Honey," she repeated, "come read this text."

I knew enough by this time not to ask twice. Grabbing my coffee and giving my wife a kiss, I sat down. The cup was halfway to my lips when I saw the return address.

Infinity Ward.

The coffee went unsipped.

"Aren't they like the *Call of Duty* people?" Ruthie asked.

Even Ruthie knew *Call of Duty*, the video game the *Guinness Book of World Records* had verified as the best-selling first-person shooter series of all time. But maybe more important to me was that the game was especially popular in the military. When I was a soldier, I saw how the game provided both morale and stress relief to our service members while deployed.

"Yeah, they're the *Call of Duty* people," I said. "They're the ones who do all the *Call of Duty* stuff." *Call of Duty: Modern Warfare, Infinite Warfare, Advanced Warfare, Black Ops, Cold War…*

"I think you should talk to them, honey."

*Oh no no no,* my frightened monster moaned.

"You know," I said, trying to sound casual, "we got a lot of other training coming up, and…"

I teach many others, but, apparently, I don't learn enough on my own—especially when it comes to Ruthie's instincts and her tenacity.

"I think you should contact them, honey."

"Oh, okay. But we have San Francisco coming up and, you know, I have to worry about San Francisco. It is going to be a private close-quarters combat training for law enforcement, where we run through a series of mazes to learn close-quarters and hand-to-hand combat."

I stopped, since what I was describing sounded like a video game—even to me. I think it did to Ruthie too.

"Okay," she said patiently. "But I think you should contact them."

"Well," I sighed, "let's go ahead and, you know, set that up."

We did. Turns out they wanted me to collaborate with them on the way I move, both with my body and my weapons. It was very flattering. I had always wanted to be in a *Call of Duty* game. But first things first. Like I said, we had a lot of other already-scheduled training to do for people who had made reservations and plans.

Soon, we were in San Francisco running with the local law enforcement through a series of mazes—running low-light tactics, which was all about when, where, and how to use low light, when to use angles, how to cross-cover, how to wear night vision, and use lasers and interlocking fire, and even teaching them how to row one's foot for stealth.

That was just one of the lessons of a ninja, which included how to move and balance weight, how to shift under cover of night, how to move from primary to alternate weapons in the dark, and how to most effectively reload.

"Honey." Ruthie's voice next to me made me look toward her. Mistake.

"Yes," I said as my night-vision goggles were completely blinded by the lit-up cell phone she was holding up to my face.

As I flipped up my night vision, I heard her say, "Infinity Ward got back to us. They want us to fly from here to LA. I think you should do it, honey."

I didn't take a lot of convincing. "Okay, honey. I'll do it."

We finished the training, then flew to LA with our gear, swords and all, to discuss the massive project. I want to tell you everything about this amazing experience, but ironically, it turns out I have to use the same approach I did with all the other secrets.

Think it's strange that I would deal with a video-game company the same way I would refer to a military operation? Well, Infinity Ward's headquarters is more secure than some of the most secure levels I ever worked with in Special Operations. I guess that's what comes of creating an entertainment company that has made more than thirty billion dollars. That's billion with a *b*.

Even so, we got to talk with co–studio head Dave Stohl and animation director Mark Grigsby, meet the entire team, and tour the facility. Then the work started. And it was a lot of work that went into making me what they call an *operator* in the game.

And not just any operator. They wanted me. They wanted Rōnin as a character. They gave me full access and control on what I wanted to do, as well as how I wanted to do it—up to and including my "finishing moves." For any readers who don't play video games, a character's *finishing move* is probably their most memorable feature. My finishing moves came from my experience in martial arts mixed with commando-style tactics.

To accomplish this, I acted out all of my—aka Rōnin's—movements for Infinity Ward's performance-capture—or motion-capture—tech, including my finishing move. They wanted something different and authentic, so I gave it to them. I gave them my all.

After mo-cap, we spent the next few days scanning my face and body for the game. It was an unforgettable experience working with Infinity Ward. The staff at their mo-cap center were incredibly helpful, not to mention kind. So kind, in fact, I don't recall my inner monster making a peep. I truly loved seeing all the results and how my character came to life.

It was all, for want of a better word, *fun*. I rationalized that it was just for entertainment, but I realized later that being able to use my knowledge of killing in a safe space, where no one—villain, victim, or innocent bystander—was actually hurt, was incredibly freeing. It was similar to how I felt about the Toughman fights but even better. I didn't get my leg or face broken in these fights. No guilt, no shame, no anxiety, no damage. I could do what I did well with almost no psychological blowback or fallout at all.

It was like a tsunami of relief that washed over me, unleashing my total talent. So there I was. Rōnin. In person for millions of players. Wow.

Once Rōnin first appeared in *Call of Duty: Modern Warfare* in April of 2020, the rise in fame for me, and the rise in success for our Rōnin Tactics, made the gratifying fan increase from *Forged in Fire: Knife or Death* look like a speed bump.

Now more and more students were coming to my training to see if I was really like the Rōnin they played with on their video-game screen. They quickly discovered that I was.

When I looked around at them, I felt an energy inspired by

pride and community in addition to fear. They felt fear because they were learning at an intense level. If you were at my classes that meant we were soon moving with speed and violence, like the stuff I was trained in. You know, at the special-operations level.

They were like the people *Hagakure* was written for—peacetime samurai who had never tasted war and were trying to put into words, thoughts, and actions what they didn't understand. And there I was, this wartime samurai looking to find my peace—trying to find my way. Again.

Ironically, it was perfect timing, because that mission was almost perfectly captured by my Rōnin character in *Call of Duty*. And my popularity only continued to grow, resulting in ways to help people I never expected.

*"Hi. Your girlfriend Nalia sent me a message on Instagram and told me that this was your birthday, so I just wanted to send out this message and wish you a happy birthday. Thank you for all your support."*

Yeah. People wanted Rōnin to send birthday wishes, and why not? Rōnin and I were not just warriors. Before *Call of Duty* happened, I might have immediately said I didn't want to do that, but the mission had changed. I wasn't here just to free the oppressed anymore. I also wanted to spread compassion. I realized that I could touch people simply with a sincere birthday wish. So why not make somebody's day?

It felt good. Now I woke up every morning, meditated, then sent a blessing to everyone who requested one…and to those who didn't but would still appreciate it. I wished everybody a great day. As I worked on myself, I was able to give that love to others.

"Hi, Mr. Tu Lam. My name's Kyle, and I'm ten years old."

Kyle was interviewing me via Zoom for his third-grade class. It was Veterans Day, so that was the excuse to let their teacher arrange to have me speak to them. Well, actually, have Rōnin speak to them. And it wasn't just Kyle's third-grade class.

There were other schools, podcasts, and all different kinds

of speaking engagements. Sure, I still spoke to military groups, and I still trained police and public alike, but now Rōnin's horizons were broadening. I found myself being an influencer—empowering people through social media. And still, that was not all.

"You want me to wear what?"

The photographer who came all the way from New York City looked like one of my students I had just asked to load and make ready. I could feel his fear.

"Uh, yes, sir," he nearly stammered. "We want...we want you to wear that." He pointed at the apparel line that a new sponsor wanted me to present in promotional ads. Yes, my wife had gotten me into modeling. I started being a brand ambassador. Crazy, huh?

But in between all this, I still managed to get up at four, work on myself, meditate, and follow it up with physical training, no matter where I was in the world. Everyone was following me everywhere—in life and online—up to and including one organization I never thought I would hear from again.

# 30

I was born in the Year of the Tiger. I was also born in the hour of the tiger. But the symbol of Rōnin is the dragon, because it is a sign of strength and clarity. The red dragon is born out of war, yet is also a symbol of finding oneself.

That's why I chose an image of the Red Dragon to represent my company, Rōnin Tactics, which was growing because of my training courses, its website, and the fame that came from *Forged in Fire: Knife or Death* as well as *Call of Duty: Modern Warfare*.

The red dragon might have been born out of war, as I was but I am still truly a tiger as my mother is. So whenever I think of the tiger, I think of her. I don't remember her from Vietnam, or even the Indonesian refugee camp. I remember her from Fayetteville.

So I thought of her as I sat in the backyard of a Fayetteville Airbnb at five in the morning.

*Smile and be brave.*

As wind swirled around me, I could smell my hometown. The scent of the pine trees where I used to run in the woods, playing commando. The smell of my mother's Vietnamese cooking, as well as the barbecue the area was famous for. And even the faint whiff of cigarettes and alcohol in the mucous of the man who had spit on me in that Piggly Wiggly so long ago.

For good and ill, I was back home. Not because my mother had called me but because the Green Berets had.

I exhaled all the odors and continued the morning meditation that I had been developing through five years of practice. I inhaled again, taking in a sense of gratitude that I had survived to live such a life. I filled myself with this beautiful moment, reminding myself that this was my upbringing, this was my hometown.

Yet there was still my old friend inside me as I exhaled. Anxiousness. After all I had survived, you'd think that it would back off. But, of course, it was made and fed by all I had survived.

As I focused on my breath, I could sense my friend beginning to grow. It knew why I was here. I opened my eyes to it, remembering that it was this morning that I had been invited to speak to more than four hundred newly graduated Green Berets. Whether I knew it or not, the Green Berets had always been following me. I was, and am, a Green Beret, so their PR teams were always following me, no matter how long ago our parting had been.

Yes, I was about to go back to the breeding grounds of the Special Forces, where I had experienced so much and trained so hard. Nervously, I looked down at my watch.

*I better start getting ready.*

I slowly made my way through the Airbnb, and into the bathroom to take a quick shower. Then came the big decision of the morning. Do I wear a tie or do I not wear a tie?

*You need to look professional, but you know how the teams are, right?*

No tie. I quickly threw on a blazer, jumped in the car, punched info into the navigation system, and drove through the dark woods toward Fort Bragg.

*Man, I don't need no GPS.* I could've gotten there blindfolded. Driving down the curvy roads, I finally made it to the main gates.

*Oh man,* I thought, *they never get it right.* There was a long line of cars waiting to get in, as usual. *You would think that they'd put more guards at the gate by now. Geez.*

I quickly reminded myself that wasn't the judgmental person I wanted to be anymore. I reminded myself that, although I was going back to familiar grounds, I shouldn't go back to the way I used to look at things.

I finally got to the gate and saw two security guards. As I handed my *Retired* ID card to one, I looked over the other. He was E-5, neatly dressed. They looked at my card, snapped to attention, and the E-5 spoke.

"Have a great day, Master Sergeant! Airborne."

I smiled as I took my ID card. "Thank you for your service," I said.

The soldier looked at me with a raised eyebrow and snapped back. "Airborne! Move along!"

As almost always, I followed orders. I drove past dark, guarded, wooded areas, toward the Special Forces breeding, training, and selection areas. I had to go through historic sections of the base to get there—buildings that dated back to the eighteen hundreds, back to the beginning of Fort Bragg, and the beginning of the Special Forces. As I admired those beautiful buildings, the navigation system spoke up.

"Arrived."

Parking the car, I shut off the engine and turned out the lights. As I sat there in the dark, I felt like I was back in an Overwatch position—like I had been during my training. I would always do Overwatch before linkup. Every Green Beret knew that tactic.

I was early, like I always was, so I sat there in the empty parking lot, taking time to look at the Special Warfare Training Center, which had been developed to combat Communist insurgency during the Vietnam War. Ironic that the very grounds where I lost my freedom became the birthplace of a special breed of warrior.

*Well, let's get on with it now.*

I got out of the car and made my way through a cluster of pine trees, moving, of course, tactically. I smelled the pine needles—a scent that was so familiar to the Special Forces. As I walked toward the building, I enjoyed the beautiful sunrise, and thought *Linkup, fifteen minutes.*

Standing at the linkup point, I observed a beautiful, larger-than-life bronze statue of John F. Kennedy approving of Brigadier General William P. Yarborough wearing the green beret during the President's visit on October 12, 1961. I read the legend etched around the base of the statue.

"The green beret is again becoming a symbol of excellence, a badge of courage, a mark of distinction in the fight for freedom."

The statue had been dedicated in 2012 during a graduation ceremony.

I smiled at the thought that my linkup point was where John F. Kennedy decided to activate the Green Berets—later signing an executive order allowing the Special Forces to wear the coveted, and now iconic, headgear. And those were the very grounds where I was going to meet my linkup.

But as linkup time approached, my old friend anxiety also approached.

*Steady now,* I told myself, then literally moved from the shadow of the statue into the light. Standing in front of this monument of Kennedy and Yarborough, two legends in Special Forces history, I read the motto I had worked so hard to achieve.

Free the Oppressed.

At that moment I heard someone call out.

"Tu!"

I turned around to see a Sergeant Major in full uniform approaching. Let's call him John.

"Hey," John said brightly, "I'm here to escort you. There's four hundred Green Berets ready to hear you talk, man. You ready?"

*Ugh. Anxiety.*

But that was inside me. Outside, my smile widened.

"Yeah, man," I answered. "I am so ready. And what a beautiful morning, is it not, John?"

He looked at me and then around. "Yeah?" he answered. "It *is* a nice morning, huh?"

"It is a beautiful morning, my friend," I told him.

Smiling even wider, John escorted me across the street along familiar grounds. I knew where I was going. The Special Forces Foreign Language Training Lab was a big building. After graduation from a long special warfare guerrilla-tactic pipeline, you went into the language training courses there. In my case, as you may remember, it was French.

The students I was asked to speak to were in the very last portion of the pipeline before they moved on to their A-Teams. But now they were waiting on me.

John's enthusiastic voice broke me out of my reverie. "Oh, make sure you look both ways, man. They're crazy driving down this street. You'd think that they could see the red lights, but still, soldiers get hit here. Crazy, huh?"

I looked at the man. I recognized this sort of talk. John had something else on his mind. I waited until he looked back at me before replying.

"Yeah, crazy."

John nodded, taking my comment as a connection. "Yeah," he said, then kept leading me toward the building as he spoke. "Oh, Tu, I wanted to let you know this, man. I've been following you."

"Yeah?"

"Yeah. And I'm at the tail end of my career now, and I've done close to thirty years and, you know, I'm lost too. You know, I did the war. I'm kind of lost, and I just wanted to let you know that you really helped me out, man."

I looked at John and nodded. "Thank you," I told him.

I had heard it many times from students, law-enforcement officers, and soldiers I had tried to help. I understood where they were coming from. It's where I was coming from as well, so as I helped myself, it was important to me that I try to help them too. Many times my fans, followers, friends, and fellow soldiers sent me messages of thanks, and I never took them for granted and always tried to respond in kind.

So this morning, coming from John, it meant a lot because I realized I *was* John. In many ways I was still lost, and I had to remind myself that everybody's loss at each stage of their lives was important. My anxiety constantly reminded me of that.

"So any advice for me, man?" John asked.

"Any advice?"

"Yeah. I'm getting out. Any advice?"

I answered his question with another question. "What do you want to do?"

"Oh," he replied, as if it was the first time he'd heard that question. "You know, I could do contract work. There's a lot of money in that. And, you know, obviously the agency is always looking for guys like us…" He seemed to remember who he was talking to, because he then said, "I mean, like, what you did is crazy."

"What do you mean?" I asked him.

"I mean," John said, "you built your own brand."

"Oh," I replied, "thank you."

"Yeah, man. You know, I would love to do that."

"Well, why don't you?"

"Oh, well, you know, I don't know… I don't know, like, how to do all that stuff."

"What stuff?" I asked, reminding him, "You're a Green Beret."

"Oh, you know, like, you know…" he stammered.

"John," I interrupted, "when I got out, one lesson helped me learn how to do all that stuff."

"Yeah?" he said. "What is it?"

"Self-worth," I told him.

"Huh?" he responded. "What do you mean?"

"Self-worth, John. You know, what are you worth?"

"Well, I never thought about that," he admitted.

"You're getting out, and you want to get into business, right?"

"Yeah."

"So if I am the president of a multibillion dollar company, and I want an hour of your time, John, what is it worth?"

"What?"

"What are you worth? What would you want for an hour of your time?"

John thought about it for a few seconds, then finally replied. "Well, Tu, if we could do like an installment plan where if he does like, you know, maybe a membership where you know, he continues to come back, you know, I'm thinking about that continuous income coming in—"

"Green Berets," I interrupted. "So intelligent, but always overthinking things."

"Oh yeah," John admitted in recognition. "Right. I do too."

"Like every Green Beret," I assured him. "We're intelligent. But the thing is, I didn't ask you about all that. All I asked is, what is one hour of your time worth?"

He couldn't tell me. So I smiled and put my hand on his shoulder. "Self-worth, my friend," I said to him. "If I was to say anything to you: self-worth. When I got out, I didn't know my self-worth."

"And you do now?"

"Hmm," I answered with a smile. "Follow me, John."

We went into a big auditorium classroom, and I could see all these Green Berets filling the place. As John walked me down to the front, I was trying to look cool and keep my composure, but my anxiety was coming on strong now. Still, I was breathing and holding it together. Self-worth.

"Hey, man," John said to me. "I want you to meet the NCOIC of the class." That was the Noncommissioned Officer in Charge.

"Hey, Tu," the NCOIC said to me, motioning to the gathered audience. "They're ready for you."

Some people think that public speaking is more frightening than death. But I kept that monster at bay too.

"Is the mic on?" I asked quietly.

"Oh, yeah, the mic is on."

"So I can just go up there and start talking?"

"Yeah."

See, we Green Berets always get our intelligence first. I had my mission, and I had my equipment. I smiled when I said "thank you," and, as I moved to the front of the class, I could feel my heart rate going up and my hands twitching.

I just stood there for a few seconds, observing the class, feeling the silence and feeding on the energy. As I took my place behind the podium at the microphone I was floating.

I just looked at them, saw myself, and spoke from the heart.

"You know, guys," I said, "I've sat where you are, and I want to congratulate you for the dedication and commitment that you and your family have made for you to be sitting here today.

"When I was sitting where you are, I was twenty-one years old, wondering what the A-Teams were all about—wondering what the Special Forces and that life was all about. Let me tell you this. There were some things I wanted to know. There are some things I wish I would have known when I sat where you are. Let me explain some things that you need to understand, that will help carry you through each evolution of your life. Not just through the Special Forces A-Teams but through war and peace. Let me tell you these elements that I wish I would have known."

And as these Green Berets looked at me, I spoke my first truth.

"You must understand your why. And I'm not talking about a why in your job, your career. I'm talking about what's your purpose, man? What's your code that you're willing to live and die for? What is your why?"

The Green Berets started to sit up.

"Let me tell you something. That why is going to carry you when you're in some country where nobody speaks your language, and you're running with rebels, and you're taking out the enemies of America. And when you're missing your family and you're missing their birthdays, and you're fighting a war or suppressing a conflict that nobody else will ever know, you better know your why."

I stared at them for a second, then my memories drove me on.

"When you're pulling your dead teammate off the battlefield. When you're standing underneath an oak tree and people spit in your face, flip you off, and say 'Thank God for dead soldiers,' and you're trying to ignore them and just watch your friend be buried in peace, you better know your why."

I lowered my head, trying not to let the memories stop me. I knew my why.

"Once the war is over and the rounds and the bullets stop flying and the smoke from the hand grenades finally clears, you better know your fucking why."

I could see something start to grow in their faces. These graduating Green Berets started to understand their why, and maybe even my Way. And, as I spoke, I could feel the anxiety retreating and energy radiating from my mind, body, and soul.

"The warrior's path is so hard. There are so many hardships. You will make your mistakes. But the thing is this: he who conquers himself is mightier than a thousand times a thousand men in a thousand battles. Have control of yourself. Don't lose yourself in the journey."

I knew what I was talking about: it was a paraphrase of a quote from Buddha, and I told them so they might not make the same mistakes I had.

"At one point in the war, I weaponized hate. Weaponizing the energy that starts war to oppress people, then change and slay people? That's hate. At one point in the war, I picked up the sword of hate. Because I, like many of my teammates, saw the worst of the world. But what happened was, when you weaponize hate, you become blind to the world. You cannot see the beauty in this world."

I could see that their faces were like John's when I first told him it was a beautiful morning. The very idea of the world's beauty was still foreign. They still had their eyes on an uglier prize—a prize they would have to fight for throughout their military careers.

"Do not lose yourself in the journey," I repeated. "Do not weaponize something that can end up destroying you."

I watched their faces. Like the wind shifting to push the gun smoke away, the Green Berets' expressions shifted.

"One moment," I reminded them, "can change a day. One day can change a life. One life can change the world."

As I stepped back, the Green Berets started applauding. I could feel their energy swallowing my anxiousness like a tsunami.

The commander stepped up. "Whoa," he said, "thank you. Oh my God. Not what I expected."

"Sir?"

"That's really powerful, Tu," he told me. "Thank *you*. Wow."

Then I heard the NCOIC. "All right," he announced to the graduating Green Berets. "Hurry up, get back to your class. Zero-nine training starts."

As the Green Berets began to fall out into formation one by one, John came up to me.

"Oh man. Whoa. Did you rehearse that?"

"No," I answered honestly. "It was just me speaking my energy."

"Your energy, huh?" he replied. "I like that, dude, your energy. Love it." Then John's attitude changed. "But before you go, you've got to link up with Bob, and Bob is going to take you upstairs. To Brian Hall."

"Excuse me?" I said.

"Yeah," he told me. "The commander wants to meet you."

Everybody, every new student, knew Brian Hall. It wasn't a "who," it was the headquarters of the special warfare training zone. Anybody who sees the top floor of Brian Hall is either A, a hero, or B? Well, let's just say that it's not a good day for B's career.

So now that I'm a civilian, why am I having anxiety about going to the top of Brian Hall?

"Ever been to the top floor, Tu?" John asked as we went up in the elevator.

"No, John," I answered. "I've never been."

"Yeah, it's not good if you go," John replied. "You know what I'm saying?"

"Yeah," I agreed as the elevator doors opened, and a young Special Forces Major, who had just transferred to Special Warfare Training Group, was waiting. I knew him as a great American, West Point graduate, and second-generation Special Forces A-Team commander, now serving in the Special Warfare Training Center.

"Hey, Tu," he said. "It's great seeing you again, man. I heard your speech went well."

The two shared a knowing look before Bob explained. "News travels fast around here. Come on, the Sergeant Major wants to see you."

Standing on no ceremony, they immediately brought me to the Command Sergeant Major of the Special Warfare Training Group. My anxiety was defeated by my respect.

Anybody who serves as a senior NCO in these positions is a legend in Special Forces. His military achievement badges and qualifications stacked all the way up to his shoulder blade. Combat diver, halo masterjumper, static line master parachutist, and more. Then I looked over at his left sleeve and there were all his qualifications—Special Forces, Ranger, Sapper, Airborne, and more.

And the first thing he asked was "How did the speech go?"

"Oh, I loved it," I told him. "Thank you for allowing me to speak."

"Our pleasure," he told me. "I heard it went great. You know, news travels fast around here."

"So I've heard, Sergeant Major," I said, glancing at Bob with a grin.

"You know, Tu, I'm about to get out and I want to go into business with my wife like you."

Even though John's questions should have prepared me, I was still surprised when a Command Sergeant Major looked to me for advice. "Like me?"

"Sure," he said. "You're a big role model, Tu. You're an entrepreneur, and you and your wife travel around the United States, so I just want to let you know I'm proud of guys like you. Successful during and after the military."

*Wow.*

Before I could think of any advice, Bob came back in.

"Sergeant Major," he said, "the Commander says he's busy, but he wants to meet Tu before his next meeting. Can I steal him real quick?"

"Yeah, sure," said the Sergeant Major.

So Bob brought me over to meet the Commander General and shake his hand before he went to his meeting. It was a pleasure because I knew how busy guys like him were.

Then the Special Warfare Training Group Sergeant Major wanted a picture with me. But first he said, "Hey, Bob, make sure you have Tu sign the book."

That stopped Bob. "Sergeant Major?" he answered with a bit of surprise.

"Yeah. Have Tu sign the book."

I looked at Bob. I didn't understand why they were looking at me for so long. Something had just happened that I didn't know about. But what? What book?

I wanted to gather intelligence on it, but the Sergeant Major took over. "Come on, Tu," he said. "We'll take the picture in front of the book."

So we all went to the hall's secretary. Well-dressed, well-mannered, she had an American flag pinned to her sweater. She smiled at me and got a set of keys to open a drawer that had another set of keys. She took that second set of keys and went to a glass display case of museum quality. Behind the glass was an old book with the word *Guests* etched on the cover.

It was the Fort Bragg Special Operations Command Guest Book—first used on October 12, 1961, on the occasion of President John F. Kennedy's visit. The visit when he and General Yarborough discussed making the green beret a symbol of excellence for the US Army again. Very few people had seen the inside of this book, and even fewer got to sign it.

They took the guest book out. I gave Bob my smartphone and he got ready to take a picture of me and the Special Warfare Training Group leader. I stood with this legend of a Sergeant Major as I got into my best pose as a rōnin...and we both gave the camera the classic *V for Victory* sign.

Bob loved that. "Let's get another one!"

So we showed the camera our finest guns...a battle of the best bulging biceps. Then I locked arms with him in a classic muscle-to-muscle "Spartan" position.

Even the secretary smiled.

"So, hey, Tu," the Sergeant Major said, "I got to run, but hey, man, thanks for what you do for the regiment, and keep on representing the Green Berets."

"I appreciate that," I told him. "Thank you."

Then back in his office, Bob smiled and opened the book to its first page. "You know, Tu," he said, "the first guests who signed this book were the Kennedys."

I looked at the names recorded there, and it reminded me of how John F. Kennedy had helped give birth to the modern Special Forces by approving the use of the green beret as the official headgear.

Then Bob turned to the next page. "And, Tu, look, here's General Yarborough."

*What a legend*, I thought. One of the founding fathers of the Special Forces. They even named the Special Forces knife after him. And there it was, his signature.

By then both Bob and I were a little giddy. "Hey, Tu," he said, "you want me to take a picture of you signing the book?"

*Hell yeah*, I thought, but I managed to keep it to a simple "I don't mind."

Bob flipped the pages, trying to find the next free place for me to sign. "A lot of historical people in here," he said as we watched the names flip past. "A lot of legends." He put the book down on the last page of signatures and made room for me. "And, you know," he said as I prepared myself, "I just want to thank you for what you do."

Then he handed me the official pen. It was made from two bullet casings. The brass and copper looked just like a bullet. It was beautiful. I took it, leaned down, put the tip onto the guest book paper—

"Tu, smile!"

Turning to my left, I gave him my biggest, brightest smile and a peace sign.

"Beautiful, man!" Bob cried, then took the picture.

Then I slowly wrote my name, the date, and my position. *Rōnin*. Only then did I sign my signature.

As I looked down at my name, recorded along with all these other people I admired and respected, I realized what an honor had been bestowed on me. Then it all came back. The birthplace. The building. The base. The book.

Now I truly was home.

My life had come full circle. So now it was time to start again. *De oppresso liber. Et ipse.*

# EPILOGUE

How? How do I free the oppressed, including myself?

As I meditated that morning, I asked myself the question again: How do I live by the soul? What does it even mean to live by the soul?

More questions flashed in my mind as I tried to exhale strong sensations of hate and regret—emotions that had surrounded me since the morning of my birth. How could I let go of all the emotions that did not serve me well?

The Buddha is credited with saying that *the root of all suffering is attachment* because the only constant is change. But how does one let go of these attachments? How does one let go of beliefs, narratives, even intellect? How can I let go of all the things that hurt me and hold me back without hurting and holding myself back?

These questions had gone from important to imperative a few months before. Things had come to a crescendo inside my brain. I had been going through a hard time, harder than any I could remember—which is saying something after all I'd been through.

But I had stepped into this mental quicksand, and I started to sink deep into a dark void. But how could that be? After my speech to the Green Beret graduating class, everybody told me I was a rising star—in business, in media, in life. I had everything I had ever wanted, and more. But still, depression was assailing me.

Physical pain, I understood. I had survived crippling amounts of physical pain. But I had discovered physical pain was little compared to mental pain. I learned my body could heal. But my mind? I knew from the Army doctors that my brain was traumatized, but there had been precious few advancements in treating that. Understanding and curing emotional trauma was still in its infancy.

On that morning, I couldn't wait for the advancement in treatment. I honestly didn't know how much longer I could take this constant, tormenting pain. Even though I followed the Bushido code and tried to give back and teach, I was stuck in a pit of seemingly endless, increasing pain.

I would keep my successful entrepreneur mask on, then go off to suffer in isolation and silence. I would wake up and try to meditate and practice martial arts, but I was getting so lost and the pain was going so deep that I didn't know what to do.

Worse, what I did know was the end game. Within the Special Operations community, especially at the tier-one level we fought at, a lot of guys were committing suicide. I did not want to be pushed over that brink, so I looked for help. Luckily, I knew one of the places to find it.

I went to Shawn Ryan, a former Navy SEAL and CIA contractor, who had me on his popular video and audio podcast as part of his Vigilance Elite company. We had become fast friends, and he revealed to me that he had been having trouble too. But he had gone to Mexico for a treatment specifically designed to manage traumatic brain injury and post-traumatic stress disorder.

According to him, it changed his life. And, as a SEAL who had completed more than a dozen deployments in more than a dozen hot spots in years of combat service, I had a lot of reasons to have faith in him.

Through this mindset, driven to finally heal myself, I found myself in a safe house near a beach in Mexico preparing myself for the most aggressive treatment to heal my past traumas. The safe house was an incredibly welcoming and peaceful place, run by people who were both caring and extremely professional.

They were a combination of doctors, nurses, scientists, and therapists who were calling on the entire history of internal healing from everywhere in the world.

After a thorough medical screening by doctors, I loaded up in a van and we made our way to a traditional sweat lodge located in a remote part of town. The clay sweat lodge was heated up to a hundred and twenty degrees, accompanied by the beating of native drums, the shaking of native maracas, and the singing of native chants.

It was what they called the first door. I had to go through that door five times. Once you enter the door, each session lasted roughly thirty minutes. That meant I could leave after each session, but I had to go back in. The heat and the native rhythms were so intense that I faded in and out of consciousness.

It was pitch-dark in the sweat lodge, and I could hear my spiritual brothers chanting and making their native music. It was so fucking hot I started hallucinating. Chanting in unison with them, I could feel my mind drift out of the physical and into the spiritual world.

The Mexican spiritual woman leading the ceremony later told me that I was very connected to my ancestors. In a weakened state, I asked her what she meant by that. She told me that she felt the presence of my ancestors in that sweat lodge.

I passed out, and suddenly it was night. My first day was over. The next day the medical staff did an electrocardiogram and blood work to see if I could handle the next treatment session. They gave me an IV and made sure I was all properly hydrated.

Then a breath coach came in. I had done a lot of what I called mindfulness meditation, but this was a different, more intense technique. The breath coach had me lie down on a meditation mat and taught me a traditional deep-breathing practice.

I saw a light. I had never seen such a beautiful light. I had never seen such colors. To this day I can't describe those colors. There are no words to describe those colors.

Others I know of who had gone on healing seminars all over

the world talk about experiences with meditation, massage, and music that had unleashed dreams of lights and colors and shapes and movement that were so psychically powerful that it nearly paralyzed them. Their treatment elicited so many emotions that they had cried for hours.

The external universe was huge, but we were all learning that our internal universe could seem as vast.

One of the treatment's healers helped me discover just that. The only way I can describe his treatment was that he entered my spirit and led me to the beginning of life. The goal was to reconnect me to my soul, and this was done through ibogaine—a powerful medicine from the iboga root of what is referred to as the tree of knowledge, imported from Gabon in Central Africa.

The night of the treatment, the sun was going down as I stood next to a fire. The wind was strong that night, and I could hear the waves crashing in the distance. The house staff of doctors, paramedics, and spiritual healers stood behind me as I read my intentions from torn pieces of paper, then threw them into a burning barrel.

Looking around, I said a silent prayer for my military brothers. I knew I was about to go into battle, only this time I would have to face my inner demons alone.

Before, I couldn't tell you certain things because they involved national security. Now I would love to clearly tell you all that happened, but it was mostly emotions, indescribable sights, and sensations beyond definition. I can't tell you what I felt. Words would not suffice. But I will try to tell you what I saw.

The treatment room was dark as I sat on a meditation mat in front of a large mirror. In front of the mirror was a burning candle, native maraca, black sand in a glass jar, a hawk feather and other secret items. The medical staff hooked me up to a heart monitor and ran an IV to keep me hydrated during the treatment. My healer gave me a high dose of medicine.

Through the illumination of the candlelight, I stared at my reflection in the mirror. I could hear maracas being shaken in unison. I joined with them as I began to transcend into the spirit world. As I shook my maraca, I began to see the image in the mirror take on a life of its own. My face started shifting and bending. It was like looking into a fun-house mirror made of moving liquid.

The dose of medicine the healer gave me made me incredibly nauseous. There was a purging bucket next to my mat. I stared at the shifting mirror as long as I could before I started throwing up. Finally, I lay down on the meditation mat and put on an eye mask. At this point, I could feel the spirit of the medicine fully enter my body. That's the best way I know how to say it. Then I blacked out.

Slowly opening my eyes underneath the mask, I found myself in a different world. I was in what seemed to be a cement elevator shaft looking up to what seemed to be infinity. I immediately started looking for an escape. And, as I looked, the shaft was suddenly full of every imaginable obstruction and obstacle. There were World War II metal X-shaped barriers, barbed wire, large metal rebar, and many more metal obstacles stacked on top of one another, making it impossible for me to escape. I do not like being trapped. I tried to look for a way out for what seemed like hours. Eventually I got incredibly frustrated.

"What are you trying to fucking show me?" I cried out.

And then a voice came to me as if in a meditation.

*Your soul is trapped.*

I can't even begin to tell you the panic I felt from that realization. But as soon as I figured out one visual clue, the spirit of the medicine took me to another visual riddle.

Just as I thought I was getting the hang of it, I was suddenly hurled into the back seat of my car. I was looking at the dashboard. The car was a rare Mercedes-AMG muscle car, a gift from my wife. It was her present to celebrate our business success. Although I love the car, I'm not really a car guy. And for some reason my mind kept flashing me into the back seat, looking at the dashboard.

*Flashing* is the best way I can describe it. It didn't slam me into it, it flashed me into it as if I was made of light. It kept flashing me into the dashboard until I yelled again.

"Why are you bringing me here? What are you showing me?"

But it just kept flashing again and again until I shouted, "What the fuck are you trying to show me?"

Only then did the answer come to me in the form of a question.

*What do you love most about this car?*

"My wife bought it for me," I immediately answered.

The reaction was instantaneous, like a lightbulb turning on over my head. The light felt like a warm presence: I could sense the light. But if I tried to look up at it, it would immediately disappear. So, I just let that light shine down on me. I don't know how I knew, but for some reason that light was my wife.

But once I accepted the light, it seemed to signal to all the powers that I was ready. What I felt next was unimaginable. I felt, and even saw, an old Asian man walking on my body. He stopped at my chest. With a sigh, he bent over, grabbed my hair, and pulled. With each pull I felt pain, anxiety, fear.

Then, for what seemed like the next thirteen hours, the old man pulled on my hair. And with each pull, I felt all the trapped emotions from my traumas, pain, and suffering played out as if I was reliving it all over again.

All my mistakes.

All the lives I took in war.

All the souls from those lives.

All the people that I killed directly or indirectly.

Military, military, military.

It got so painful.

I felt the hate in myself and in others.

The souls from all my enemies appeared, whispering and wishing me death from the shadows.

I felt the pain of judgment from others and in myself.

I heard billions of voices screaming in every crevice of my brain.

It was so painful that if I'd had a gun, I would have ended it right then and there.

I had never felt so much pain.

The only thing that gave me relief was that car dashboard. And with it came thoughts of my wife and the love she had for me. As I focused on her, I could feel the warmth from the light hovering over my head.

So I kept my mind on the love of my wife as the pain ripped and rippled through my body. It was the pain of pure suffering, far deeper than the skin.

With each pull I could feel the emotions. It felt as if that old Asian man was a gardener tending to his plants, picking out the growths that did not serve me well.

It was as if he was purging my negative thoughts, pulling out all the agonizing emotions that had taken root in my brain. With a sigh, he would rip them out like weeds.

It was so painful, and I could literally taste the dirt.

One after another, in the thousands, I saw, smelled, and felt the weeds being torn up over and over again, from my childhood, through my military career, to now. And with each pull came a painful emotion.

One of the medicine's side effects was that it made you nauseous, so in between reliving all my traumas, came many purging sessions. That's a nice way of putting it. But at least this gut-wrenching up-chucking was purging out all the evils that had taken root in my mind and body.

Finally, *finally*, after who knows how long, I floated back to some sort of physical reality. When I managed to slowly open my eyes, I could actually see steam rising from the ground and my body. I felt energy radiating through me. I looked down and actually saw my dragon tattoos moving around me like a suit of armor, protecting me from demon spirits. I felt as if my body had just come back from battle.

Have you ever seen movies where someone deals with a ghost and they come out drained? That's how I felt. Like I had walked through the spirit world and survived the draining of my energy to come back to this dimension.

Then I had to, once again, purge. I had vomited so much throughout the night that I had nothing left in me except dry heaves. Then, the only thing I had the strength to do was lay my head on the rim of the purging bucket and pass out.

Finally, the healers helped me up to my room after I don't know how long. I lay down. The windows were open. I could hear the waves. I could smell the beach.

Then I cried. I cried so hard and so long the pain was magnified a hundred times over.

The spirit healer came in. "How you feeling?" he asked. I mean, what else could he say?

I told him what I just told you and then said, "I feel like shit."

Disappointed, I told him that I didn't think it worked. I mean, I felt far worse now than I ever had, and the negative voices in my head were even louder.

"Tu," he said kindly, "the treatment is still working. It's still going through your system. You'll feel better tomorrow," he promised. Then he left me to try to sleep, but stopped at the door. "You know, Tu, Shawn was a lot worse off than you at this point."

"Really?" I said.

"He was," the healer assured me. "Oh yeah, a hundred percent."

Hey, I hate to say it, but that gave me hope. I love Shawn, so if he could take it, I could. Especially since the pain played out all day and all night. I had come out of my spirit world at nine in the morning. Sixteen hours later I was still awake in my room with the pain.

The staff called the doctor to give me a sedative. It didn't take much. My body was so weak I basically passed out.

Sometime later I opened my eyes. The sunshine was pouring

in my window. I blinked, realizing something was different. I lay there trying to figure out what.

It was the voices. The voices were gone. I didn't hear them anymore. The voices that I had heard through my entire life. They were gone.

I couldn't believe it. I jumped off the bed, then immediately had to grab the wall since I was so dizzy. I held on, opened up the window, and looked at the beach. The beach was even more beautiful because now my mind was present. So were my senses. The air was so silky, so clean.

An incredible sense of relief washed over me. Believe it or not, memories of watching *A Christmas Carol* came to mind. Like Scrooge waking up from his nightmare, I ran and saw two cooks making breakfast and hugged them.

A healer came into the kitchen, recognized my reaction, and cried "Perfecto!"

I ran outside. The warmth of the sun embraced my body, and the beautiful grass embraced my feet. I felt connected to it all.

The caregivers soon reminded me that this was not a miracle cure. It was a process that continued, like everything else in life.

Sure enough, eventually the voices started coming back. Like it or not, they were a part of me. But I knew them now, and I started to focus on them rather than try to run from them. I tried to understand and accept them rather than fight or destroy them. They were still there, but they weren't so controlling anymore.

"How you feeling, Tu?" asked my spiritual healer.

"I can still hear the voices," I replied.

Smiling, he told me that the next session would clean it all out. The next session was to inhale 5-MeO-DMT—or as it is also known, toad venom. This venom is used in Indigenous ceremonies and has been referred to as *ego death*. It is also known as the most powerful psychedelic on the planet, and it is said that, once inhaled, it provides a gateway to communicate with a higher order, a divine consciousness.

After a quick video explaining the medicine, we made our way downstairs. The spiritual healer took me outside. After what seemed like forever, I made my way to where I would be given the toad venom.

The warm sun was comforting as I sat on the grass overlooking the nearby beach. I could hear the waves crashing as my spiritual healer prepared the venom. A team of healers, doctors, and paramedics stood behind me as I began my twenty-second-long deep inhale.

I will tell you what I felt and saw, even though its power is almost indescribable. As I inhaled, I felt the slow death of my physical existence. It was a feeling of nonexistence. And I saw a light approaching me.

I could hear my spiritual healer telling me to let go. So I did as I fell back onto the grass. I felt the fear of death as my body shook uncontrollably. I could feel trapped trauma surfacing throughout my body.

My muscles shook as a tunnel of light quickly approached, then engulfed me. And then I felt my soul shoot through the tunnel of light—leaving this physical world.

Next came a feeling of oneness, warmth, and love. Love that I had never allowed myself or experienced before. There was no judgment, just acceptance, and a peace that I have never gotten to experience in my lifetime.

As I sat with this higher order I felt oneness with all things. A true love for humanity, our planet, and myself. Then just like that, I could feel gravity pull my soul back into my physical body.

The thing about 5-MeO-DMT is that it's fast-acting and lasts around twenty minutes. Slowly, I opened my eyes. The sky was so beautiful and blue. I could hear the birds in the sky and the wind fluttering the palm trees. I slowly sat up and looked out into an ocean of energy. I saw these waves of energy dancing as they crashed onto the shore.

I felt a oneness with life and all things.

Then again I cried. I cried from the depths of my soul. I cried so hard that I started hyperventilating. Finally, after my emotional downpour, I turned around and saw the love on the faces of all the healers, doctors, and paramedics. Behind them I imagined all my spiritual brother-warriors. All the ones who had suffered, and were still suffering, what I had suffered. Now we were one.

I was sitting outside, looking at the waves crash, when I was informed that my ride had arrived. It was the van taking me back across the border into California. As I slowly stood up and stared at the beach, I felt grateful for life and this opportunity.

I came back home to Colorado feeling the way Shawn had—not only that this treatment had helped but it could truly help all the team guys who were suffering. Yes, it had become vitally important to help myself, but also to help all of us win our internal war and to choose love over hate. We could deliver a message that could help others remind them of our true selves, which is God and love.

But where to begin? That was the question filling my mind as the sun broke over the beautiful Colorado landscape. I finished my morning meditation and exercise, still pondering how best to proceed.

It had been three months since my treatment in Mexico. How could I take what I had learned and help make things better for myself and others? How could I lead my students to live by the soul and walk in the way of heaven?

Then I heard my wife call out.

I straightened and turned my head toward the sound. I had heard the same excitement in her voice when she had seen the emails from the History Channel and Infinity Ward.

"Honey," she cried. "Oh my God. Honey!"

I almost tripped as I quickly ran to her.

"Are you okay?" I asked.

"Yes," she said. "Yes. Read this email."

My eyes widened when I saw it was from the founders of an organization that provided grants for hundreds of US Special Operations veterans. They were the ones whose mission was to end veteran suicides.

"'Hi, Tu,'" I read. "'Thank you for everything you do. We are praying for you and your journey. Thank you for being brave enough...'"

Okay, that was all well and good, but their next sentence really floored me.

"'We would love for you to be the guest speaker at our Gala this November...'"

The timing was amazing, impossible, even though I was the guy who was sure nothing happened by chance.

Wow! Well. What a blessing to be given this opportunity. What a great honor to be a voice to help my fellow warriors and their families in Special Operations, and all those who had served, fought, and were now suffering.

I said *yes* at almost the same moment Ruthie said, "Honey, you should do it."

I looked at her, smiling. I kissed her.

But inside, my monster friend had his own old song. He gave me his usual gift: doubt.

*How are you to do this?* it sneered. *How can you make your words impactful? You know, you're speaking to the top tier of Special Operations. Who are you to speak to them?*

But as you know by now, I had met the monster many times. In training, on the battlefield, on the sound stages, on the motion-capture sets, on the sidelines of many training sessions. I had faced it in Mexico. It had been with me for a long time, but I knew who it was now. I had always known.

It was me, and everything I had been taught.

*Who am I?* I asked it. *Who are you? We are one and the same.*

It was my doubt, my insecurity, my anxiety—everything I had faced and fought from the moment I was born. The odds against me had always been big. I was never sure I could survive against bullying, abuse, hatred, and war.

But I did. I survived. I strived. I thrived. Living under the monster's shadow was rarely a pleasure, but it had never stopped me. And I wasn't going to let it stop me now.

The anxiety didn't drive me away. It inspired me to meditate for many days. Those days turned into weeks. The light shone through the dark clouds—always with the same words.

*What does it mean to live by the soul?*

I started trying to answer that question on paper, changing the words every minute. I was drafting the outline of my speech for the gala every chance I got. What some call *rewriting* my monster called *doubt*. What some called *changing the words*, my monster called *worry*. What some called *memorizing their lines*, my monster called *insecurity*.

But that wasn't the biggest issue. I had the speech. The words really flowed after meditation. I just wanted to make it as good as it deserved to be. So at this point in my healing process, I started studying the subconscious mind. What made us who we are? How does one study?

I studied by thinking and writing everywhere. I rewrote the speech. I read the speech. I recorded the speech. I listened to the speech on my headset. I listened to the speech while I practiced martial arts. I listened as I dressed up as Rōnin the video-game character. I listened as I posed for a *Call of Duty* photo shoot. I meditated on the speech, and, as I did, I tried to descend into a lower frequency in my brain.

The only time I didn't listen was when I was teaching.

As the gala date drew near, I was in the heat of Baton Rouge, Louisiana, then Dallas, Texas, running and gunning, shooting and moving, training. Even then I was still studying the developing speech while on a plane flying to another city, to another town, or at night, often passing out with my headphones on. I would wake up at four in the morning, still programming the speech in my subconscious.

It was a month-and-a-half blur. I could not—would not—waste this opportunity. It was too important to me knowing my words could help save so many lives. Finally, the day came.

"Honey, are you ready?"

I was standing in a beautiful cottage overlooking the beach in San Diego. It was the training grounds of the Navy SEALs.

My wife took my hand. "Are you ready?" she repeated. Smiling, I thanked my wife for sharing this moment with me.

A private golf cart met us at the cottage and drove us to the entry of the gala. It was obvious how hard the staff had worked to make it this amazing.

The gala was decorated with a purple theme, the color associated with higher self. Within this mix of successful businessmen, doctors, politicians, and monks there stood some of the most dangerous men in the world, beside their spouses who had helped them through their journey, as mine had helped me. Spiritual healers stood side by side with Special Operations warriors.

One doctor approached me. "I studied with the Shaolin monks," she told me, "and I've been following you on social media. A lot of things you say really resonate with me. Do you train in kung fu?"

"Excuse me?"

"Do you train in kung fu?"

"No," I answered honestly. I had learned that martial arts were only a part of kung fu. "I train in gun-fu," I told her, half-jokingly. She laughed. I took her hand. "No, I don't. Humbly."

"Well," she said, "a lot of your teachings are very internal. You know, I was a drug addict at one point in my life."

"Excuse me?"

"Yes. I went to China, and there were monks who helped. They brought in practitioners who would teach us how to breathe. And a lot of the practices have the spirits that you had in Mexico."

I looked forward to knowing more, but first things first.

Slowly, we made our way into the main room with the more than seven hundred other people who were there that night. My wife and I were sitting next to an admiral, who was sitting next to an ex-teammate I had known since I was twenty-four. He was now on the same spiritual journey I was.

Looking around the room I saw more warriors, philosophers, and doctors. Everyone was so accomplished.

*And who are you to sit with this crowd of people? Do you really think that that subconscious training really works?*

My monster friend was making its presence known, like a drunk at a party.

*Too little*, I thought back at him. I was already there, whether I deserved to be or not. *Too late*, because one way or another, we would find out if it worked. And if it didn't, we would keep trying until we found something that did.

My true adversary that night was not my sabotaging subconscious, it was Father Time. I found out my speech was at the end of the night. I had to sit there for hours through musical and artistic performances I would have normally really enjoyed. Instead, I went over and over the speech in my head.

My anxiety kept me company, but so did my wife. She held my hand when it started to shake.

*Why is this speech, among all the others you've given, so important to you?* my monster demanded.

*I'm here to help save lives, if I can.*

*Oh, you're going to go out there and flop. You're going to forget your lines.*

*Thanks*, I thought. That only made me go over them more.

Finally, the time was up.

Ruthie looked at me. "Honey, you ready?"

I looked into the monster's mirror and saw myself. Myself— the one who kept me on my toes by whispering doubts.

"Yes," I said and kissed her.

As I walked backstage, preparing to enter the spotlight, a video played.

*"Who is Tu Lam?"* I heard myself say. I had worked with a very talented crew to prepare this video introduction. It showed the audience my story, accomplishments, and hopes, among other things, as I stood offstage, trying to breathe.

I heard another voice.

*Focus, Tu*, it said. I guess it was my newly born healer voice, as opposed to a monster voice. *Focus.*

Well, I always listened to my monster, so why not give my healer equal time?

I inhaled. I exhaled.

I heard yet another voice. One I totally recognized. It was my voice.

*Nothing happens by chance in this universe*, it said. *Surrender and flow with the energy of what has always been.*

I felt calm, yet energized.

As I stepped up to the podium, I looked under the lights and to the people. I saw my wife, my ex-teammate, and all the rest.

Focusing in on my breath and finally exhaling, I spoke.

"Can you imagine what it took for heaven and earth to align for us all to be sitting here tonight? I mean in this endless space of the universe?"

I was off and running—something I had been very good at for a very long time.

I spoke of the impossible odds of the universe that we were all gathered there tonight on that common ground.

I spoke of my journey.

I spoke of jungles and mountains.

I spoke of seeing the worst of the world and the search for meaning there.

I spoke of losing myself to find my true self.

I spoke of Lao Tzu and of the eternal energy of what has always been.

I spoke of Musashi Miyamoto and his search for truth and meaning.

I spoke of oppression and how that energy was needed for me to free the oppressed.

I spoke of the battlefield within.

I spoke of people and life and rebirth.

I spoke of my treatment and how it broke the grip of my ego.

I spoke of land mines and pencils.

I spoke of the impossible possible.

I spoke of the peace that only love can generate.

I looked out on that crowd. I saw myself in their eyes, and I saw them in mine.

"As a child born in war," I told them, "I've searched for the meaning of living. Out of oppression, I rose to free the oppressed while searching for the meaning of life and who I am. In the end, the answer was found within me. Tonight, on this common ground, let us stand united and create a better world for all the generations to come."

And, as I looked at that applauding crowd, and saw them reflected in me, I spoke my truth with an open heart, open mind, and all my soul.

"And remember this. One moment can change the day. One day can change a life. And one life can change the world. God bless our troops. God bless America.

"God and country."

As I stepped back, I exhaled. And the crowd, all seven hundred of them, stood up and cheered.

I was in a grateful haze as I looked at my beautiful wife. She was crying, looking at me proudly, and giving me the double thumbs-up. I walked off the stage into the dark, then into the hallway, and tried to catch my breath.

Then the crowd started pouring in—all smiles, nods, and high fives. As I tried to make my way outside just to get some needed fresh air, I could see the wives and warriors.

"That was amazing."

"You're a freaking beast."

Beast is a compliment from a commando.

As I made my way through the maze of people, they wanted to share their journeys with me and how my words reminded them of their soul and how to live better.

Finally, I broke free into the cool San Diego night. I looked down at my watch. It was around ten thirty. I walked behind the building and thought about what had just happened. I was trying to process it all, you know.

What an amazing experience, and how blessed I was to be a part of that after all the pain, anger, and hatred I had suffered.

Walking back to the entrance after catching my breath, I looked up at the stars. The rest of the universe, and my life, lay beyond.

I listened for my monster, but all I felt was contentment. And why not? After all, my monster was me.

"Honey?"

I turned to see my wife. As always, she knew how to find me.

"You okay?" she asked.

I walked over to Ruthie, seeing her love and strength. Hugging my wife, and finally feeling the peace I never had, I stayed in this center of the universe and opened my mouth to answer her question.

And as I did, my ego spoke in harmony with me to the greatest love of my life.

"Yes, honey," I said. "I'm doing well."

★ ★ ★ ★ ★